MARJORIE TOO AFRAID TO CRY

Marjorie
TOO AFRAID TO CRY

A Home Child Experience

PATRICIA SKIDMORE

DUNDURN
TORONTO

Substantive Editor: Jane Gibson
Copy Editor: Jennifer McKnight
Design: Jesse Hooper
Printer: Webcom

Library and Archives Canada Cataloguing in Publication

Skidmore, Patricia J.
        Marjorie too afraid to cry : a home child experience / Patricia Skidmore.

Includes bibliographical references.
Also issued in electronic format.
ISBN 978-1-4597-0339-1

        1. Arnison, Marjorie. 2. Home children (Canadian immigrants)--British Columbia--Biography. I. Title.

HQ792.C3S55 2012   362.7'7912092   C2012-904605-1

1   2   3   4   5   16   15   14   13   12

We acknowledge the support of the **Canada Council for the Arts** and the **Ontario Arts Council** for our publishing program. We also acknowledge the financial support of the **Government of Canada** through the **Canada Book Fund** and **Livres Canada Books**, and the **Government of Ontario** through the **Ontario Book Publishing Tax Credit** and the **Ontario Media Development Corporation**.

Printed and bound in Canada.

Unless otherwise stated, all epigraphs are poems written by Patricia Skidmore.

Front Cover:
Top photo: Marjorie arriving at the Prince of Wales Fairbridge Farm School. *Courtesy of the Skidmore Family Collection.*
Bottom photo: The children being picked up by a bus on their way to the Prince of Wales Fairbridge Farm School. *University of Liverpool Archives, Special Collections Branch, Fairbridge Archives, D296.F4/1/1/268.*
Back Cover:
Top photo: Marjorie Arnison's Middlemore Emmigration Home file photo. *University of Liverpool Archives, Special Collections Branch, Fairbridge Archives, Arnison Family Records, D296.E1.*
Bottom photo: Marjorie and her brother David visiting their parents' graves in 2011. *Photo by Patricia Skidmore.*

VISIT US AT
Dundurn.com | Definingcanada.ca | @dundurnpress | Facebook.com/dundurnpress

Dundurn	Gazelle Book Services Limited	Dundurn
3 Church Street, Suite 500	White Cross Mills	2250 Military Road
Toronto, Ontario, Canada	High Town, Lancaster, England	Tonawanda, NY
M5E 1M2	L41 4XS	U.S.A. 14150

This book is dedicated to my mother, Marjorie Skidmore (née Arnison), who let me believe that I was the driving force behind unlocking her story. I thank her for taking me back to her lost childhood. She always was — and still is — a much stronger woman than I can ever hope to be.

In 2007, sisters Joyce Earl and Marjorie Skidmore revisited the Whitley Bay sands of their childhood days. This was their first return to their place of birth since being removed from their mother's care in February 1937, over seventy years earlier. The experience allowed for some very curative memories to surface.

Table of Contents

Foreword

This is an important book telling a life-changing story, and its publication is long overdue.

When, in February 2010, I made a formal full and unconditional apology to the victims of the child migrant program on behalf of the U.K. government, it was with the story of Marjorie right at the forefront of my thoughts.

It was right that we said sorry to Marjorie and all those truly let down. Sorry — as I said then — that she and so many others were allowed to be sent away at the time when they were most vulnerable, sorry that instead of caring for her and thousands more, this country turned its head and their tears were not seen and their cries for help not heeded. Sorry also that it has taken so long for the day of atonement to come, and for the full and unconditional apology that is justly deserved to be given.

In addition I am delighted that Marjorie was able to be reunited with her brother as a result of the family restoration fund we set up with a £6 million grant.

I am humbled by the determination of Marjorie and all former child migrants to have the failures of the past acknowledged, I'm inspired by her and their refusal to be victims, and I'm inspired also by the strength of her spirit. The actions we took in government cannot change the past but can go some way to easing even a small amount of the pain Marjorie and child migrants have endured for many decades.

I believe that *Marjorie, Too Afraid to Cry* will also play a role in helping share with the world an astonishing story of courage in the face of unthinkable hardship. Courage is the greatest quality of all, for on it everything else depends — and Marjorie has shown a courage that all should applaud.

Former British Prime Minister Gordon Brown

Preface

This is a story of my mother, Marjorie, who was one of the thousands upon thousands of children who were removed from their families, their communities, and their country to be placed in one of the British colonies to provide "white stock" and cheap labour for that colony.

As a child, it angered me when I asked my mother about her past and she would not tell me. The anger stemmed from fear, as I imagined the many horrid secrets that she was keeping from me about her past. I felt such a strong sense of not belonging that I told the other children in my school that I came from Mars. We had no past. There was nothing to root me to my birthplace. I did not understand why my mother was so vague about her family and why they all lived in England while we lived in Canada.

It took me many years to discover why my mother would not tell me about her childhood family — it was not because she was keeping a dark secret, but because she had lost her roots.

By 1937, Marjorie's family had been living in Whitley Bay, in northern England, since the early 1920s. Unemployment there was high, and Marjorie's father had left his family and the area to look for work. He did find employment around London but had not returned home for the past four years. From time to time he sent some money to his wife and their nine children, but it was rarely enough to sustain them.

In February 1937, with the permission of Marjorie's father, Marjorie, two sisters, and a brother were removed from their mother's care by one of Britain's many emigration societies, the Fairbridge Society. (Kingsley Fairbridge started the Society for the Furtherance of Child Migration to the

Colonies in 1909. It was soon shortened to the Child Emigration Society. In 1935 it was renamed the Fairbridge Farm Schools Incorporation, and by the early 1950s it was renamed again to the Fairbridge Society Incorporation. For the purposes of this book, the "Fairbridge Society" will be the main title used.) The society placed the four children in the Middlemore Emigration Home, over two hundred miles southwest of Whitley Bay, in Selly Oak, Birmingham. There they waited their turn to be tested to see if they were mentally and physically fit enough to be accepted for emigration to Canada.

Six months later, ten-year-old Marjorie and her eight-year-old brother were sent to the Prince of Wales Fairbridge Farm School on Vancouver Island, British Columbia. Marjorie recalled that when leaving Liverpool on the *Duchess of Atholl* she physically pulled an "imaginary cloak" of protection around her as the shoreline slipped away. For this ten-year-old, forgetting her past, her family, and England was the only survival tool she had to enable her to face her frightening and uncertain future. She and her brother were separated and continued to be so until they were well into adulthood. Two of her sisters were at the Middlemore Emigration Home and her beloved mother was in Whitley Bay with her other siblings. She had no one.

Their younger sister was sent out eleven months later, but the older sister, Joyce, was left behind at the home in Birmingham. She was deemed to be too old for the Fairbridge farm school scheme. She was only twelve, but her records incorrectly showed that she was thirteen.[1] Her loss was as great as her siblings'. They were simply gone one day, and she was not even allowed to say goodbye to them when they left for Canada. Joyce stayed at the home until she was sixteen, then was sent back to her family.

I started my research with a small handful of my mother's early memories, mostly from her childhood at Whitley Bay: she recalled swinging on an old rusty gate, yelling to her mother for a half penny. It was her tenth birthday. She eventually ran off across the alley to school without so much as a farthing. She also recalled playing on the sands at Whitley Bay, the Spanish City Fun Fair at the north end of the town and walking over to St. Mary's Lighthouse at low tide. I had a photograph of my mother (see top front cover and page 172), although it would take finding several other pieces of her journey before we recognized this as a photograph from the day she arrived at the Prince of Wales Fairbridge Farm School. She had vague memories of Canada House in London and of leaving Liverpool. The rest was locked away.

I was determined to unlock her hidden past. I contacted the Whitley Bay School District. They still had records from the 1930s, and I was not only able to discover which schools she attended, but also the dates she attended and the addresses she lived at while at each school. I tracked down the only home where they lived, across the alley from a school: a brownstone house on John Street. I stood and imagined her swinging on a rusty gate and running off to school. I walked the Whitley Bay sand and imagined her playing there as a child. I visited the lighthouse and the old fairgrounds. I walked the same streets that she did as a child.

When I felt that I had found what I could of her first ten years in Whitley Bay, I brought my mother back to the little seaside town of her birth in 2007 to share with her all that I had found. Her big sister Joyce came with us. Seventy years had passed since the sisters had seen Whitley Bay. They both said that they did not remember much, but I walked quietly behind them, with a notepad, as memory after memory poured out.

Together, we walked from the last flat they lived in with their family, on Whitley Road, to the train station — the very station the children left from in February 1937. We stood by the new gate at the John Street brownstone and imagined the squeaky, rusty old gate and ten-year-old Marjorie running across the lane to Cullercoats Primary School. It was torn down years ago, but standing there I felt I could see Marjorie running across the alley to the school. Marjorie and Joyce stood by the Rockcliffe School, the last school they attended in Whitley Bay, and memories of skipping school and running to play on the beach came back to them. We visited the other houses where the family had lived and the other schools the children attended.

A fuller picture of her childhood slowly emerged. Together we pieced her last few months at home with her mother, and then her journey from the Whitley Bay train station to Newcastle upon Tyne, down to Birmingham, and eventually to London, and finally up to Liverpool. The crossing of the Atlantic aboard the *Duchess of Atholl*, landing in Montreal and the train ride to Vancouver, the ferry to Nanaimo, and finally the last bus ride to Cowichan Station on Vancouver Island. These events all had dates attached to them now. We had a framework to work from, and with it details of her childhood and her journey to Canada emerged.

The pieces of the puzzle were coming together to portray a picture, each piece helping to unlock her painful past. But there was still one pain that needed addressing: the feeling of betrayal towards her mother that Marjorie had carried for seventy years. By the time Marjorie turned ten, she had not seen her father for almost four years, thus, removed from her mother's care, it was natural for her to blame only her mother for sending her away and not keeping her safe.

My grandmother managed to get to Canada for a brief visit with her "Canadian" children in 1969. It would be the only time after being sent away that Marjorie would see her. It was not a successful visit. Marjorie wanted answers and her mother could not give any. My grandmother returned to England, the bond with her daughter still as broken as ever.

During our visit to England we were able to visit my grandparent's grave. They are buried at the Greenwich Cemetery on Shooters Hill, Eltham, London. As Marjorie stood by the grave, she was able to tell her mother that she forgave her and that she finally realizes, after all these years, that it was not her mother who sent her away. Marjorie had been told so frequently by her English family members that it was to her mother's "eternal distress that she lost her children to Canada." To know that they both shared this "distress" at being parted helped Marjorie's healing and allowed her to forgive.

In February 2010, Marjorie received a call to be present at the formal apology that the then-British-prime-minister, Gordon Brown, was scheduled to give to all child emigrants sent from Britain to the colonies from 1619 to the 1970s. The 350-year history of child migration was finally being recognized for what it was for so many of the children — a shameful part of British history. Marjorie waited for seventy-three years to hear it. In her heart, she knew from the start that it was wrong to separate her from her family and send her to the colonies.

When the prime minister took Marjorie's hand during his very personal and individual apology to each of home children present, he looked directly at Marjorie and said to her, "I am truly sorry." I sensed that she fully believed that he was sorry for what happened to her and even appeared to be a little shocked at the whole phenomena of child migration. With that recognition and understanding, she was finally able to shed the last of her shame.

This is Marjorie's story. It is a story of a little girl who learned at a very young age that it would do no good to cry, no matter how frightened she was. The only person who could stop those tears was 6,000 miles away. When Marjorie was removed from her mother's care, they not only took her away from her family, her community, and her country, they took away the love of the most important person in her world — her mother. It is a story of loss and a story of discovery. It is a story of healing and of forgiveness.

This is also my story. As a little girl I struggled to accept my mother — this woman without a past. As a teenager I simply left. After my first son was born, I wondered how I could be a good mother if I couldn't be a good daughter. It took many years to find a way to walk together with my mother. I needed answers and it was not until I fully understood that she wasn't keeping anything from me, that we could truly communicate. She had lost her past. Together we went and found it.

What's in a Name?

Many of the British child migrants sent to Canada between 1833 and 1948 are known as "Home Children" or "British Home Children." Marjorie was one of the 329 children sent to the Prince of Wales Fairbridge Farm School, near Cowichan Station on Vancouver Island, British Columbia, between 1935 and 1948. This group — the only British child migrants sent directly to British Columbia, Canada — most often refer to themselves as "Child Migrants" or "Former Fairbridgians." Children sent to the Fairbridge farm schools in Australia and former Rhodesia have been called Child Migrants or Former Fairbridgians, but most frequently "Old Fairbridgians." The narratives have changed over the centuries, from ridding Britain of its "idle young people" (see chapter 13, note 1), to child rescue and Empire settlement. Stories of the kidnapping of children run throughout most of the history of child migration. Today, even though many migrants were happy to be sent to the colonies, there are numerous stories that centre on *loss*: loss of county, loss of records, loss of family and roots. Regardless of what the stories are or what these children are referred to as, they were all part of the British child migration movement, which went on for over 350 years — from 1618 to the mid 1970s.

One

BUTTERFLIES PREVAIL

Nervous. Pacing. Wandering abroad.
Wondering what? Wondering aloud ...
If there can be a resolution in this clime
For this loss carried over a lifetime?

WESTMINSTER PALACE, LONDON, ENGLAND, FEBRUARY 24, 2010

Emotions hung heavy, like late fall fruit dangling precariously in a forgotten orchard. Faces open, fearful, waiting; cheeks glistening with the ancient tears of pain held for years. For some, this pain was the only connection to their past.

Sixty-five or so men and women had been brought to London — back to their land of birth. They had waited a long time for this moment — their moment. Dressed in their town clothes, they mixed and mingled, nervously sharing bits of their stories. I, too, was there, having accompanied my mother to England.

"I was five, but my papers said I was three, and they changed my name. It made it hard to find my way back, you know." One woman offered me this bit of information.

"Yes, I can only imagine." I wanted to provide more, but what could I give? Besides, the woman had already moved away. It was an apology she was looking for, not my attention.

PHOTO BY PATRICIA SKIDMORE.

British Prime Minister Gordon Brown presenting a personal apology to the former child migrants brought to London for this occasion, on February 24, 2010.

"They sent me to Australia and my brother to Canada. That wasn't right you know, to split us up like that." The man wore his uneasiness like a shield. "I had no one," he muttered as he too walked away.

"I know. It happened too many times," I replied after him.

I walked by an elderly man, cradling a framed photograph, his face lined with a record of a life long-lived. "It's me mum," he told me, pushing back a tear. "It took me twenty years to find her, and I only saw her just the once before she passed. Just the once."

I found it difficult to know what to say. Others talked to me, but only in passing while they paced about. Wandering, waiting, wondering. Would they finally find what they were looking for? The room seemed crowded, but this group represented just a tiny portion of the whole number of children and families affected by Britain's 350-year policy of migrating children to the colonies. Even though I knew better, I still found it difficult to believe that, at fifty-nine, I was older than some.

I kept my eye on my mother. Marjorie looked regal in her burgundy brocade jacket. Patient. She had been waiting for seventy-three of her eighty-three years for this moment. Nervous, stomach full of butterflies.

Of this present group, it was just her and one other Canadian child migrant, along with three offspring and two spouses, invited to represent the more than 110,000 child migrants who had been shipped to Canada between 1833 and 1948.

The tone shifted and those in the room paused. I looked over as British Prime Minister Gordon Brown walked through the door.

FEBRUARY 9, 2010

I had arrived home in the evening to my partially packed house after a long, fruitless weekend of searching for a new home, to find an unexpected urgent message from Dave Lorente, the founder of Home Children Canada. "Can you come to the formal apology that the British prime minister, Gordon Brown, is giving to all British child migrants? It is just two weeks away. We need an answer tonight."

The apology was an important issue for me, but never in my wildest dreams had I imagined that I might actually be present for it. I knew the event was imminent, because it had been announced the previous fall that Britain would follow the lead of the Australian prime minister, Kevin Rudd. In November 2009, Rudd had given a formal apology for the wrongs experienced by all children, including the child migrants who found themselves in his country's care between the 1920s and the 1970s. I had been waiting for the date of Brown's apology to be announced, but Dave's call made it so that my mother and I were among the first to hear about it, since the event had not yet been formally publicized.

"Well, yes, I could go." I heard myself say without hesitation. I could drop my house search, my packing, and everything else, and go to London. I listened intently to the details, then recalled that my passport was due to expire. I cradled the phone on my shoulder and dug through my papers searching for it. Just as I thought, it would expire before our return date. My mind immediately started to make lists. First, forget everything and race to the passport office in the morning, then …

"Pat, are you listening? Can you bring a home child?" Dave's tone urged me to pay attention.

"A home child?" His question caught me off guard since I had always called my mother a "child migrant." It was the children sent to the provinces in eastern Canada who were most often referred to as home children. But child migrants and home children were really one and the same. I came to my senses. "My mother?"

"Your mother! She is still with us? Can she still travel?"

"Oh yes indeed!" I didn't know whether to laugh or cry.

"Absolutely perfect. The British High Commissioner here in Ottawa will be in contact with you in a day or two." I listened to another twenty minutes of details, all of which I really wanted to hear, but I also wanted to hang up and phone my mother before she went to bed.

"Why are you phoning so late?" Marjorie sounded cautious, perhaps afraid of bad news that prompts calls in the dead of night.

"You will never guess. We have been invited to go to London to hear the British prime minister's apology."

"London, England? You are pulling my leg."

"No, seriously, it is true. At least I think it is. It does seem a little unreal, doesn't it?"

"Well, I can't go. No. No, I just can't drop everything and go. I have too many commitments. When does this take place?"

"It is scheduled for the twenty-fourth, which is two weeks tomorrow. We would have to leave by the twenty-first to have time to settle in before the big day."

"No, I can't." Her voice determined.

"Well, can you at least think about it?" I begged, even though I found it difficult to be persuasive when I felt so uncertain myself.

"Yes, I will think about it. Goodnight."

An email flashed on my computer as I hung up. More details of the trip, making it seem very plausible. I forwarded the email to my mother. Ten minutes later the phone rang.

"Okay, I will go."

I had always hoped for some formal recognition for the thousands of child migrants or home children sent to Canada. It was a little-known part of Canadian history. At one point there were up to fifty sending agencies in Britain shipping children overseas. While the numbers most commonly used for child migrants sent to Canada's have varied widely from 80,000 to 100,000, Dave Lorente of Home Children Canada has pointed out that the Library and Archives Canada now has a list of 118,000 home children taken from ship lists that date back to 1865 at *www.collectionscanada. gc.ca/databases/home-children/index-e.html*. Many of the children had a difficult time accepting their new lives and all too often they found themselves in communities that did not fully accept them. A belief that the child migrants were of inferior blood led some of the new communities to not want these children to mingle with their own children. Home children were sent to Canada to work and then to find their own way once they were adults. It would not do to coddle them.

The farm school that my mother had been sent to was named the Prince of Wales Fairbridge Farm School. "Prince of Wales" was for the support the Fairbridge Society received from Edward, the Prince of Wales, and "Fairbridge," after Kingsley Fairbridge, a man who advocated for the migration of Britain's pauper children and for training them to become farmhands and domestic servants in the colonies. This farm school was established near Cowichan Station on Vancouver Island, British Columbia. The children were housed in cottages that held between twelve to fourteen children. Each cottage was headed by a cottage "mother," and the boys and girls were separated. Between 1935 and 1948 the farm school received 329 child migrants.

A number of these Canadian Fairbridgians claim that being sent to Canada was the very best of luck, however many of them do not hold that sentiment. As a daughter of a child migrant, and thus having experienced firsthand the effect it can have on families, I believe the system of migrating children to be fundamentally flawed. The family is the nucleus of our society, and it was precisely the family support system that was torn away from many of the children and replaced with something quite inferior.

Isobel Harvey, a B.C. child welfare worker in the 1940s, visited the farm school in 1944 and presented a nine-page report on the conditions she found at the Prince of Wales Fairbridge Farm School at that time. The cottages were, in Harvey's opinion, "planned on an outmoded plan which allows the cottage mother little opportunity to foster any feeling of home … most of the children appear in aprons designed by the school clothing head, one might imagine they were residents of an orphanage in the last century."[1]

Harvey's report was written almost two years after they sent Marjorie out to work as a domestic servant. It appeared that life at the farm school had not improved since her departure. For many of the children, the farm school cottage life did not provide a real place of belonging. The various cottages Marjorie was housed in and the numerous cottage mothers she was placed under were a poor substitute for her own family.

Letter from Malcolm Jackson, branch secretary, Fairbridge Farm School, June 11, 1940, to Marjorie's mother. Jackson claimed that Marjorie asked for her siblings to join them at the farm school. When Marjorie saw this letter in 2009, she vehemently stated that she would never have said anything like that.

I wondered what effect an apology would have on my mother. Marjorie and three of her siblings had been removed from their mother's care in early 1937. She strongly believed that removing her from her family and sending her to Canada as a child had not been the best thing for her or for her family. I tried to envision how it would be for my mother to actually be present when Gordon Brown gave his formal apology. Would it hold meaning for her? Would it speak to her "heart," the heart that was broken nearly seventy years ago? Would the spokesperson, the British prime minister, be able to speak for the heart of Britain? After all, Gordon Brown himself was in no way responsible for the years of child migration.

I was aware that I had persuaded my mother to make this journey and if she could not find any meaning in Brown's apology, then this trip could cause more damage and not bring her any resolution. It was not Brown who sent her away. Would his words be sufficient? Could his words touch her heart?

In the days leading up to our departure to London, I was asked numerous times: "What does this apology really mean? After all, it will only be a group of words uttered by a government spokesperson — it is nothing really concrete. It doesn't change anything. It is a waste of money, time, and words."

I never failed to reply, "If you are not the recipient, then how can you understand or begin to judge its merits or its effects on those who are directly receiving the apology?"

As for my mother, I truly wanted to believe that it could become a final resting place for her childhood grief, a time to replace any leftover stigma with a sense of pride, and a time to really see herself as the strong survivor that she was forced to become at such a young age. But there were no guarantees. I could just remain hopeful.

Others were stunned when I told them why Marjorie and I were going to London. Often they replied with something like this: "I consider myself well read and knowledgeable but I have never heard of child migration." I would explain that the story of child migration had not been properly documented, nor taught in history classes. Many child migrants felt such shame that they would not talk about the circumstances of their removal from England and their subsequent childhood experiences. Individual instances are tragic enough, but strung together over centuries, the stories becomes unpardonable.

FEBRUARY 21, 2010

Marjorie and I boarded the plane in Vancouver, British Columbia, in the early evening of Sunday, February 21, 2010. We would arrive in London mid-day on Monday, giving us time to recover from our jet lag before the Tuesday evening reception, hosted by the Child Migrants Trust. We should be well rested and ready for the big day on Wednesday. My eighty-three-year-old mother, Marjorie, was a trooper, but this would be a taxing journey for her, especially as there had been so little time to prepare.

I sat next to my mother, tingling with anticipation. I had warned her that I wanted to share the manuscript I had written about her journey as a child migrant with her during this journey: our journey. Uncertain as to where to start, I decided to wait until the plane was safely in the air before beginning.

A CLOAK OF SHAME

As the plane flew into the evening sky, I mulled about what this apology might mean to me. I was tired of feeling ashamed. As a young child, shame had buried itself into my very core before I was aware that such a thing was possible. For years I had been ashamed of my mother. She was ashamed of herself. We were nobody. We didn't belong. The shame was so heavy that, as a child, I felt it covering me, my head, my shoulders, even obscuring my vision. I felt it was probably passed on to me in the womb. Shame had grown to be such a part of me that I had a hard time telling where it ended and where I started. I had struggled with it most of my childhood and was certain I had "daughter of a child migrant" stamped across my forehead for all to see. I could not erase it. My mother's shame was my shame. Her rejection was my rejection.

I felt certain that Marjorie was hiding something from me. I hoped that it was for my own good. Up until I was a young adult, some part of me believed — the child in me perhaps — that if I tracked down where my mother came from, I'd discover that she was not my real mother and that I was someone else's daughter. My real mother would come for me one day and all would be made clear. I just needed to be patient. That was my childhood fantasy. Certain that there must been have been a mistake, I expected the truth to come out one day. My survival depended on it. How could I belong to this family? We had nothing in common. I needed roots and I found none. My mother was no role model for me. I blamed her for not teaching me how to hope, to trust, to reach for the stars. I felt cheated. No one came to rescue me. My mother failed me. I was afraid of my future.

Regrettably, my fear came out as anger, and the distance widened between my mother and me. Now I wanted her to know that my childhood anger stemmed from fear, fear of the empty past she presented to me, and not from a lack of love for her. My anger, rooted in fear, was blinding and isolating. They say the truth will set you free, but it is not an easy process.

I looked over at my mother's calm hazel eyes. She hated flying. It terrified her, yet you wouldn't know from looking at her. It had taken me forever to recognize her calmness as one of her strengths. It would not be true to say that nothing fazed her, but, when threatened or attacked, she usually stood her ground without needing to lash out. I think she knew that my love for her ran deep, even when I did not know it myself. Writing her story has brought us closer.

Realizing the difficulty I had chipping away at my own locked-up childhood helped me to gain a better understanding of why it was so complicated to pull out my mother's hidden past — her buried memories and her painful secrets of rejection. She had years of experience to harden her

PHOTO BY PATRICIA SKIDMORE.

The Whitley Bay sands with St. Mary's Lighthouse in the background. Memories of playing on the sands and walking over to the lighthouse never left Marjorie.

past behind her cloak, to lose them, to act as if they didn't exist. But it was her past, her childhood, that I wanted to know about. I wanted her to take my hand, to walk with me down that road, to show me, even at the risk of distressing her or finding the wrong things. I wanted to go back with her to revisit what it was like for her to be removed from her family and deported to Canada. I wanted to find the childhood that she had blacked out. I needed her to do this for me, with me, and I hoped that at the same time, she would find some healing as well.

Marjorie was born in Whitley Bay and lived there for the first ten years of her life. Whitley Bay is a seaside town on Britain's northeast coast, just east of Newcastle upon Tyne. I wanted to go there, as I needed to imagine my mother as a little girl. I wanted to see where she was born, where she lived, where she went to school, and where she played. The first time I saw Whitley Bay, I thought it was beautiful. It must have been a grand place to grow up. The sand is spectacular. It is a seaside playground, and a far cry from the picture of a desolate slum that many sending agents claimed they saved the children from.

My mother — *as a little girl* — that part of her had eluded me for so long. I needed to see her as a whole person, someone with a life and past beyond me, and not just as *my mother*. When I began to have a picture of the little girl, the teenager, the young woman, who took the new life that was forced on her and did the best she could with the hand that she was dealt, it changed everything for me.

I sat with my thoughts and hugged my manuscript. It had taken me my entire life to gain an understanding of my mother and her story. It was important not to make any more mistakes. I glanced over at her. Her tightly curled hair, not nearly grey enough for her eighty-three years, framed her face. I looked for the child in her. I was beginning to see my mother with patience for her life that I knew I could never attain. And, even more remarkable to me, was that she accepted me: the demanding child, the stormy teen, and then my angry rejection of her as I chose to head into adulthood without her. She waited while I travelled through my early twenties, finally finding my way back to her. She had always accepted me. Why had I not been able to do the same for her?

The bond I felt now seemed new, yet I realized it had been there all along, buried safely, but often unreachable. I had learned from the best. Bury what you cannot understand. She had given birth to me, yet I felt I was not of her. Her answers were not right for me, so I rejected her. I was content to leave it that way for a long time. Then, with children of my own, my perspective on motherhood and family changed. How could I be a mother if I did not know how to be a daughter? I knew that if I were unable to accept my mother fully, I would not get to know her, or myself, not in the deeper way I needed. And then it would be perpetuated, as my children wouldn't know me, not the whole me, which included my mother, their grandmother, with her child migration baggage unpacked and properly sorted.

My mother broke into my silent ramblings, "Can you start at the beginning?"

"The beginning?" I murmured.

"What did you say?" My mother's hand went to her ear.

"Do you have your hearing aid turned on?" I raised my voice, feeling annoyed. She had the hearing aid, but all too often she turned it down because the amplified noise bothered her. I hated repeating myself. I hated that she was showing signs of her age. I hated that I had lost so much time wrapped up in my own anger.

I watched as she fiddled with the remote control device for her hearing aid. She winced. "There — are you satisfied? It's on loud and clear."

What had it been like for my mother as a child? She was sent away permanently from her family, from her country, at such a young age and expected to be grateful for such an injustice. The numerous sending agencies responsible for migrating children gave little thought to the fact that they were taking those children away from their families, not just their mothers and fathers, but all of their relatives. Dr. Alfred Torrie, a British psychiatrist, argued that "a bad home is better than a good institution."[2] He thought that the evacuation of many thousands of children during the war years had shown some of the dangers of breaking up a family. The children he studied likely came from the wealthier families whose children were returned to them after the war. Nevertheless, it reinforces my belief of the importance of family for all classes. "Family" is not just a phenomenon set aside for the wealthy to enjoy.

I clung to my manuscript. I felt hesitant, shy even, to show my mother what I had written. I had carefully gathered the bits and pieces from her childhood in Whitley Bay and then little snippets from her six months at the Middlemore Emigration Home in Birmingham. I had reconstructed her journey from this home south to London, then up to Liverpool and over to Canada in September 1937. I gathered as much information as I could from her, from her brothers and sisters, from other former Fairbridgians, from school and government records, and from newspaper articles, in order to reconstruct what her journey to the Fairbridge farm school might have been like.

It was difficult to pull any memories out of her at first. It was as if her childhood was a black hole. When I was growing up, my frustrations stemmed from this blank area of our lives and that helped keep barrier between us. It took me ages to understand that my mother wasn't simply keeping things from me, but that she had effectively blocked out so much of her childhood that she couldn't find her way back there. It was as if our little family was starting from scratch. We had no past. Nothing to anchor us. This journey has helped me to deal with that. It is a coming to terms with things. It is an acceptance of my mother, and of me, instead of always wishing that it could be different. As a child, I longed to believe in a "switched at birth" story. As I grew older, my life and family did not seem to "fit" me. I wanted to wipe the slate clean and imagine any past but my own. Now I feel different, especially with a greater understanding of what my mother went through, what her childhood was like, and why she blocked so much of it out.

I wanted to tell her that I was proud to be her daughter, but the words were difficult to say. It has been a long journey, the countless hours in the bowels of the archives, the prying, digging, and uncovering information, piece-by-piece, transcribing interviews, writing numerous letters, searching on the internet, and emailing and writing to obscure places in England — always hoping for some response, some little piece of the puzzle. I often wonder what was driving me to figure it all out. And I know my mother has wondered that herself. I was aware of treading on territory that she had buried for a reason. However, I knew my mother was pleased about the newfound memories because, for the most part, they were good ones. Even the bad memories that I stirred up were easier to look at now, from this distance.

The turning point happened when I finally visited the Fairbridge farm school grounds near Cowichan Station in 1986. I had driven up and down Vancouver Island dozens of times, but it never occurred to me to take the road in to see where the school was located. I didn't realize that I had a picture in my mind of the place, an image leftover from my childhood, and when I stood on the former Fairbridge farm school property, I was speechless. The vision of the farm school that I had in my mind was simply that of a gravel pit. I carried that image for years. I never questioned it. I was surprised to see such a beautiful valley before me. I suddenly realized that it was not *where* my mother grew up that left this image with me, but it was *how* she grew up. Her loveless childhood, her lost family, her state of mind, and her feelings about being taken away and having to grow up in this institution.

Whenever she would talk about the Fairbridge School, all I took away was a stark image of a desolate and lonely place. It was still not easy for me to explain to her how scary the stories of her childhood were for me. One of the most valuable things about my research is that, by finding out about my mother's childhood, I have been allowed a parallel journey into my own. As I started to figure out who my mother was, what her childhood was like, what her mother was like and her brothers and sisters, I finally acquired a sense of family. I had found a place where I belonged. Suddenly, I had to have all the details about her. I needed to know exactly where she lived, what schools she went to, what streets she walked on, where she played. I needed to find out about the gate she recalled swinging on while she yelled out for a half penny on her tenth birthday. For me, all the magic of England is wrapped up in that one half penny.

"Are you telling me you wrote my story around a half penny?" My mother laughed when I told her.

"A half penny started it all, yes." I admitted.

"And I would have settled for a farthing, but I didn't even get that." The sparkle in her eyes told me it was okay to keep going.

I began to see who I was. I was no longer the daughter of a child migrant; I was a daughter of a child migrant with a family history. I saw what she had been through, and my shame of being her daughter turned to feeling a tremendous pride. She survived her ordeal. She came away from it intact. They did not break her. They didn't give her much education or feelings of self worth and they had deeply instilled in her that she was a British guttersnipe, but she kept going. And she kept her children going and she kept us together.

I was going to ask my mother to read my manuscript, her story, but I realized that I wanted to read it to her, with her. A sudden shyness almost overwhelmed me. I held my manuscript, hesitant to open it — to share it, even with this newfound friend of mine.

"I call this chapter 'Winifred's Children' and it starts while you were still living with your mother in Whitley Bay. I wished I got the chance to know my grandmother. I think she must have been a strong woman to pick up the pieces and carry on the way she did."

"I forgive her, you know, now that I realize that she didn't just throw us away. I still blame my dad, though, and the government and the Fairbridge Society. How could they send us away?" Mom asked, obviously not expecting a satisfactory answer.

"This is the story I am going to tell to your great-grandchildren. I want them to know what it was like for you. You are an important part of Canadian history. Your experience and the experiences of the child migrants should be in the school history books." I cleared my throat and prepared to present my findings.

A British half penny dated 1937, the year Marjorie left Whitley Bay and was sent to Canada.

PHOTO BY PATRICIA SKIDMORE.

Two

WINIFRED'S CHILDREN

Winifred's children
Screaming — they came
Into this world
One after the other
She loved them all

SEPTEMBER 21, 1936

"Mum, Mum, can I have a half penny? I want a half penny! I won't go to school until I get one!" Marjorie put one foot down and gave herself a push. The screeching worsened with every swing of the gate. The back door to their brownstone house remained closed. Her mum peeked through the hole in the curtain. Marjorie persisted, her voice becoming hoarse.

It was no use. She would not get a half penny, not even today. What to do? Her school friends expected her to have money for her birthday. She pictured herself walking into the shop after school and picking out a tasty sweet. Her first choice would be a bag of lucky tatties[1] — just like the other kids bought. The taste of the powdered cinnamon sugar as it melted on your tongue was divine. Each one had a prize in it. What would her prize be?

A sudden gust grabbed her demands and sent them scuttling up the lane with the other bits of debris. The gate's old rusty hinges creaked once again as the school bell rang. Marjorie jumped off and ran across the lane to the schoolyard. She thought of going to the beach instead of

Marjorie is standing in front of the John Street brownstone house in Whitley Bay in 2007. The Cullercoats School that Marjorie attended in 1936, now demolished, was across the alley from the house.

PHOTO BY PATRICIA SKIDMORE.

to her classroom, but she had on her new birthday dress. A new dress was something to show off. With a quickened step, she headed for the girls' entrance.

The second bell rang out. Oh no! She should be sitting in her desk. Marjorie tore across the rest of the deserted yard, running like the wind. Seagulls circled overhead, playing in the incessant breeze. Their raucous cries seemed to mock her: "Late again! Late again!"

Why should she care if she was late today? It was her tenth birthday — double digits! She stopped to smooth the dress her mum gave her that morning. It was wrapped up and sitting by her feet when she awoke. It had a pocket that would be perfect to keep a half penny safe until after school. Sadness came over her when she realized that she would not be able to show everyone the treasure in her pocket. Her friends might ask to see her money. What can she say — that she lost it? No, she would say she already spent it. Yes, yes, that would be better. She would say how the tasty sweets melted in her mouth. That was why she was late this morning. Yes! She went to the shop before school.

———————————

Winifred Arnison sighed as she watched her daughter cross the school-yard. The fall term was still new at the Cullercoats Primary School. Her children were finally settling in. Moving so often was not easy for them, and moving schools only added to their distress. And it distressed her because she didn't know how to explain to them why she was not able to provide them with any security. And now she would have to tell the children that they would be moving yet again. She would try her best to stay in this school district, but she knew she could not promise anything. They all needed some stability in their lives, but there had been no word from her husband for a long while.

———————————

Marjorie grabbed at the old brass door handle with two hands as she skidded up to the girl's entrance at the school. She swung it open and flew in. There were other times when she snuck into her desk after the bell and avoided punishment. Would today be a lucky day too? She dashed down the hallway. Almost safe. Then, yelling out in surprise, she found herself flying head-first down onto the freshly polished floor. Her teacher was about to close the door when the noise in the hallway caught her attention. Marjorie grinned up at her.

"Marjorie! Get up. You are late again! Go to your desk!" The teacher was not impressed. But, really, she thought, what was the use? There was no one to encourage the children in this family to come to school. What can you expect? Many families were in the same boat. It is not the children's fault. In these troubled times many of the men had left the area to look for work elsewhere. The council had informed the school that Marjorie's father had deserted this family. Maybe they were better off without him.

She wanted to help these families. Their children were so thin and they had a hungry look about them. She watched Marjorie slip her slight frame into the desk. There was a pleased manner about the girl today. Was it because she avoided the strap? The girl had on a different dress, but her feet were bare and her straight dark hair could use a good brushing.

As Marjorie's teacher, she had taken it upon herself to contact the local attendance officer during the first week of the fall term — something had

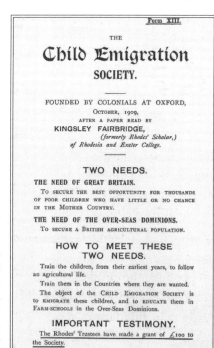

The front cover of a six-page Child Emigration Society (Fairbridge Society) pamphlet, dated December 1912, which appears to be among the first appeals for money made by the Society. The need "To Safeguard the Empire" is stressed throughout. According to the pamphlet, Britain's poor and orphaned children are the little soldiers for the job.

Form XIII.

THE

Child Emigration

SOCIETY.

FOUNDED BY COLONIALS AT OXFORD,
OCTOBER, 1909,
AFTER A PAPER READ BY
KINGSLEY FAIRBRIDGE,
(formerly Rhodes' Scholar,)
of Rhodesia and Exeter College.

TWO NEEDS.
THE NEED OF GREAT BRITAIN.
TO SECURE THE BEST OPPORTUNITY FOR THOUSANDS OF POOR CHILDREN WHO HAVE LITTLE OR NO CHANCE IN THE MOTHER COUNTRY.

THE NEED OF THE OVER-SEAS DOMINIONS.
TO SECURE A BRITISH AGRICULTURAL POPULATION.

HOW TO MEET THESE TWO NEEDS.
Train the children, from their earliest years, to follow an agricultural life.
Train them in the Countries where they are wanted.
The object of the CHILD EMIGRATION SOCIETY is to EMIGRATE these children, and to EDUCATE them in FARM-SCHOOLS in the Over-Seas Dominions.

IMPORTANT TESTIMONY.
The Rhodes' Trustees have made a grant of £100 to the Society.

to be done — but not a word had come back to her yet. She wondered whether it would be appropriate to approach him again. The pamphlets sent to the school by the outfit called the Fairbridge Society[2] intrigued her. Their emigration scheme was very compelling. With the backing of the Royal Family, it had to be a sound program. The Fairbridge Society was one of the many sending agencies emigrating England's poor children overseas to a better life in the colonies, and the Tyneside area was a good place to gather up children. The high rate of unemployment in the area had taken its toll on many families. Imagine the luck for these children — the opportunity to begin a new life in the colonies, away from their poverty-stricken parents and their bad habits. The Fairbridge farm school scheme was a good one, too. It would give the boys a good education in basic farming and teach the girls all they would need to know about domestic duties.

She had attended the meeting held in Newcastle last September,[3] and believed them when they said that Britain's big cities were overpopulated, but Whitley Bay certainly was not. However, it rang true when the society's representatives talked about the devastation of the high unemployment for the area. They argued that Empire migration was the only solution to this unemployment crisis. The Fairbridge Society brochures showed photographs of the already emigrated children living happily in their new countries. Once she saw the pictures, she was certain that it was the right thing to do. She was satisfied that without this type of scheme, some of these Tyneside children would never find a chance to break free from their backgrounds and get out of the slums. Since the Fairbridge Society could accept only those children of good mental and physical standing, they requested the help of the teachers because of their unique position of being able to identify the brighter children of the poor and bring them to the attention of the local council authorities.

Looking down at Marjorie, she felt sure that the children in this family would do just fine if they could get one or two square meals a day and a proper routine. The family moved too often, which simply was not good for the children. When she spoke to the attendance officer, she had assured him that there was nothing wrong with the minds of the children in this family. And, with a good diet and a healthy environment, such as the colonies could offer them, she was certain they would simply flourish. She heard that the families rarely gave up their children on their own — at least, not without a lot of encouragement. Really, she thought, it was the right thing to do. It was her duty to report these children. It did seem like a drastic step though, removing children not only from their families, but from their communities and their country as well. Still, she hoped that she had done the right thing.

Marjorie's bare feet convinced her. It *was* the right thing. Winter was coming fast, and barefoot children had a harder time getting to school. She turned to the class and said, "Children, if you have any extra wellies at home, can you please bring them in?"

Marjorie's cheeks flushed and she felt everyone looked at her, and then at her big sister. It was the first time that she noticed Joyce in the back of the classroom. She tried to hide her feet. Audrey and Kenny were in the infant classes and she expected they would all be teased about their bare feet at recess. It never occurred to Marjorie, however, that her family was not the only one with bare feet or that many of the children with shoes had cardboard placed carefully to cover the worn-out soles.

All too soon, the bell rang to signal the end of recess. Marjorie and Joyce looked at each other. They dropped the skip rope and instead of running to the classroom, they tore down John Street, past their house, hoping their mother wouldn't see them, and made a beeline to the beach to spend the rest of the day. It was Marjorie's birthday and they needed to celebrate it properly.

FEBRUARY 2, 1937

Marjorie hung around the school after her detention. She did not feel like going home just yet. She sat on the brick fence and tossed her schoolbook on the ground, still hopping mad because the teacher refused to believe that her mum threw away her homework. Well, she tried. That story often worked at her last school, and that was another thing that she did not like about this new school. Her teacher made her stay after school and finish her work. Her Cullercoats teacher had never made her finish her work. She looked up at her new school. Rockcliffe School was quite a large brick building. It looked so solid and strong. Her mother had told them all to come straight home after school, but she was already late from her detention so she didn't worry about dawdling now.

A group of older girls pranced out of the girls' entrance and stopped to play jump rope. They were the smart girls who never got into any trouble and they were the teacher's favourites. Their proper shoes and socks and their neatly plaited hair, tied with pretty ribbons, caused a bad feeling to surface in Marjorie's stomach. Sometimes she hated her family for being so poor.

She remembered their leaving the John Street brownstone house; her family snuck out in the middle of the night. They went out by the side garden, and in the quiet of the night its squeaky gate seemed loud enough to wake the entire neighbourhood. Marjorie, roused from her sleep by a sudden noise, heard her mum tell her big sister Phyllis to hurry and get the younger ones dressed.

"What are we doing? What is going on?" She heard her sister whisper.

Her mum's voice was low. "The landlord is coming in the morning to kick us out if we don't have the rent money and I don't have the money, so I am going to save him the trouble. Now, will you please help me?"

That move brought them to this Rockcliffe School, but they missed days and days of school. Marjorie had crossed her fingers and imagined really hard that they could stay at their Cullercoats School or even go back to their Whitley Park School, but it wasn't to be. Her mum had left them all with different neighbours and friends while she looked for somewhere else to live. She finally found a place on Victoria Avenue, but it meant changing schools. Marjorie didn't care too much by then, as she hated having to be away from her mum and all that was important was that they were all back together again. She told her mum to never leave her again.

Rockcliffe School looked the same in 2010 as it did when Marjorie attended in 1936–37.

PHOTO BY PATRICIA SKIDMORE.

The children had been at the Rockcliffe School since the beginning of November, and, just after Christmas, they had to move again, this time to Whitley Road. Marjorie wanted to stay at their house on Victoria Avenue. It was easy to skip school from there. They would just walk down Victoria Avenue to the promenade and then, instead of turning right and going on to their school, they would run down the path to the beach. She and Joyce or Kenny and whoever else skipped school with them would stay on the beach the entire day. Playing down on the beach was so much nicer than sitting in school. No matter what they played at, they would always keep their eyes open for lost money and other pickings.

Marjorie was happiest at the beach. Sometimes they would walk all the way to St. Mary's Lighthouse and if they found a low tide, they would walk over to the island and explore around the lighthouse. Her big brother Norman went over one day, and he forgot to pay attention to the tides so he had to stay overnight until the tide was low again the next morning.

The beach was the best place in the world. No matter where they moved to in the area, Whitley Bay or Cullercoats or Monkseaton, they always stayed close to the beach. Sometimes they would build sandcastles, and at other times they played pirates. They would climb on the cliffs, even though their mother said they would get a whipping for even thinking of going near the cliffs. Kenny slipped once and tumbled down almost to the bottom. Terrified, Marjorie had scrambled down to get him. What if he was dead? By the time she reached him, blood covered his face. She dragged him home, watching his face, and hoping that he would not die. When they got to the door, her mother had a fit. Kenny wailed when he heard his mother's voice.

"What happened here? Where were you two?" she yelled at Marjorie. "Why aren't you in school?"

"We were up on the cliffs at the sands and Kenny slipped," Marjorie blurted, even though she was afraid of a whipping. Her mother grabbed a cloth. She wiped the blood away from his face. Marjorie could see that it was just a large scrape above his forehead. None of his brain stuck out. He would probably live.

Her mother was more sad than mad. She scolded them for climbing on the cliffs and warned them again to stay away from that part of the beach because of the danger. She asked them what would they do if the tide was in and he fell in the water and drowned. Marjorie and Kenny did not have an answer. They just shrugged their shoulders. She gave Kenny a clean rag to hold on his cut and when it stopped bleeding she told them to go outside and play, as it was too late to go back to school. She told Marjorie to take the two little ones and look after them and reminded them to be careful, since they could not afford the doctor.

Marjorie and her sister Joyce are standing by 106 Whitley Road. The upstairs flat, located above the brick wall, is where Marjorie was living in February 1937. From there, it was just a quick run down to the beach.

That had happened at their Victoria Avenue house. Or, was it at the Victoria Terrace house? Their many moves made it difficult to remember which house was which. She liked the Victoria Avenue house because it was much bigger than the flat they lived in now. They didn't have much furniture to put in it but that gave them lots of room to play. Her mum pawned most of their things just so they could get by.

It was cold at their old Victoria Avenue house though, especially when the winter wind blew off the ocean. The inside of their house never seemed much warmer than the outside. They had to plug money in the gas meter to keep warm, but they rarely had any coins. Once when the meter man came by to collect the money, Marjorie heard him mutter that they must have found a way to get the gas heater to work without money. She wanted to tell him that he was wrong, that they just put all their clothes on and tried to keep warm by running through the rooms playing tag or hide and seek. The worst part though, was when they had to go to the outhouse in the back corner of the yard, especially when the wind was blowing and it was teeming with rain.

The main room of their new flat, above the butcher's shop on Whitley Road, was warmer because the front of the building faced away from the ocean. There were good things about living here. Sometimes the butcher gave their mum some bones for soups and a couple of times there were bits of meat left on the bones. Whitley Road was a busy road and there were always exciting things happening along it. The best part was they did not have to change schools with this move. Now they lived closer to Rockcliffe School, and it was easier to get to school on time.

"Hey!"

Marjorie jumped down from the fence. The fancy girls were walking towards her.

"Why are you just sitting there? Are you staring at us? What are you looking at?" The biggest girl glared down at Marjorie.

Before Marjorie could answer, a pretty girl, her long plaits swinging from side to side, sneered at her, "Ooh, let's get out of here, my mom said her brothers are in jail. We don't want to talk to her!" She made a horrible face, turned up her nose, and walked away. The other two tossed their ribbon-clad heads and followed her.

Marjorie stared after them. "They are not! They are at a different school. It's not fair. You are horrible!" She hissed at the girls and quickly ran off.

The clouds flying overhead caught her attention. They blotted out the light and made the sky black. They were so low that she felt she could reach up and touch them. The ever-present gulls swooped and played in the wind. They seemed to be touching the clouds. Oh, she would love to fly like the birds. The gulls never seemed to mind the weather, except when it really blew. Even then, Marjorie thought they seemed to enjoy visiting with each other all lined up along the rooftops or when they huddled together in their nests along the rock wall by the promenade or hobnobbing down on the shoreline.

The beach was the best when it was windy. Marjorie could sit all day in the shelter of the rocks or up on the lower promenade by the paddling pool if the tide was high and watch the huge waves as they came crashing in on the beach. She liked to watch the gulls while they hung around on the protected bits. Sometimes she would run and break up their little party. They would all fly up, but not very high and then they would settle down again a few feet away, screaming at her. She watched the way the young gulls followed their mothers squawking for food. It amused her that these big birds still expected their mothers to look after them.

"When I get bigger," she yelled up to them, "I will always be a helper. I will not cry after my mum to feed me all the time!"

The sky was darkening as she headed up Edwards Road. There was a chill in the air. When she arrived at her flat, she hesitated on the stoop for a bit. She had no desire to go upstairs. She wished her father sent her mum more money, but he never did, so she knew they would have very little for their tea today. She was hungry but there was no reason to hurry inside.

As she sat down, she grimaced. Her boots were already getting too small and she would have to pass them down to one of the younger ones very soon. She would probably have blisters after running from those rotten girls. Pulling her boot off, sure enough, the skin had rubbed off her left heel. She would not complain though, because it was too cold to go barefoot now. Dropping her boots beside her, she groaned and realized that in her hurry to get away from those girls, she forgot her schoolbook. She stood up to go back, but changed her mind and sat down again.

People hurried past her on the sidewalk. A tram rumbled by. She leaned against the door and watched. Her father popped into her mind. She tried to picture his face, but she could not remember what he looked like at all. She wished he would come home. Maybe they would not have to move so much if he stopped at home. She wished for the hundredth time that her big brothers, Norman and Fred, hadn't been sent away. She felt safer when they were at home. They were the family's protection. When their mother couldn't put food on the table, they could. They never let them down. And her mum was happier when Norman and Fred were at home. Her brothers were really good at finding ways of making money. Norman and Fred would sometimes sell firewood to people and also gather mushrooms and sell them at the local grocers. Norman also helped a farmer down at Dalton Fields. The farmer had several donkeys and, during the summer months, he would hire Norman to give donkey rides to the tourists down on the north end of the Whitley Bay sands. Even her sister Joyce helped with the donkeys.

Her brothers had been doing other things too. Marjorie had secretly followed them a few times and she saw them pinch beer bottles behind the local pubs, and then walk boldly through the front door of another pub and dump the bottles down on the floor as if they had carried them all the way from home. She wanted to help too, but they told her, "Nah, girls can't help with this." Sometimes she got so frustrated about that. She wanted to make her mum happy too.

Norman and Fred spent a lot of time at the Spanish City fun grounds near the north end of town. Marjorie often looked for them before she went to the beach to play, but her brothers usually headed straight for the gaming machines. Marjorie wondered how they found the money to play. Once, when she and Kenny were on their way down to the beach to pick winkles for their supper, she saw Norman standing nervously by the gaming section. She sent Kenny on ahead and told him to get started. She promised that she would catch up with him in a minute as she handed him her pail and told him to scoot.

Marjorie snuck up on Norman. "Boo!" She hollered as she grabbed onto his back. He did not even flinch. He calmly asked her to get lost. He refused to talk to her, so she threatened to tell her mum about how he nips the bottles.

Norman turned to his sister and warned her that if she told, she was really going to get it. He made her cross her heart and spit and told her that he was serious. He warned her that if she told anyone that he would lock her under the cupboard again and Jack the Ripper would get her this time for sure. The memory made Marjorie wince. Fred and Norman were minding her and Kenny one day when they suggested playing hide and seek. The kitchen cupboard was the best hiding place. Marjorie and Kenny both got to the cupboard at the same moment and scampered inside, closing the door behind them. When the latch slipped across, they knew they had been tricked. Kenny started to kick at the door, but Norman's threat of Jack the Ripper stopped him, and they both remained still until their mother returned and let them out. Marjorie shuddered at the memory and agreed not to say anything. She crossed her heart and spit.

Norman shook his head and called his little sister a pest. He looked around, and lowered his voice. He told her that there was a little hut in the centre of the gaming section. He stopped, his eyes darting around.

"I know that," Marjorie said, thinking he was going to try to get out of telling her.

"Gor blimey. Will you quit yer yammering and just listen!" He said that a man sits in the hut and if people want a shilling's worth of coins to play the machines that is where they have to go. The man changes your money for tokens and they work in the slot machines. He told her that he has seen rich people take a pound worth of tokens at one time. Norman paused, anxiously looking behind him. He told her that Fred saw that this man heads out for lunch at the same time every day and he comes back at the same time. Fred found out how to get in there and he fills his pockets with tokens.

Marjorie's eyes grew wide and she sucked in her breath. "Really? For true?"

"Don't look so gobsmacked, Marjorie. We're only doing what we can." Norman gave her a little push.

Marjorie's stunned face suddenly beamed with the pride that she felt for her two big brothers. They were so brave and clever. Norman told her that he was the lookout for Fred and that he makes a whistling sound if he sees any trouble. He told her that they only use the tokens and never bet with any of their winnings. That was the way they could sometimes bring home as much as five shillings or maybe even more.

Marjorie asked if they kept any for themselves and Norman looked crossly at her and told her that wouldn't be right. He assured her that they bring it all to their mum. He told her she could stay and watch, but she better not get in the way, or let Fred know she was here. She stood in the shadows watching her brothers go round to the machines and play with the nipped tokens. She jumped and had to cover her mouth to stop her excitement from coming out when they won and the money clanked down. They both carefully slid the coins into their pockets. Those were the best nights. They would all head to the store and pick out some fresh bread, and sometimes they would even buy some meat and have money left over for treats and sweets.

Fred and Norman were leaving the gaming area, so she scampered off towards the beach. She noticed that Fred was wearing her favourite Sunbeam[4] tunic as a shirt again. She had told him a hundred times not to wear her tunic. But it was hard to stay mad at Fred. She looked up to both her big brothers and would do anything for them.

She thought about her Sunbeam meetings. They always sang the Sunbeam song together. Sometimes she could remember all of it. As she skipped along she tried:

> See the Sunbeams march along
> Listen to our Rally Song.
> Every girl of eight or nine
> Come with us and learn to shine

Marjorie tried to remember the rest of the song but gave up when she noticed Kenny playing in the shallows, totally engrossed in making a large sand castle. His pail was filled with sand, and her pail was empty, lying on its side. She yelled at him and told him that it was getting late and they'd better hurry and fill their pails with winkles or they were going to get into trouble and have nothing for their tea.

Kenny reluctantly dumped the sand out of his pail and slowly walked to the water's edge to give it a wash so the winkles wouldn't be sandy. Marjorie called him to follow as she ran down the beach towards the rockier parts where she knew the winkles liked to hang on. As she picked, she noticed a small corner of something sticking out of the sand just below the surface of the water. She quickly grabbed it. It was a half penny from 1926, the year she was born. What a lucky day! She would give it to her mother, then she could be a helper too. She quickly tucked it safely into her pocket.

"Come with us and learn to shine," she sang happily while she filled her pail. As the winkles plunked in the bottom of her pail Marjorie thought about the dinner they would have that night. She loved to sit around the pot of cooked winkles, digging out the meaty parts with a pin. They were best with some butter, but it had been a long time since they had butter. But with Norman and Fred's winnings and her half penny they just might have some that night.

The Fairbridge Society wrote "This is a consent" across the letter received from Thomas Frederick Arnison, Marjorie's father, thus sealing her fate.

Marjorie leaned back against the door on the stoop. She rubbed absently at her blistered heel. Her feet were getting cold. Oh, the feast they had for tea that day, she could almost taste it. Their pails were filled to the brim with winkles. Norman and Fred waltzed in with some bread and butter and some chocolate. Her tummy growled in remembrance. Maybe she should run down to the beach now to look for winkles. No, it was too late as it would be dark soon.

An odd noise from their flat distracted her, but she tried to ignore it. It kept getting in the way of her remembering the better times. It was the same feeling she had when she woke out of a nice dream and tried to go back to it, but couldn't because whatever woke her up was too noisy and demanding.

Numbly, Winifred clutched the letter. She watched one of the men as he questioned Joyce, while the other, a medical examiner, she was told, took Kenny aside. She thought of her two older sons. Where had she gone wrong? They were good sons. They really helped out with the family. But when Fred got caught stealing they sent him away to Borstal.[5] *He doesn't belong in a boy's detention home*, she thought. Her son was only trying to help her. She had argued with the man who took him away, but to no avail. The officer left her with a bad taste and a sense that she, too, was "bad" for depending on her older children. But all the families hereabouts did the same, especially the ones who had lost their husbands — through death, or desertion, or like her husband, who left to look for work elsewhere. Really, it wasn't their fault that there was no work here. It was difficult to survive. They couldn't just sit by and starve.

Deep down, though, Winifred blamed herself for not stopping her sons. She knew she encouraged the two of them by taking the money they brought home. She never asked where it came from. She did not ask and they did not tell. It was their silent agreement. What else could she do? Without their help she would have given up long ago. There was no steady work for her boys. They had to do whatever they could. There was no way she was able to feed her nine children, keep clothes on their backs, and put a roof over their heads with the little money her husband sent home. The daily shame was hateful. She had to lie about the number of children she had before a landlord would even consider renting to her.

The last move had been the hardest. She was at a breaking point. It was just after Christmas — what had happened to the charitable Christmas spirit? No one would rent to her. She was desperate and so swore to the owner of this flat that she only had three children. She recalled one other time that she had to send Fred, Norman, Phyllis, Joyce, and Marjorie away, with strict instructions to wait until after dark before sneaking back to their new home. She could always count on Fred and Norman to take care of the younger ones in those times. It was harder to expect the girls to do things like that. It was a sad day when they took her older boys away.

Winifred could not imagine what that was like for Fred. Norman was sent away shortly after Fred. Norman was sent to a farm school. It was better than being put in Borstal. They took him down to Castle Howard,[6] near York. That was not too far away, maybe only about a hundred miles, but it might as well be at the other end of the earth. She knew that she would never be able to find the money to visit him.

Norman sent a letter home right away saying that Castle Howard was like a huge beautiful palace. Imagine, they gave him all new clothes and boots — nice new working clothes and a new suit for Sundays. He wrote that he was enjoying learning about farming. She had a difficult time believing him though since Norman was always trying to make everybody happy. She could tell that he missed his family, and she missed both her boys, more than anyone would ever know.

Winifred's worst fears had come true, and a shudder went through her when she thought of how she had lied to the landlord about having only three children. Was this God's way of punishing her? Could her lies have anything to do with making it come true? How could this be happening? Losing six of her children in just under a fortnight. It wasn't fair. She simply could not make ends meet with Fred and Norman gone. It pained her to see her children's hungry faces, their bare feet and their ragged clothes. Something had to be done, but what could she do? Nothing. Not by herself at any rate. She needed help, but they were offering her the wrong kind of help. Maybe her children would be better off, but it did not seem right.

"Okay, Audrey, come over here, it's your turn." The man's voice showed his impatience as he turned to Winifred, "Where is your other daughter? Marjorie, isn't it?"

Winifred sighed, "Yes. She should be along any minute."

"Well, for your sake, she better be," he snapped at her, flaunting his authority. "I told you to have them all here! The medical examiner has taken out time from his busy schedule."

Winifred's voice cracked as she assured this nasty man that she told her children to come straight home after school. She turned and asked Joyce to run along and see if she could find her sister. Joyce started to get up, but stopped when she heard the door. Winifred looked down and saw Marjorie standing at the bottom of the stairs.

———————————————

Marjorie had been sitting on the stoop, unaware of what was going on in her flat. Something was different about this day, though. It was hard to place at first and then she realized — it was too quiet. Lawrence and Jean were usually playing noisily, running up and down the stairs to the flat, shrieking with laughter, happy that school was out and everyone was coming home. Kenny often played on the sidewalk or in the back alley with some of the neighbourhood boys. But no one was around today. She turned the door handle, expecting the little ones to charge down to greet her; instead, as she stepped over the sill, the sound of strange men's voices startled her.

Maybe it was her father! She could hardly remember the last time she saw him. It was years ago, she was probably only six or seven. A funny feeling erupted in her stomach and made her head spin a bit. Would she like her father? Would he like her? She could barely remember him. Would he recognize her? She did not recognize the strange voices. Maybe this was not her father. Maybe it was the landlord and they have to move again. She liked it here now and the possibility of changing schools again made her mad. As Marjorie closed the door and stepped inside, she thought of turning around and running away and hiding until the coast was clear. She could see her mum at the top of the stairs. Lawrence and Jean were clinging to her skirt. Her mum's face told her that something was terribly wrong. Marjorie reached for the door handle.

For adults, married or single, male or female—sixteen years of age or over—
and those under sixteen not accompanied by parents.

COMMONWEALTH OF AUSTRALIA
MIGRATION & SETTLEMENT OFFICE.

MEDICAL EXAMINATION.
Instructions to Medical Examiner.

In cases where the Medical Examiner is unable to describe the applicant as being in good health,
he should state under "REMARKS" the exact nature of the defect which he finds and whether it is of
a temporary or permanent nature. Any disablement received on Active Service or otherwise should also be
noted and commented on, and if a Pension is received the amount of it should be stated.

The presence of Pediculi or Nits should be noted. In the case of married women, if pregnant,
please note the fact in "Remarks" column, and state number of months.

CERTIFICATE.
Replies by Applicant to Questions.

NAME *ARNISON, MARJORIE.*
(Full Name in Block Capitals)

ADDRESS *106 WHITLEY ROAD, WHITLEY BAY.*

1. Have you ever had any serious illness or surgical operation? *No*
2. Have you or has any member of your family ever been in a Sanatorium or other institution or
   attended thereat for the treatment of Tuberculosis? *No*
3. Have you ever had Enuresis or any sign of disease of the Genito Urinary Organs? *No*
4. Have you or has any member of your family ever suffered from mental disease or epilepsy or been
   treated in an institution of any kind for these Diseases? *No*
5. Have you required medical attention during the last twelve months? *No*

Results of Medical Examination.

A. Heart *Normal*

B. Lungs *Normal*
   (Particularly Tuberculosis)

C. Nervous System and Mental Condition *Normal*

D. Intelligence *Bright*

E. Digestive Organs *Normal*

F. Genito Urinary Organs *Normal*

G. Sight {without glasses / with glasses (if worn) (Snellen's Type)}

H. Hearing *Good*

I. Physique *Small for her years*

J. Skin *Normal (nits in scalp)*

K. Number of vaccination scars and date of
   operation *4 — infancy*

L. Teeth *Satisfactory for her age*

REMARKS (include particulars of any departure from normal conditions not fully set out in answer to
above questions)

AGE *11 yrs* HEIGHT, in Boots *4' 1"* WEIGHT, Clothed *5 7 lbs*

Having read and made myself conversant with the instructions contained in Form KA, supplied
me, I certify that I have this day examined the above-named and am of opinion that *she*
is in good health and of sound constitution, and not suffering from any mental or bodily defect which
would unfit *her* for earning *her* own living as a *domestic*

Date *2-7-37* Signature and Qualifications

Address

I hereby certify that the information supplied by me to the Medical Examiner is correct in every
particular :—

Signature of applicant which must be made
in the presence of the Medical Referee. } *Marjorie arnison*

TO :—

THE DIRECTOR,
MIGRATION & SETTLEMENT OFFICE, AUSTRALIA HOUSE, STRAND, LONDON, W.C.2.
(FORM K.)

PLEASE TURN OVER.

Marjorie's Commonwealth emigration form. Note Marjorie's own signature on the bottom of
the sheet.

"Is that Marjorie?" The strange voice filtered down to her.

"Yes, it is," Winifred replied. "Marjorie, come up here will you?" Her mum's tone left no room for argument. Marjorie slowly climbed the stairs. The tension in the room was familiar yet it held something different.

"Marjorie, come over here." The speaker's gaze made her nervous. "I need to ask you some questions."

Marjorie slowly walked over towards the man, but stopped a few feet away from him and dropped her boots. Nervously, she demanded to know what he wanted. She looked around the room. Joyce and Phyllis were sitting on the mattress. Kenny was lying on his stomach on the floor, rolling a marble against the wall. Back and forth it went, over and over again. Audrey sat quietly in the corner on the orange box, hugging her ragdoll. She was talking to a second strange man. He had a black bag beside him. Lawrence and Jean quietly clung to their mum's skirt. For a brief moment, the only noise in the room was the sound of the marble.

"Well, come over here!" The man's voice made Marjorie jump, and she walked over to him. "Do you wear eye glasses?" he asked her.

"Well, you can see for yourself that I don't." Marjorie was having trouble understanding what he wanted.

"Marjorie!" her mum snapped. "You don't need to be rude. Just answer his questions."

"What is your school standing?" he continued. Marjorie noticed that he was writing her answers down on a long form.

She told him it was 4C and asked again why he was asking her these questions. Puzzled, Marjorie wondered if he going to make them move to another school. She shouldn't have yelled at those girls at her school. He looked at her and continued his questions. Marjorie bravely approached him and glanced at the long form in front of him.

She could see her name and birth date at the top of the page. She immediately told him that he had her birthday wrong. That it should be 1926, not 1925. She looked at her mum for reassurance, and told him that she was ten on her last birthday and that she would not be eleven until September.

Again, he did not answer her but kept on writing on the forms. Marjorie started to remind him that her birthdate needed fixing, but he told her to go over and see the doctor. When the doctor finished, he asked

Marjorie's Fairbridge farm school emigration form. Marjorie's mother was forced to "hereby hand over the child Marjorie" and thus had to give up her custody of her daughter.

Marjorie if she could sign her name. She told him that of course she could, she was not a little kid. He handed her a fancy fountain pen and urged her to do a good job and not to smudge the ink. The pen had little bands on it that looked like gold. She had never touched such a beautiful pen before.

The doctor passed the four medical forms over to his associate, who then walked over to Winifred, shuffling his papers, "Just your signature now and I'll be gone. Can you sign your name?" He handed the papers over.

"Of course I can. I may be poor, but I am not stupid." Marjorie was alarmed by the change in her mother's face.

"Where?" Winifred's voice cracked as she blindly looked at the pages.

"Here, and on the bottom of all four — in the same place." He grabbed up each paper as she finished. He told her that was all he needed for now. He bid them all good day and warned Winifred to make certain that she put the children on the train on Monday morning. He told her that a sister would meet them under the main clock in Newcastle's Central Station. He tossed an envelope at her as he left the room.

He took the stairs two at a time. The doctor quickly followed. The children charged after them. Marjorie ran onto the sidewalk. She could see them walking quickly up Whitley Road, their heads together looking at the papers. Kenny flew out behind her trying to get a better look, but ran into a shopper and knocked her grocery bag out of her arms. Kenny said he was sorry as he bent down to help her, but she was angry and just yelled at him to watch where he was going. She told him to get away from her and that she would pick up her own things. She called him a "little heathen" and shooed him away and threatened to call the police. Kenny glared at her and said he was sorry again. People stopped and stared at the children. Marjorie asked them what they were looking at. She hated the look in their eyes. Well, she did not care today. She just wanted to get back inside.

Malcolm Jackson whistled as he looked through the Arnison applications. It had been a good day. He was lucky to get the medical examiner on such short notice. Now, he could write to Gordon Green at the Fairbridge Society's headquarters in London as soon as he got back to his office and tell him — mission accomplished — four more youngsters for Fairbridge. It was not a moment too soon, as far as he was concerned. He was happy that headquarters listened to his letter recommending they let him remove the children as quickly as possible. He smiled to himself. He liked rescuing the area from the children of Tyneside.

Three

Adrift

Take them away! Take them away!
Out of the gutter, the ooze and the slime,
Where little vermin paddle and crawl,
Till they grow and ripen into crime ...
Take them away o'er the rolling sea![1]

FEBRUARY 8, 1937

Early the following Monday, the four children watched the platform in dismay, their little faces plastered on the train window. The train chugged out of the Whitley Bay train station, taking them away and leaving their mum and their older sister, Phyllis, standing on the platform. Where were they going? Why did their mum send them away? Had they been bad? It frightened them to watch their mum wipe at the tears running down her cheeks. Marjorie's own tears were impossible to stop. She watched the two figures grow smaller and smaller until she could not see them anymore.

Would they be going to the same place as Norman and Fred? She would like to see them again. They would help. She hoped that her brothers were together. Some of the kids at school told her that Fred had gone to one jail and Norman to another. Maybe those kids were right. Maybe her brothers were in jail. Maybe they were going to jail too.

Marjorie turned to Joyce and asked if they sent kids to jail. Joyce looked alarmed and said no, she hoped not, her voice betraying her panic. She gave

Marjorie a warning look and told her not to be so daft. She assured her sister that they were not going to jail, then and nodded towards the two younger ones. Their eyes had begun to open wide with this new fear.

Marjorie rubbed her cheek, leaving a smudge of tears. She looked to Joyce for answers. "Well, smarty pants, where are we going then?" She challenged, but Joyce didn't know. They huddled together — clinging in fear and grief.

Audrey wiggled away first, pulling her doll out from under her coat. She held it close to her. Wiping at their tears, the children turned to look out the window again. Kenny pointed to the sheep in the fields. They had been told that Norman was sent to work on a farm. Kenny suggested that maybe they sent Norman to that farm. But no, Joyce knew he was sent much further away. The new sights distracted them, and, for the moment at least, they forgot their plight.

Two elderly women sat across the aisle from the children. Mary,[2] the stouter of the two, was keeping a close eye on the children. Her glasses were perched on the bottom of her nose and she looked over the top of them as

PHOTO BY PATRICIA SKIDMORE.

The entrance to Whitley Bay train station, shown as it looked in 2007, has altered little since 1937. During their visit, Marjorie and Joyce walked from 106 Whitley Road to the station and caught the train to Newcastle upon Tyne, just like they did in February 1937.

her knitting needles automatically clicked out "knit two, purl two." She put her knitting down and asked the children where their parents were and why were they travelling alone. The four children looked over but turned back to the window without answering.

Her companion, Dora, a thin, nervous woman, implored her to not talk to the tatty children. But Mary did not listen as she tried to find out their story. "Look at them," she told Dora, "the oldest cannot be more than nine or ten years old and the youngest bairn is just a wee whip of a thing." She could not for the life of her understand why they were on the train by themselves. She shook her head in disbelief.

Dora looked up from her knitting and suggested that the children were probably up to no good. She said to Mary, her voice high, "See what happens when you try to save a few bob! If we'd got first-class tickets like I wanted, we would not be sitting in this third-class coach. We will get nits from them for sure. Look at that one scratching at her head! Just ignore them, Mary, please. They probably do not have any tickets. The ticket man will take care of them." She shook her head, making no effort to keep her voice low or to hide the distaste she felt at being so close to the little group.

Mary would not let it go. She told Dora that the children did have tickets because she saw their mother hand them to the older girl. She tried to illicit some compassion from Dora, so she asked if she saw the fuss the little girl made. The older one had to clutch her and pull her onto the train. Tears were flowing from everyone. But Dora said she hadn't noticed anything. Mary continued, stating that she simply could not understand it. The girl on the platform looked positively heartbroken. "It was quite a commotion, I tell you, Dora. This world is coming to no good. Imagine sending little children off alone."

Paying no heed to her friend, Mary stared over at the group determined to find some answers. She asked the children again, a little louder this time, why they looked so sad and why they were travelling alone. However, the children turned away again and said nothing.

They found some safety in looking out the window, and kept their eyes glued to the view and watched their world whiz by. The trip to Newcastle did not take long and soon the buildings were closer and closer together. Audrey was the first to point out the huge church steeple.

Just before the train pulled into the station, Mary and Dora put away their knitting. Dora started to get up, but Mary grabbed her arm, nodded towards the children, and told her that she was going to wait to get off after the children because she wanted to see what they did when they got off the train. She wondered what they would do if there was no one to meet them. She couldn't bear to think of them stranded in the busy train station. Dora shook her head, and muttered that she could not understand why her friend concerned herself with things that were not her business. These children were not her responsibility, but she knew that once her friend had made up her mind to get involved there was no stopping her, so she sat back down.

Their train entered the enormous station and squealed to a stop. They heard the announcement — Newcastle Central Station. Joyce turned to her siblings and told them that they were to get off here. Joyce's voice had a new edge to it. Their mum had told them that someone would meet them on the platform beneath the big clock. She said that the clock would be easy to see. Joyce hesitated, then quickly stood up and told everyone to follow her. Marjorie dawdled, as if she did not want to leave the train but followed when Joyce yelled at her to come along. Besides, she did not want to be left alone.

The children stood for a moment and looked around. The busy station overwhelmed them. People were rushing everywhere. Trains roared in and out. For a moment, they were lost in the noise and excitement, then remembered that they had left their mum behind, and all at once panic spread through the little group. The three younger children looked at their big sister. Joyce, remembering her promise to her mum, tried to hide her own fear.

It was this fear in the children's eyes that affected Mary. As the train stopped, they looked so frightened and unsure of what to do. As Mary got up to follow, she noticed the grubby little doll lying under the seat. She gingerly picked it up on her way out. She stepped onto the platform, and called out to the children, holding up the doll. The littlest girl looked horror-stricken and ran back to grab her treasure.

Marjorie was the first to point out the big clock. Joyce directed the children towards it. As they stood there, Marjorie noticed the two women from the train watching them. They had black coats on. Hadn't they

PHOTO BY PATRICIA SKIDMORE.

Marjorie and her sister Joyce stand under one of the clocks in Newcastle Central Station in 2007. Retracing their 1937 journey from Whitley Bay to Newcastle upon Tyne brought back a flood of memories.

been told to look for someone dressed in black? For a moment, Marjorie thought that it might be nice to stay with them. They looked like her friend's grandmother and she liked the idea of having a grandmother.

Then someone shouted out, "Are you Winifred's children?" The sound stopped Marjorie in her tracks, her pondering shattered by the shrill voice. Mary had been about to approach the little group, when she heard them being called. She turned to her friend, shaking her head — perhaps these children were orphans after all. Maybe that was not their mother in Whitley Bay. Mary looked back at the children, at their pinched shoulders, saw the fear in their faces, and intuitively thought that something was just not right. She watched them timidly head over to the nun. They reminded her of animals at her old uncle's farm on their way to the slaughterhouse.

There was little about the woman with the long black robe to reassure the children. Her thin face didn't smile and the wart on her chin made them think of a witch. Their hearts sank when she told them that she had been sent to pick them up. She told them to call her "Sister" and ordered them to come along, stating that she didn't have all day. "Hurry up. Follow me and don't get lost." Her unfriendly greeting matched her unfriendly face.

The children crowded together and followed her out of the station. When Marjorie looked back, she could see the two women from the train walking away. She wanted to run after them. She should have talked to them on the train. She did not trust this unhappy sister.

The children struggled to keep up with their leader, but the busy sidewalks made it difficult. People pushed past and knocked into them. Lorries and trams raced close by, adding to their distress. Joyce grabbed tightly at Audrey and Kenny's arms while Marjorie clutched at the back of Joyce's coat and hung on.

The sister marched ahead unconcerned that the children were having problems keeping up with her. She turned to the little group and snarled a second time for them to hurry up. She called them "little guttersnipes" and told them that this country would be better off when the likes of them were all gone. Then she turned and walked even faster. The look in her eyes sent a cold trickle of fear running down Marjorie's back. What did she mean? What did they do to make her so angry? She turned to Joyce for answers, but Joyce snapped at her, and told her to hush up and just do as she says and to hurry up. Then she asked Marjorie to help her to remember the streets so that they could find their way back to the train station. "This is Neville Street," Joyce said under her breath.

Neville Street. Neville Street. Marjorie chanted it to herself. The sound of Joyce's voice worried her. It sounded just like her mum's voice last week when those horrid men yelled at her. Something told her that they would not be going back home. Ever. She was becoming more and more frightened. She wanted her mum.

Marjorie's tight ill-fitting boots cramped her toes and rubbed her heels, setting her old blisters on fire. Every hurried step was agony. She tried to remember the way in her mind. Neville Street, then Mosley. No there was another one too. She could not keep the names straight in her mind. She read the next street sign — Dean Street. Neville Street, Mosley, then Dean Street. Maybe if she remembers some, Joyce will remember the others.

They turned down a steep street. A train chugged noisily on the high arch bridge at the bottom of the hill. The group stopped at Number 35.[3] They did not stay long, thank goodness, because she saw one of those horrid men who came to their house last week. He smiled as if he was happy for everyone. Marjorie shook her head at how mixed up adults were at times. How could he tell them that they should be happy and grateful? Grateful for what? All she wanted was to go back home to her mum.

They soon found themselves being led out of a different part of the building and they could see the steeple of the church they passed on Mosley Street. Or was it the other street? Marjorie felt really turned around now, but she was certain it was the same church. She was trying to keep track, just in case but felt hopelessly lost. The children were taken to the far side of the building, away from the steeple, and led through a doorway into a long, dark hallway. Immediately, someone whisked Kenny away. He reached out and called for Joyce and she tried to run after him, but the woman in black pulled her back. The three sisters watched helplessly as Kenny's frightened face faded down the hallway and up a flight of stairs. The remainder of little group carried on down the opposite hall and through an archway.

The girls were escorted into a large room. There were several washing tubs along one wall. Large drains ran down the centre of the floor. Laundry, hanging on racks suspended from the low ceiling, dripped silently. Little rivulets made their way to the drains and disappeared. Even though there was a large wood boiler crackling away in one corner, the dampness of the room nipped at their bare legs and sent a chill through the children.

Sister said, "Okay girls, they are all yours. Clean them up."

Marjorie jumped when a voice shouted out at them to take their clothes off. The children stood still as three big girls walked towards them. For a brief second the sisters hoped for some friendship, as the girls appeared to be about Phyllis's age, but they soon found out that they were meaner than any schoolyard bullies they had ever encountered.

They slapped the frightened hostages and called them "filthy heathens," as they removed their clothing, tossing everything towards the boiler. Marjorie reached out for her dress. It was a present from her last birthday. But one of the girls slapped her again. She stood there stunned and shivering in the cold February morning. Audrey whimpered and reached out for her doll. Marjorie started to tell them how important that doll was to Audrey, but she stopped when she saw Joyce. She shook her head and mouthed "No."

Trembling with the cold and her anger, Marjorie looked to see if there was a way to scoot out and get Audrey's doll. They couldn't do this to them. What right had they to take their things? She stepped forward, but one of the girls abruptly stopped her. *Slam!* A hard metal thing landed on her head, knocking her off balance. Her shorn hair soon fell to the floor. It was the same for Joyce and Audrey. Marjorie wiggled, trying to get away, but the cutter snarled that she better keep still because if she got poked with the scissors, it would be her own darn fault. The girl cutting Joyce's hair yanked at a clump and told her to watch it or she would cut her ear off. Audrey stood still, too terrified to move.

All three "cleaners" laughed at the sisters as tears streamed down their cheeks. When it was over, their tormenters stood back to admire their handiwork. They praised their good work, and told the sisters that they now looked quite bonny.

Marjorie stared at her sisters' spiky short hair. She reached up to feel her own. Before she could, one of the bullies began to scrub her scalp with horrible smelling black soap. Some of it got into her eyes and it stung. She cried and wiggled trying to get free, but all she got for her effort was another slap and a mouthful of the vile stuff. Then, without warning, cold water rushed down her back. She sucked in her breath and tried to stop from crying out. They scrubbed her skin until it screamed.

Audrey sobbed loudly. Marjorie glanced at Joyce. Her miserable face frightened her. Why were they doing this to them? What had they done wrong? Joyce cried out and asked what they had done with their brother. But they told her it was none of her concern. But he was their concern, Marjorie sobbed to herself, he was their brother.

After a thorough scrubbing, the sisters stood shivering while combs ploughed through their hair. A chorus of "ow" echoed off the clammy walls. A slap on the head warned them to shut up. "We have to get all the nits and dickies out — afterall cleanliness is next to godliness. It is bad enough that we have to put up with you lot for a couple of days, but we don't want to catch the vermin you carried as well." Marjorie's comber sneered at her when she tried to get away again and gave an extra hard yank at what was left of her hair.

Quietly, the three sisters put on the clothes they were given. The rough material scratched at their raw skin. They wanted their own clothes back, but the girls laughed and asked if they were daft. "We've burnt them," they mocked, as they pointed to the boiler and said that they were not even good for rags. When Audrey cried for her doll, she was told that she was really a thick one. "Can you not hear properly? We burned that too." Audrey's wail brought shrieks of laughter.

The Arnison sisters spent the rest of the afternoon in the kitchen scrubbing dishes and peeling vegetables. Audrey started to say that she was tired and hungry, but cook stopped her, telling her that if she was hungry, then she better get used to working for her food. "Get your chores done first. You will be fed when it is time," she told her. Cook softened slightly when Audrey's tears slipped down her cheeks. But she quickly demanded the tears to be wiped away and assured Audrey that she was telling her this for her own good.

Joyce watched her little sister. Her odd haircut and her funny fitting clothes made her almost unrecognizable. She had always come to Audrey's rescue; it was second nature to her. She told the cook that Audrey was just little, that she had just turned seven. She offered to finish peeling Audrey's potatoes for her.

Cook would have none of it. She turned to Joyce, and told her that now she would have extra chores and maybe that will teach her not to coddle her little sister. Audrey needed to learn to fend for herself. She looked squarely at Audrey, then at Joyce, and warned that she will not be helping her little sister if she always did her work for her. "She needs to toughen up or she won't survive."

The sisters looked at each other. What was the cook saying? What did she mean? The fear in their eyes came spilling over. It had been growing steadily throughout the day. They had no one to turn to and no one seemed to care how they were feeling. Quietly they went back to their chores, sucking back their tears.

Marjorie fell into her cot that evening, numb and exhausted after the long day but unable to fall asleep. Audrey hiccupped as she sobbed. Joyce tried to comfort her. She was crying for her doll and could not seem to understand that it was gone for good. She kept asking Joyce to go look for it. Marjorie's own tears were flowing, but like her mum and now Joyce, she too was learning to keep them silent.

Marjorie thrashed about, trying to get comfortable in her unfamiliar bed, searching for a spot on her lumpy mattress not soaked with salty tears. Would she ever see her family or Whitley Bay again? It felt like she had been away for ages, not only since this morning when her mum and Phyllis put them on the train. It was impossible to make sense of everything. Where were they? Who were those strange men last week? They must have made their mum do this. They had seen her upset before, many, many times, but this was very different. Her mum was afraid. She had heard it in her voice.

As Marjorie lay in her cot, she thought about how she had run back upstairs that day, hoping her mum would tell her what those men wanted. All she got from her mum was a sharp retort making it clear that she did not want to talk about it. The sound of her voice stopped Marjorie in her tracks. Phyllis was standing behind her mum and she put up her hand and shook her head, as if to say "Don't say a word." Marjorie would have to wait until she got Phyllis or Joyce alone.

Marjorie finally got a chance after they had settled in their bed that night. But her sisters could not tell her very much. Joyce whispered that one of the men shouted at their mum and said that she had no choice but to sign the papers. Phyllis said he passed a letter to their mum. It was supposed to be from their father and he said it gave him permission to take the children. Joyce said that letter really made their mum cry. Phyllis asked to see the letter, but her mum said no. She told Marjorie that their mum just kept shaking her head and saying, "He was our last hope and now even that is gone."

Phyllis told them that when their mum wouldn't agree to sign the papers, it made the man really mad, and then he yelled and said she better do as she was told, or they would take away all of us, even the babies. Then he said that she was fortunate that the society wanted her children. He told her that we would be much better off anywhere but here.

What society? And why did it want children? Phyllis didn't know but she wished that she had closed the door and locked it and not let those horrid men into their flat. They all knew that their mum did the best she could.

Phyllis choked back tears as she admitted that she didn't know what to make of it all. She hoped they would get a post from their dad or that he would come back and now look what he did. Phyllis whispered, "You should have seen Mum's face when that nasty man said 'Look around you, woman! What kind of a place is this to bring up children? You don't have any furniture, you use old jars to drink out of, and the children are thin and hungry and dressed in rags.' Then in a mean voice, he said, 'This is no home, this is a disgrace!'"

The girls knew their mum struggled. But, this was *their* home. It was *their* family. They had each other. Their mum loved them. She would give them anything she could. They just did not have very much. They had seen their mum go hungry and give up her own food to the little ones. She always told them that one day their father would come home and then everything would be okay. Marjorie had waited and waited for that day.

Lying in this unfamiliar cot, away from the warmth of the big bed they always shared and miles from home, Marjorie realized that day would never come. She had waited for almost four years and now he had abandoned them again.

Now what? What was going to happen to them? No one told them anything. Not even their mum.

Marjorie tossed and turned, her new bed becoming more and more unfriendly. The events of the past few days reeled around in her head. She could not shut them out. She slammed her head into her mattress, but the picture of her mum, sitting on her old wooden orange box would not go away. Her mum had sat there all night last night. That morning Marjorie wanted to find some answers but she felt she dare not ask. Her mum's face told her that questions would be futile. They ate their morning porridge without a sound. Afterwards, no one seemed to know what to do. Joyce moved first and picked up the baby, hugging him so close that he squealed to be let down. Kenny and Jean moved away from the table and sat quietly in a corner. Phyllis was doing her best to help.

Their mum finally spoke. Her voice held a sadness that made it unfamiliar. She simply asked Phyllis to help her get them ready. Marjorie's head screamed, "Ready! Ready for what?" She wanted to know, but the words wouldn't come out. Joyce found her voice and asked what they were getting ready for. Phyllis whispered to her little sister that she had no idea. She said they were getting ready to go on a trip.

Marjorie shouted out, "Where? Who? We never go on trips." When no answered her, she let out a loud wail. Her mum interrupted her wailings and told her to run outside and ask someone on the street for the time.

"Go! Now!" she demanded when Marjorie stayed put. Marjorie wanted an explanation, but the unfamiliar tone in her mum's voice made her head towards the stairs. She leapt down taking two at a time, swung open the door, and ran onto the sidewalk. Whitley Road was strangely quiet, but she noticed a man entering a building a few doors down. She ran up to him and asked him for the time. She watched as he slowly reached into his trouser pocket and pulled out a watch. He told her it was almost eight o'clock and suggested that she should be running along to school. Thinking he might be a truant officer, she quickly turned and ran back without a thank you.

Marjorie pushed open the door and yelled up that it was about eight o'clock. Winifred gasped, and hurried everyone.

"We will miss the train," she told them. "Now let's go. Get your coats on. Out the door!" She turned to her four-and-a-half-year-old daughter, Jean, and told her to stay put and mind her little brother, Lawrence. "Do not go outside. Do you understand me?" she yelled back as she hurried the children down the stairs without waiting for an answer.

Jean had never been left in charge before. Proudly, she took Lawrence's hand, but a loud wail followed them before the door slammed shut. Jean yelled again asking them to come back, but Winifred was too intent on her other four children to even notice her cries.

Winifred leaned on Phyllis as she rushed the group along Whitley Road. The four children followed closely behind. Joyce held Audrey and

Kenny's hands. Marjorie lagged a little behind. She wanted to run off and go to school. She would be late. Her teacher probably wondered where she was. She could not remember ever wanting to go to school so badly before. The punishment for arriving late today and the strap for not going to school all last week would be worth it. A cross teacher would be easier to bear than walking any further into this unknown. But she followed when her mum turned up Station Road. The Whitley Bay train station was just ahead.

The train station — that was where it all started this morning, even though it was all set in motion last week. Everyone was so upset after the visit from those awful men. Nothing had been the same from that day on. At first, Marjorie thought it was odd that their mum did not make them go to school. She said that she wanted to spend more time with them. She told them that school could wait. Instead, they spent the afternoons down on the beach. Their mum seemed sad and distant, but the children busied themselves with exploring and running after seagulls and watching waves crash on the shore and they were able to forget the sadness for a while. That had been Winifred's hope.

No one had said a word on the walk to the station. It was pointless to demand answers. Nothing made any sense to Marjorie. She did not run off though, she had just followed along and walked past Clarence Crescent, Algernon Place, and all the familiar alleys, and walked right up to the train station and now here she was — lying in a cot in some strange and scary building.

Marjorie could not settle her mind. She looked over at Joyce and watched her get up and gently put Audrey back into her own cot. Audrey had finally fallen asleep. Marjorie called over in a choked whisper as Joyce climbed back into her bed. The look Joyce returned stopped her in mid-sentence. Joyce told her to hush, since she was afraid of waking up Audrey and of getting caught talking. Strict warnings had been given as to not make any noise after the lights were out.

Tossing with exhaustion, Marjorie wondered what would happen tomorrow. These people terrified her. They had not seen Kenny since they arrived. Where was he? Was he okay? She made up her mind that she would run away. She had no idea where she would go, but she would find Kenny and the four of them would run back and try to find the train station. She was certain she could remember the way. Neville Street, Neville Street played in her head. They should not ask for directions. It might seem suspicious. Maybe they would find the nice old woman at the train station. Maybe she would help them get back to Whitley Bay. This thought eased Marjorie's mind enough that she was finally able to drift off into a fitful sleep. In the middle of the night she yelled out for her mum.

Joyce rubbed her back as she told her it would be okay. "Wake up," she whispered, and assured her sister that she was just having a bad dream. Joyce climbed back into her cot and choked back a sob as she lay in the darkness, wishing it were just a nightmare and that they would all wake up in their own little flat. "Oh, Mum, I need you."

Four

WINIFRED'S SORROW

Where are my children?
I want them home!
Where are you taking them?
They must feel so alone.

FEBRUARY 8–9, 1937

Winifred felt the eyes of her children glued to her as the train pulled away. The brave face she worked so hard to keep fell to pieces once the door shut after them. When the train pulled away, it wrenched something deep inside of her and the tears followed fast and furiously. She did not want her children to see her like this. She had been holding herself together for days, fighting to curb the growing feeling of defeat. For the sake of her remaining three children, she had to find the strength to continue. If they took them away too, then there would be no point — no fight left in her. She tried to be brave so they could remember her that way. Lord knows, they would need to be brave.

Winifred watched the train disappear. In her heart of hearts she felt it was the last time she would ever see these four. It was bad enough when they took her older sons. No one told her the worst was yet to come. At least she had a chance of seeing her boys again. Fred and Norman were in the country somewhere, but these four would not be staying in England. She tried to find a way to explain to her little children what was going to happen to them. But it was beyond her understanding why her country would ship young children so far away. She had struggled over the past week for the right words, the right time, but when she started, she faltered. The words stuck in her throat. She was a coward, afraid of what her own failure would look like in their eyes. In the end, she thought it was best not to tell them, that way she could pretend it was just a nightmare, at least until they left.

Winifred stood on the platform and tried to see the purpose of everything. The horrid man told her that the children would stay in Newcastle for a day or two, and then they would send them to the Middlemore Emigration Home in Selly Oak on the outskirts of Birmingham. She wrote that down right away, not wanting to lose track of where they were. Birmingham was so far away. She would never be able to visit them. She wanted to smack that man when he told her that it was men like John Middlemore that made this country great. He told her Middlemore's first home for children had opened in 1872 and they had been emigrating children of the poor ever since. He told her that Middlemore Homes now worked closely with the Fairbridge Society and assured her that Kingsley Fairbridge's plan was sound. He opened a book and read from it:

> Every year tens of thousands of boys and girls seek admission to the labour market only to be told that there is no need of them, and they are flung back on to one or other of the great human scrap-heaps which lie at the gates of every one of our great cities — derelict little vessels on the Ocean of Life, children doomed to a blind alley existence and the squalor of the slums.[1]

He said her children would go "from these slums to sunshine." The man was daft. Obviously, he had never seen her children play in the sun down on the Whitley Bay sands — a site to gladden any mother's heart with its fresh air, sea breeze, sun, and sand. Her children had all the ingredients for a healthy life; she just needed a little more help from her husband. That damn letter — that was not the kind of help she needed.

Winifred could have strangled that wretched man too, when he told her, "Your children are being given a chance." His lip curled as he continued.

"Children like yours have no future here. The country has no need of all this flotsam and jetsam. It is the best thing for the children, your family, and the entire country. Do your duty, woman."

The Prince of Wales is featured in this Fairbridge Society appeal for funding, which appeared in the *The Times* on March 11, 1925. This funding was to provide "for intensive training of 200 happy little embryo Empire builders."

A Christmas Charities poster that appeared in *The Times*, December 14, 1931.

It is not our fault that we are poor, she thought, her frustration growing by the moment. There are no jobs. Maybe they would have a better chance; there was little work around here for their men, let alone their children. That was her only hope, that he might be right. Will they keep their promise and send her information on where she can write to them? Would the Fairbridge Society send her children to Canada or to Australia?[2]

He had spat out that this was a chance of a lifetime for her children and it was selfish of her to think only of herself.[3] He had the authority to take the children anyway, with or without her say, because her husband had given his written consent. She felt bullied and pushed around by that man. Cornered. How can she forgive her husband for deserting her now — to leave her alone and penniless with their nine children and then a simple letter from him takes away years of her hard work and struggle? She only hoped that one day her children would be able to forgive her and understand that she ran out of options. How could she let them know that she never wanted to let them go? She would do her best to get her babies back. But how could she get them back if they were in Australia or Canada? She prayed for them to stay together. If they had each other they might not be so afraid.

It was with misgiving that she took Joyce aside just before they left the flat and told her that it was up to her now to look after the little ones. Did she do the right thing? Her urgency, her tone of voice, had frightened Joyce, she could see it in her eyes. Joyce would have to grow up quickly now.

Phyllis gently took her mum's arm and pulled her back across the platform through the station building and down Station Road. Winifred's eyes glanced down the tracks one last time before she followed her daughter. She leaned heavily on Phyllis. Their wet cheeks glistened in the February morning sun as they plodded down Whitley Road and opened the door to their flat. Side by side, they trudged up the stairs. Jean and Lawrence's red eyes stared from the far corner of the room. Lawrence jumped up and ran to his mum. Jean did not move. "Where are they? What have you done with them?" She cried out from her corner, but the sharp look from her mum hushed her.

Phyllis tossed and turned that first night. She missed the comfort and the warmth of her younger siblings. Were they okay? She tried to imagine where they could be, and what they were doing but simply could not. Her mum had said very little ever since they stood together, watching the train pull out of the station. She felt shame when she remembered that for a second she was jealous. For ages she had wanted to get out of Whitley Bay and momentarily was envious of her younger sisters and brother.

HIS friends have gone; will YOU help him to join them? It costs £30 — a Christmas gift that lasts a lifetime!

This appeal is made through the generosity of a friend to extend the work of the Society.

THE FAIRBRIDGE SOCIETY

President :
H.R.H. THE DUKE OF GLOUCESTER, K.G., K.T., K.P.

Director : W. R. Vaughan, O.B.E.

38 Holland Villas Road, Kensington, London, W.14.   Tel : Park 6822

One of many Fairbridge farm school appeal posters. This one appeared in newspapers such as *The Times* and the *Illustrated London News* from 1954–55.

Phyllis glanced over at her mum sitting on the orange box, staring off into space. Phyllis thought of getting up and trying to get her to bed, but the look on her face made her change her mind. She looked lost, worn out, but mostly unreachable.

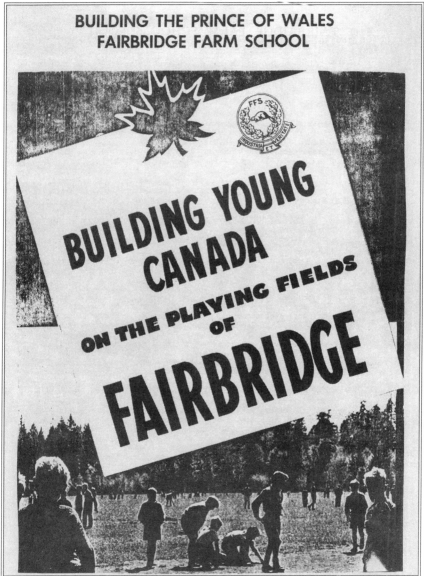

A poster for the Prince of Wales Fairbridge Farm School, reproduced from Fairbridge publicity materials. Perhaps this was meant as a reference to "The Battle of Waterloo was won on the playing-fields of Eton," as said by the Duke of Wellington, Arthur Wellesley.

Phyllis looked through the pamphlets that had been left. They claimed that the society was giving children the chance of a full and happy life in the British Commonwealth. Her brother and sisters would be trained in countries where they were wanted. Why didn't England want them? Why would they take little children from their families? Why would her country choose to send little children so far away? If they could find money to ship her brother and sisters off to another country and care for them there, why then, they should give that money to her mum so she could take better care of her children. At home, where they belonged! Children should not have to grow up away from their mother and their families. Phyllis could not understand the logic.

Her mum seemed so miserable that it scared Phyllis. She hoped that her father would stay away for good. It was his fault that they were in this situation. She had her sixteenth birthday a few weeks ago and would try to find a job and help. Maybe they could get enough money and bring the children back home. Phyllis closed her eyes and pictured her three sisters. She did not want to forget their faces; she was already having trouble remembering Fred and Norman. Then she thought of her little brother, Kenny. He was so young, and he would be so alone. At least the girls had each other. Would they forget about her? She wiped at her tears and tried to be quiet so as not to disturb her mum or wake up Jean or Lawrence, the two little ones snuggled closely beside her. Phyllis finally fell asleep, but it was a restless sleep.

Winifred sat on her orange box for the second night in a row. She felt drained. Her heart burdened her with its weight. It seemed like it could fall right out of her chest and crawl down Whitley Road after her children. It required too much effort to move. She hoped she was dreaming. Maybe she would wake up and she would find her little ones all tucked in, asleep, where they should be. Her tired mind convinced her that if she did not move, everything would be normal.

By dawn's early light, she was cold and stiff. She could plainly see that her four little ones were not there. They were gone. Gone. Where did they spend the night? Where will they be tonight and tomorrow, and all the other tomorrows? Sadly, she climbed in beside Phyllis. How could one body feel so drained, yet still carry the weight of so much sorrow. As she fell asleep, she wondered where the strength would come to cope with this latest loss.

Phyllis felt her coldness. It would take a long time for her mum to warm up. It would take forever to forget.

Five

MIDDLEMORE EMIGRATION HOME, BIRMINGHAM

Far-away
Nothing is familiar,
They hang on with woe.
If they saw their chance,
Where would they go?

FEBRUARY 10, 1937

The train picked up speed as it pulled out of Newcastle Central Station. As the children watched Newcastle disappear, they abandoned any shred of hope for finding their way home. Restlessness and worry became their constant companions. Fear kept them speechless. The train rolled down the track, taking them further and further away from their family and everything they had ever known.

They had barely left the station, but it felt to them that they had been travelling for an eternity. Birmingham was their destination, but where was that? The four of them sat together on a bench. Sister sat behind by herself where she could keep an eye on all without having to sit with them. This was an unpleasant task for her and she would be glad when it was over.

Kenny peered out the window, watching the world go by. The drizzle had steadily increased as they travelled south and now it was raining hard. The wind splattered the raindrops on the window. He watched the droplets gather and run in little muddy streams. Seeing past the dirt and the rain was difficult, so he decided to find a better seat. "C'mon," Kenny motioned to the others to follow.

Sister immediately reacted and told them to get back to their seats and stay there. She told them that they could not be running all over the train and if they didn't behave she will put every one of them off at the next station and they would be lost forever. Kenny quickly scrambled back. He pushed Marjorie out of the way, reclaiming his window seat. She was about to push back when Sister's face stopped her. The thought of standing on a strange platform and watching the train go on without her gave Marjorie such a fright that she quickly moved and gave the window seat back to Kenny.

The unfamiliar landscape sped by. Around noon, Sister passed the children some bread. The train's rhythmic motion lulled the children, and, having eaten, they curled up on the bench and one by one, fell asleep. As Marjorie slept, she dreamt of Whitley Bay and when this train blew its whistle, she dreamt that she was hearing the train coming into their Whitley Bay Station.

"We're almost at Birmingham New Station, wake up. We have to change here for the Selly Oak train," Sister said as she shook each child. Marjorie jumped when Sister touched her and nearly fell off her seat. She gasped, ready to bolt, but when she opened her eyes she realized where she was. The other three woke up, cranky from their uncomfortable sleep. Audrey cried out for her mum. Joyce tried to distract her by reading the sign as they pulled into the station. "Look Audrey, it says Birmingham New Station."

Audrey punched at Joyce and said, "I don't care. I hate everyone. I just want my mum. I want to go home."

Sister scolded both girls and said that good little girls did not talk like that. She looked at Audrey and told her that she could forget about going home and it would be best if she could forget about seeing her mother, as that would not happen. "The sooner you accept that, the better it will be for everyone." Sister ignored Audrey's wail and demanded that everyone stand up; it was time to get off the train.

The four children stumbled onto the platform, feeling overwhelmed and disoriented. This station seemed as busy as the streets of Newcastle. Sister shouted above the din for the children to follow her, proclaiming that if they got lost she would not waste her time looking for them. They quickly found the platform for the Selly Oak train and quietly climbed aboard when their train arrived. It seemed that they had barely been on the train when Sister said to get ready to get off. Their stop was the next one. They stood on the platform looking at Sister for instructions, but she turned from them and marched on, then, after a moment, stopped to see if they were following. The girls bumped into her. "Pay attention. Now, where is the boy?" She demanded.

A streak of panic went through Joyce. "Kenny!" She yelled out. "Kenny, where are you?" Looking after the younger ones and herself was proving to be a trying chore. She told Marjorie to hold Audrey's hand and to stay put while she ran back towards the tracks. Kenny was standing there, totally fascinated by the trains, not even aware that he was lost.

"Kenny, you gave me a scare!" Joyce grabbed him and told home to stay with her. She will leave you behind, she warned, but Kenny did not seem to care. He told her that he was just watching the trains. He pointed to one and said that he bet it was going to London.

Marjorie, waiting with Audrey, didn't like the looks of Birmingham. It was so far from Whitley Bay. She could find her way all around Whitley Bay, but in these past few days they had travelled so far and through such huge places she hardly knew which way to go. It would be impossible for the four of them to walk home now. In Newcastle, when they told the children that they were leaving for the Middlemore Emigration Home[1] in Birmingham, she had hidden some of her bread in her sleeve, but they found it and took it away. She thought she could use the bread

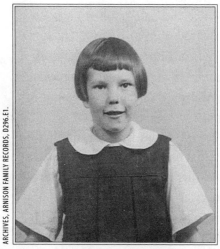

Marjorie Arnison is shown in a photograph taken at the Middlemore Emigration Home for the Fairbridge Society Files, circa summer 1937.

like Hansel and Gretel and find the way back to her mum, but it would be impossible after today's long train ride. She would need a thousand loaves of bread, maybe even a million. She had no idea that England was so big. The train had raced by town after town, field after field. It made her head dizzy.

Joyce ran back with Kenny in tow. Sister warned, "You there, hold onto the boy's hand and don't let go. Do you understand?" Joyce nodded as she grabbed his hand.

Marjorie took a long look at the station as they walked away. The sign said Selly Oak. It was the only way they would ever get back to Whitley Bay, but which train would they catch and where would they get the money for the tickets?

"Ow! You don't have to squeeze so hard," yelled Kenny. He wiggled as he tried to get free, but Joyce only held tighter. She was not taking any chances. Joyce snapped at Marjorie to grab Audrey's hand and warned her not to let go. Marjorie decided not to argue. The forlorn little group followed as fast as their feet would allow. They walked across a little bridge and carried on up the road. The cold February rain began to wick its way up their socks. Their shoes made little squishing noises as they marched along.

They crossed a busy street and continued up Bristol Road. Sister turned around to make sure she hadn't lost anyone. With a sigh of relief she saw all four trailing after her, so she told the children that it wouldn't be long now as they were almost at the home.

Excitedly, Audrey let go of Marjorie's hand and grabbed Joyce's coat. "She said we are going home, Joyce."

For a moment, that was what Joyce heard too, and then she remembered the nuns had said they were going to *the* home and she knew it was not *their* home. She had to tell Audrey that they were going to a different home, not home to their mum and their Whitley Bay home. Tears welled up in Audrey's eyes and were about to come spilling out when Sister noticed. She told Audrey that she had enough of her nonsense. She looked at the group and told them all that they must learn to be good little soldiers for the King, and warned the children that "brave little soldiers do not whine and cry." She needed to deliver the children to the home and have nothing stand in her way of catching the train and returning directly to Newcastle. She did not want to waste her time wiping their tears and she did not want to walk into the home with a group of blubbering children.

Marjorie glared at Sister. These last couple of days had been the worst days ever. She just wanted to know what was going to happen to them and when they would get to go home but she could not find her voice to ask. In Newcastle the nuns kept them busy with chores during the day, but the nighttime was different. She lay in her little cot on the second night, and the loneliness and coldness crept in that would not leave. Fear overtook sleepiness. If the nights scared her, she thought, then what was it like for Kenny? He was all alone.

They had not seen Kenny until they were ready to leave for the train that morning. He was so happy to see them, and choked back tears as he grabbed Joyce's hand. Marjorie noticed that he held on until they were on the train. When Joyce asked him where he had been and if he was okay, he just looked at them, his frightened eyes telling their own story.

They had lots to eat at Newcastle. Still, Marjorie wanted to go home. She wanted her mum. She would rather be hungry and be with her. Homesickness and fear were leaving little room for anything else inside.

Sister interrupted Marjorie's thoughts as she yelled for the children to come along and not dally. As they plodded up the road, above them the low thick clouds made the early afternoon an eerie darkness. The light drizzle was turning to slush, and then to snow. The cold crept in and threatened to create a mutiny among the children. Audrey sat down and refused to walk anymore. Joyce pleaded for her to get up, telling her that she was getting all wet. But Audrey would not budge. Joyce reached down, picked her little sister up, and tried to carry her, but she was too heavy. When, after a short distance, she put her down, Audrey just stood, stubbornly refusing to move. Joyce pulled at her, trying her best to get her sister to keep walking. Kenny piped up and told her that the bogeyman will get her, or maybe Jack the Ripper! His warning had the desired effect. Audrey squealed and looked behind her. She demanded that they stop teasing her, but she walked on, keeping close to Joyce, just in case.

They turned down a little lane. At the end was a tall church spire. As they approached the church, they veered off on a smaller path. Marjorie read the sign by the church fence: THE CHURCH OF ENGLAND, ST. MARY'S

PARISH CHURCH, SELLY OAK. Sister announced, with noticeable relief in her voice, "We are almost there."

The children peered through the falling snowflakes at what was to be their new home. Snow sticking to the ground around the grim grey building made the dreary scene look even more uninviting. It was so much bigger than their Rockcliffe School. Joyce whispered that it looked like a hospital. They walked along the side of the building to the main entrance and followed quietly into the building. Shaking the rain and snow from her coat, Sister whispered, "Now you four better be on your best behaviour, or else."

Marjorie hoped that Sister would leave right away. They were supposed to call her Sister but she was not their sister, and Marjorie did not even like her. It was easy to see that she did not like them either. She always yelled at them for no reason, and that made Marjorie nervous. It angered her that during lunch Sister kept all the soft inside parts of the bread and passed the hard, burnt crusts to them. Their mum would never do that. They shared everything and if there was not enough, their mum would divide her share too. But it was more than that. It was the little things. She missed her mum's smile and her warm eyes. Sister's eyes were icy-cold, just like the snowflakes.

PHOTO BY PATRICIA SKIDMORE.

Joyce, Audrey, and Marjorie returned to the Middlemore Emigration Home in Selly Oak, Birmingham, in August 2001, over sixty years after they had been placed there. The top floor of the wing on the left of the photograph was the girl's dormitory. The building was demolished circa 2005.

The group followed cautiously into the foyer. The hallway, which travelled the entire length of the building, bustled with children. Kenny, curious as ever, started to explore, but Sister grabbed him by the collar and pushed him ahead of her, motioning for the girls to come along. They stood on the threshold of a large office. A lamp lit the desk but cast eerie shadows over the rest of the room. As their eyes adjusted to the light, they were drawn to a rather large man sitting behind the desk. He did not look up but continued to write in his notebook. Smoke from his pipe disappeared into the darkness above his head.

Sister cleared her throat and excused herself, telling the man that she had the four children from the Fairbridge Dean Street office in Newcastle. As she handed him an envelope, he put his pen down and looked up at her and then at the envelope. Sister whispered, "You were expecting us, weren't you?" Her meek voice caused Marjorie to look up and stare at her.

Without a word, he took the envelope and pulled out its contents.

"Please, sir," the Sister implored, "everything is in order, I hope."

He puffed away on his pipe as he looked through the papers without answering her. At one point, he gazed up over his spectacles and stared long and hard at each child. His bushy furrowed eyebrows, along with the pipe smoke curling up past his nose, had Marjorie struggling to contain a fit of the giggles.

Sister hissed through her teeth for the children to stand up straight and to be polite. Marjorie choked back a giggle just in time. She concentrated on paying attention and tried not to move about, but it was not easy. Edgy nerves were hard to control. Looking at one spot sometimes helped, so in desperation she looked at the floor by her feet. Her shoes were leaking and her coat was leaving a circle of little droplets. The two puddles ran together and disappeared under the desk. She longed for her mum. The room was hot and stuffy. A strange feeling came over her, starting with a tingling in her scalp and snaked its way down to her toes. The room swayed. His voice intruded into Marjorie's world of worries when he announced that everything appeared to be in order and said to take them away now.

"Come along with me." The children had not noticed the woman in a white uniform somewhat like a nurse would wear standing behind them. When the children remained fast to their spots, she urged them to follow her. She chatted kindly to them suggesting that they must be tired after their long journey. She pointed to a rather large cupboard in the hallway, lined with rows of hooks and told them to hang their wet coats there. As they did so, they were told that, first, she would quickly show them around the home and then they could get out of their wet shoes and socks. She told them to call her Nurse and asked them for their names.

She had a nice voice, even if the girls had a hard time understanding exactly what she said. Joyce spoke first, "I'm Joyce, and this is Marjorie and Audrey. We're sisters and Kenny is our brother."

Nurse smiled and said, "Well, I'm pleased to meet you. Let's go this way." She started walking towards the centre of the building. When the girls looked back for Kenny, they saw Sister leaving the office and marching quickly towards the door. Marjorie said *good riddance* under her breath. Nurse turned and asked, "Pardon me?" but Marjorie stammered that it was nothing, she was just wondering about Kenny that was all.

"The boy's nurse will show him to his dorm. He'll be fine. You don't need to worry about him." The tears in Kenny's eyes moved down his cheeks as she escorted him away. The separation in Newcastle had terrified him, and now it was happening again. Joyce knew she would not be able to help him much, but she boldly questioned where they were taking their brother. Nurse assured the sisters that he would be looked after. She hurried the girls along, and told them that it would soon be teatime.

Marjorie commented on the number of children who were visible as they walked down the halls. She asked if they all lived here or were they getting ready to go home after school. Nurse told them that they had quite a large family at Middlemore and that all the children belonged at the home. She explained that they do not have their school classes here but go out to the local schools during the day. They climbed up the middle stairs and turned down a hallway. Nurse pointed out the dining hall where they should go for their tea when the bell rang. As they walked on into a warm steamy kitchen, Nurse said, "Cook, we have three new girls."

Over the stove stood a rather stout short woman, wearing an apron that was smudged across her middle. She stood on her tiptoes and steadied herself with one hand on the counter's edge while in the other hand she held a wooden spoon that seemed to disappear inside a rather large pot. Cook shouted a jolly greeting at the girls as she stirred.

"Agnes, Betty, and Margaret, these are the new girls — Joyce, Marjorie, and Audrey. I expect you to make sure they settle in and help them out if they need it." The three young kitchen helpers stopped cleaning up potato peelings to stare at the newcomers.

"Yes, ma'am," they assured her.

"Ello, Awdery." Agnes smiled.

Audrey looked at Agnes and said, "You all talk funny." Joyce thought Audrey was going to get into trouble again, but Cook had a lot of fun with that.

"Well, well, me dearie." She laughed, "I reckon you sound funny to us as well. It won't take long for you to understand us and for us to be able to understand you Geordies."[2] She explained that children come to the home from all over England so they were used to the new children's response to their Birmingham accents. She told the girls that they have had quite a few Geordies from the Tyneside area lately, so have had a bit of practice with their lot now.

Nurse whisked them from the kitchen and showed the girls the toilets and the bathroom. There were rows of towels, bathtubs, and sinks.

"Joyce, there's no privacy anywhere," Marjorie whispered.

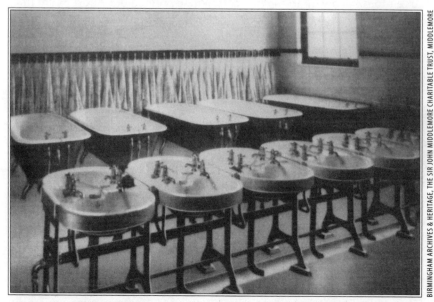

This image of the bathroom facilities, known as "Splash House," was published in the Middlemore Homes Annual Report, 1934.

BIRMINGHAM ARCHIVES & HERITAGE, THE SIR JOHN MIDDLEMORE CHARITABLE TRUST, MIDDLEMORE FONDS, MS 517/25.

This image of the girl's dormitory at the Middlemore Emigration Home was published in the Middlemore Homes Annual Report of 1934. Marjorie recalled the long rows of beds with their grey blankets.

The girl's dorm came next. The girls were shown to their beds in the large room filled with individual cots. Nurse pointed out Audrey's cot first. Audrey sat on it, delighted that it was softer than the one in Newcastle. Her face dropped though, when she saw Joyce's cot so far away from hers and then Marjorie's cot clear across the room. Audrey began to shake, but there was no time to worry. Nurse left the room and beckoned them to follow her to the room across the hall. Rows of little cupboard doors covered the wall at one end. Nurse said these were lockers where all the girls kept their clothing.

"Now, here is a locker for you, Audrey. Marjorie and Joyce you can have the lockers next to hers." Marjorie was about to say that they didn't bring anything to put in the locker, when Nurse unlocked another cupboard and inside the girls saw rows of clothes, all neatly folded — tunics, blouses, skirts, jumpers, socks, shoes, bloomers, coats, and pyjamas — everything a little girl would ever need. The sisters' eyes grew large, and they stood quietly and stared, not daring to hope that they would be getting some of these fine clothes. While Nurse was busy digging through the piles of clothes, Joyce whispered to her sisters asking them if they thought they might get to keep the clothes.

Nurse heard the girls but she did not answer right away. She was used to this reaction from the new children. They usually came to the home wearing threadbare hand-me-downs and were pleased when given a set of good clothes as well as a set of play clothes, even if they were already well worn and not brand new. Most of the children who went into the home were getting their first pair of shoes with the soles intact. In no time, the three sisters each stood with a pile of clothing bigger than they ever had before.

"These are for us? Just for us?" Audrey sighed.

"Yes, that's right," Nurse replied. "Now put your white blouse and tunic on as quickly as you can and come straight to the dining hall. The bell will ring shortly. Don't be late." With that, she was gone.

Their ill-fitting Newcastle jumpers and skirts were quickly tossed into a heap in the corner. Marjorie did not mind about losing her mum's dress anymore. She was so proud of her dress on her last birthday, but now she had something that was so much prettier.

Joyce whispered that the people seemed nicer than those at Newcastle. The sisters nodded in agreement. Marjorie whispered back, "But Audrey's right, they talk funny! I don't know what they're saying!" The three girls grinned as they put on their new socks and shoes.

Audrey smiled as she twirled around, "Don't I look nice?"

"You look very smart, Audrey," Joyce replied.

"How do I look?" Joyce turned around.

"Grand," giggled Marjorie.

Real shoes, Marjorie thought, not hand-me-down boots with the soles already so thin that they had to put cardboard in to keep their feet from sticking through. Now the kids at school could not make fun of them. She imagined walking into her classroom with her new clothes, but then she remembered where they were. Would they ever be going to school in Whitley Bay again? It was too frightening to think that they might never go back.

Joyce heard the bell first and hurried her sisters along. It was impossible not to find the dining hall — all they had to do was follow the throng of children. The three sisters stood at the doorway of the noisy hall and peered in. They could hear the clanging of cups and plates as children set the tables. Children were everywhere. They charged down the hallway, pushed past the newcomers, and scurried for a seat. Kenny was across the room with a group of boys. He was laughing. He looked smart in his new clothes. A nurse, noticing the newcomers, waved them in and found them a place at one of the tables.

That night, Marjorie, exhausted after her long day, crawled into her cot. Why were they separated at night? Joyce had asked the night nurse if they could put their cots closer together, but the answer was not much help.

"No, we have placed your cots apart for a reason. It is important that you all become self-reliant."

What did that mean? When Joyce said that Audrey just turned seven and she was afraid of the dark, the nurse told Joyce not to coddle her. That was the second time since leaving Whitley Bay she'd heard that word. Marjorie did not know what it meant, but she suspected that maybe she and Joyce should not look after their little sister. That was silly! That was what big sisters did. Marjorie started to say that it was not fair but was silenced by Nurse, who made it clear that it was bedtime and there was to be no more talking. With a firm "good night," the door closed.

Marjorie's frustration kept her from settling down. They had already separated them from their mum, and now they separated them from each other as well. And Kenny — where was he sleeping? He was all alone. Was it harder for him? She remembered seeing him at teatime but was not able to talk to him. He looked as though he was already making friends with the other boys. Maybe he was all right.

Marjorie wriggled onto her side. Propping up her head with her hand, she surveyed the room. Two long rows of little cots, all with the same grey blankets. She could hear Audrey crying. Her sobs grew louder as everyone settled down. A girl yelled out that she could not get to sleep with all the racket. Another muffled complaint found its way out from under someone's covers. A third voice yelled from across the room for them all to be quiet. The commotion brought Nurse. She was quickly told that it was the new girl.

"Audrey, we will have to put you in a room by yourself if you don't stop this nonsense. You are keeping the other girls awake. You must be quiet!" Nurse scolded.

Joyce sat up, and, attempting to rescue her little sister, said, "Ma'am, I think she's crying because she has a toothache." This explanation had worked at Newcastle. She did not want Audrey put in a room by herself, but there was no sympathy. Nurse warned Audrey again that there was to be no more noise.

As the dorm door shut, it took away the light from the hallway. Marjorie's eyes took a little while to adjust to the darkness. Across the room, she could make out Joyce's shadow as she silently snuck out of her bed and tiptoed towards Audrey's cot. Some of the other girls were whispering and pointing. Marjorie heard one of the girls say that she was going to tell.

"You better not! I'll whip you if you do!" Marjorie warned, surprising herself, but she knew she needed to stand her corner if she was going to survive in this place. She meant it. She would whip her.

The little girl in the cot next to Marjorie whispered, "Good for you. I'll help you. My name is Olive. I just got here today. How long have you been here?"

"Thanks. My name is Marjorie. I just got here today too."

"Hush all of you, or Nurse will come back." A voice whispered out of the darkness. Marjorie thought it sounded like one of the big girls from the kitchen. The whispering stopped, but all eyes were on Joyce as she crept across the dorm. She stopped at Audrey's cot and carefully scooped up her sobbing sister, who quieted down immediately as her arms went around her big sister's neck. Joyce carried her back to her own bed and they snuggled down together. Marjorie thought that it was too bad that those awful people in Newcastle had burnt Audrey's doll. She always slept with it at night. Adults did not seem to know what was important to kids.

Joyce was knackered, but fought away her sleepy feeling. They must not catch her with Audrey in her cot, but it was taking ages for Audrey to fall asleep. When her breathing finally became quiet, Joyce counted all the way to one hundred. Then she counted again, before she was really convinced that Audrey would stay asleep when she moved her back to her own cot.

Moving as quietly as she could, Joyce climbed out of bed and picked her up. She prayed that Audrey would not wake up crying again. She wondered why they had to put them so far away from each other. Audrey was afraid of being alone, and even though they said she would get used to it, it didn't seemed right.

When Joyce settled back into her cot, her thoughts jumped to Phyllis and Jean and she pictured them in their bed. They would have a lot of room now. It would not be so crowded, but it would not be as warm and cozy either. Then her thoughts jumped to Kenny. Joyce was afraid that it would be impossible to look after him, but maybe not as difficult as it had been in Newcastle.

As time went on, the girls learned to communicate with Kenny without talking. Their eyes met when they saw each other. Sometimes it was across the dining hall or when they passed each other walking to their day schools or when they walked down the pathway to the church. Marjorie thought that his eyes always looked a little sad. Nevertheless, before long, they began to fit into their new lives and they stopped complaining about what had happened to them — outwardly at least.

It didn't take long to learn that their complaints and questions would get them into trouble; it was better to keep quiet and hold on to their feelings. Their instincts, with the experience at Newcastle still frighteningly fresh in their minds, told them that it could get a lot worse. They tried to be good and not make any fuss, fearful of the possibility of being sent back to Newcastle.

Six

FADING MEMORIES

Spring had faded
Into the summer.
Memories were fading
Into the past.

SUMMER 1937

Days turned into weeks, then into months, and any plans for finding a way back home slipped into the background of Marjorie's new life. Her days had fallen into a busy routine with a rigid schedule and at times she hardly remembered how she arrived at the home. Whitley Bay was fading and so was her mum's face, but her love for her never lessened, even when her anger towards her grew so sharp she could taste it.

Marjorie snuggled into her cot. She was thankful that most everyone was nice to her at the home. She had quickly learned how to avoid the cranky matrons, and they were given lots of food to eat every day. She never had to worry about that at all. Memories of her mum would often come to her at mealtimes and she wished she could find a way to send some food to her. Her face used to light up with a beautiful smile when Norman and Fred brought home food or money. They would all dance around singing for joy and it would be just like a party. Maybe it would have been different if she had learned to bring home some money to her mum. Maybe then they would still be at home together. Marjorie treasured the idea of them all at home again and hung on to her wish with desperation. In her daydreams she was always helping, just like her big brothers.

Sometimes Marjorie worked with Joyce in the kitchen. Once she slipped a few potatoes and carrots into her pocket for her mum. What a treat! Her mum would be very happy and surprised! She might see what a good helper she was and bring her back home. Marjorie had planned to put them in the post, but when the nurse asked her why she wanted a little box, she had to say that she didn't need it anymore. They might punish her for stealing even though there were so many potatoes and carrots. Surely, they would not miss a few.

Washing the never-ending mountain of dishes and peeling the heaps and heaps of potatoes and carrots made Marjorie's hands ache. The best and freest place to be was down on the playing fields. She did not know how Joyce could stand working in the kitchen day after day. After the summer Marjorie would be eleven. She wondered if she would have to work all the time like Joyce, or go to the day school as she had before the summer break.

It was not so bad here, really. Audrey's giggles came from across the room. When they first got here, Audrey cried a lot and Joyce had to be brave and sneak Audrey into her cot every night to settle her down. One night Joyce fell asleep and when the night nurse found Audrey in Joyce's bed, she smacked Joyce, not Audrey, with a slipper, and it was Joyce who lost her Sunday sweets. Even so, for ages, her big sister risked the night nurse catching her rather than let Audrey get a whipping for crying. Night time was easier for Audrey now that she had settled in and made some friends.

Marjorie wiggled and punched at her pillow until it felt cozy. It was her one place to be alone. Funny, that in a room full of girls, she could still feel alone. At first the loneliness threatened to overwhelm her but now, once the light was off, the darkness surrounded her and she felt free. Thoughts of her mum snuck into her mind. She tried to quickly get them out because they always made her feel sad — and now it was not only sad but also scary because most of the time she could not remember what her mum looked like. If only she had a picture of her. If only her mum would come to visit them or even send a letter to them. She wished, oh she wished, not for so much, but for the one thing that the home would not give her, to be back with her mum.

In the back of her mind, Marjorie believed it when the older girls at the home said that no one would be going home — not ever. But she vowed that she would never give up hope. Some of the girls had visits from adults and one girl danced and skipped down the hall holding onto her mother's hand. She never came back. She must have gone home. Marjorie dreamed of doing the same thing. She would be so happy to see her mum that she would not even tell her how mad she was at her. She would just hug her and hug her.

Marjorie wrestled with her cover. She had to stop thinking about her mum. She tried to go back to thinking about some of the good things at Middlemore. There was a special Saturday that popped into her mind. It was her turn to mop the floor in the girl's dorm. She and her new best friend, Olive, were laughing and having a contest to see who could mop to the middle of the room first. She started at one side of the room and her friend at the other. That, of course, was not the special part. It was while they were racing towards the middle that Audrey pranced into the dorm.

"Marjorie! Marjorie! Look at me!" she yelled. Audrey was dressed in a new summer frock and had a wonderful panama hat on her head. "Don't I look smashing, Marjorie?" Audrey asked.

Immediately Marjorie asked her where she got the clothes. Marjorie and Joyce's job of keeping Audrey out of trouble had not lessened in the past few months. Marjorie grabbed her and told her to quickly get them off and put them back where she found them. But Audrey twirled around, her skirt swirling beautifully, and she laughed and told them that everyone gets a new outfit for summer. She told Marjorie that she could find her new outfit in the locker room and ran off to tell Joyce next. As she skipped away, they could hear her laughter as she disappeared down the hall.

Marjorie remembered how proud she had been of her new dress on her tenth birthday. She remembered swinging on the gate. She was so hopeful that she would get a half penny to buy sweets. Now she had sweets almost every Sunday. And the clothes were so nice — much better than they ever had. If they outgrew something, they got another, just like that. Now that summer was here, everyone had a new summer outfit. She would love to walk into her old classroom at Rockcliffe School now. They would be so jealous.

Her new school was not the best. Every weekday morning they would march out two by two all the way to the Ilmington Girl's School. It was a long walk, especially when the weather was bad. The best mornings were when Olive was her partner. The two girls talked about being life-long friends and that they would help each other find their families when they got away from

CITY OF BIRMINGHAM EDUCATION COMMITTEE

ILMINGTON ROAD SENIOR GIRLS' SCHOOL

Term ending _July 22nd 1937._

Name	Marjorie Annison.	Number in Class	36.
Age	11 yrs 10 mths.	Position in Class	19th
Class	I-D.	Times absent	1
		Times late	2.

Examination Results

Subject.	Maximum Marks.	Marks Obtained.	Remarks.
NGLISH :			
Reading	Fair		
Speech	Fair.		
Composition	100	36	
General (constructive)	100	62	
ARITHMETIC :			
Mental	100	70	
Written Rules	100	40	
Problems	100	48	
STORY			
GEOGRAPHY	100	55	
SCIENCE			
DOMESTIC SUBJECTS	Fairly good		
NEEDLEWORK	Poor.		
HANDWORK	Poor.		
MUSIC			
DRAWING	Poor.		
PHYSICAL TRAINING	Fair		

GENERAL REMARKS

I feel that Marjorie could do better. She is rather fussy and talkative. Her writing needs to improve now considerably.

P R Gray. _Class Mistress._

F Hawkins _Head Mistress._

A school report from Ilmington Road Girl's School, which Marjorie attended while at the Middlemore Emigration Home. Note the incorrect age at the top left side, which identified Marjorie as a year older than she was.

the home. It made the walk go faster and it was less lonely having a close friend especially when being teased by the other children at this school. Some of the children at the school would call the home kids bad names, but there were enough children from the home so they could take care of themselves. What frustrated Marjorie the most though, was that no one, including her teacher, would believe that she was just ten and not eleven.

"Your records show that you are eleven, almost twelve, so you belong in this group," her new teacher told her.

"But, ma'am, I'm not eleven! I am ten!" Marjorie stubbornly stated.

"Enough of this nonsense! Records do not lie but it appears to me that little girls do! To your desk please. Now!" Her teacher pointed to Marjorie's desk, clearly expecting this to be the end of the conversation.

"But I really am ten." Marjorie whispered under her breath as she walked to her desk. So much seemed unfair and confusing. Since they were living at the home, other kids treated them differently. A few times Marjorie overheard the girls in her class talking about having sleepovers and parties, but no one from the home was ever invited. She pretended not to care because she knew that children from the home would never be allowed to go even if they received an invitation.

Sundays were definitely the best days at the home in Marjorie's mind, even if they had to go to church three times that day. Their mum hadn't made them go to church in Whitley Bay because they didn't have any Sunday clothes and she told them that she felt too embarrassed to walk into church with barefoot children. But she was proud that she had her children baptized, most of them at St. Paul's in the heart of Whitley Bay. At the home they went to church first thing in the morning, then Sunday school in the afternoon, and then off to church again in the evening. It was a lot of church going for one day, however, they only had one chore for the whole day and that was to make their beds.

And Sundays were sweet days. Only the kids who had been really bad missed their sweets. After the morning service, they quickly changed to their play clothes, collected their treat, and ran out to the fields where they could play until the midday meal bell, and if the weather was nice they had free play again in the afternoon after church. Marjorie missed the beach though. Playing on the field was not the same as playing on the beach. She missed the sounds and the smell of the ocean.

A photograph of St. Mary's Church in Selly Oak taken in 2010 and the church with the three sisters, Joyce, Marjorie, and Audrey, in the doorway in 2001. This was the church they attended while at the Middlemore Emigration Home.

PHOTO BY PATRICIA SKIDMORE.

Marjorie tried to be good. Pulling her covers over her shoulders, she snuggled down and felt happier than she had in a long while. The home was okay for now, but she would never stop dreaming of finding her way back to her real home.

It was different for Joyce. She looked across the room, shouted goodnight to her younger sisters, and pulled her covers up. Like most of the older girls, she worked in the kitchen during the day and was used to it now, but when she watched the younger ones running out in the field she felt jealous. Joyce did not mind working in the kitchen instead of going to school, but working there now that it was summer break did not seem fair.

Joyce's thoughts turned to Kenny. She had watched the boys having a race in the afternoon. Kenny was one of the fastest runners and definitely the fastest for his age. She was happy to see Marjorie jumping up and down, cheering him on, and wished she could be out there with them. There were only a few times when the boys and girls could play together and the playing fields were the only place they could really talk to each other.

Joyce loved her kitchen window. It was her portal to a bigger world where she could look past the playing fields and watch the horse and the donkey grazing on the far side of the fenced-in field. There were fences even beyond where they kept the animals. Joyce thought it was to keep the kids from running away, but if they were really determined to go, they needed more than these fences. What stopped most of them from going was having nowhere to go once they got beyond the fence. As Joyce peeled vegetables she schemed of ways to get them all back to their mum.

Joyce's best friend had run away earlier in the summer. She wanted Joyce to go with her, but Joyce told her she had to stay because of her sisters and Kenny. Then her friend called her a chicken, a baby, and other names too, but Joyce stood her ground. As the girls readied for bed, Joyce noticed that her friend's cot was empty. She casually walked over and lumped up her pillow under the blankets to make it look like she was sleeping, just as she had promised to do. No one said a word as the girls walked past the empty cot. There would be trouble the next day. After the lights went out, one of the girls whispered to Joyce, "Where is she? Did she really run away?" Joyce was too afraid to answer, so she pretended to be asleep.

Cook was everyone's friend, but she made certain the chores were done on time. "Joyce! Stop yer daydreaming and get that peeler working. The meal will never be ready on time." That was Cook's favourite saying, and Joyce grinned to herself. Cook scolded everybody. She was nice though, and never really got mad at anyone.

Joyce could talk to Cook about most things. She asked her about the small groups of children who sometimes marched down the path, with a nurse or a master in the lead. She never saw any of the children return. She always got a funny answer. It was still hard to understand her accent. It sounded like she said Canada or Australia, but Joyce knew that was wrong. There were no places with those names in England. She had seen Canada and Australia on the huge wall map of the world in one of the schoolrooms and those places were clear around the world. The kids would not go there. Maybe they were getting to go home, but then they should have looked happier. The faces of some of these children reminded Joyce of her friend after they found her and brought her back — as if they were afraid about what was coming next.

Her friend had been back for a few days before Joyce had a chance to talk to her. "Where have you been? How far did you get? Why haven't you been in our dorm at night?" Joyce's questions came tumbling out. She admired her friend and wished she had some of her courage. Her friend's troubled eyes glanced at Joyce and she walked away. Later that day, when Joyce tried to talk to her again, all she got was an angry retort: "Stop pestering me! Leave me alone! I hate you all!" Her friend's words stunned her.

She pulled her covers up over her shoulders and closed her eyes. Would it have been any different if she had run away with her? Would they still be friends now? Friends were important here and losing one was hard.

The summer of 1937 moved along. The children in the home were kept busy with their daily chores. Marjorie looked forward to Sundays because of the little bit of freedom it afforded her, and she took the opportunity to go off by herself whenever possible. One warm sunny day in late July, Marjorie was out of bounds, exploring the graveyard down by the church. As she looked through the old graves she found herself thinking of Joyce. She wished her sister could be out with her instead of always working in the kitchen. The only good part of it was her big sister usually managed to sneak them some extra treats. The best treats were the cookies that Joyce took from the special jar — the jar that the kitchen helpers were not supposed to touch. Joyce knew how to rearrange the jar so that no one could tell that some cookies were missing. Many of the kids were jealous that she had a big sister in the kitchen, but she did not care, that only made her happier to have Joyce.

As she examined the graves, she felt a tingling go up her spine. It was spooky and exciting at the same time. She especially liked the old gravestone with the anchor on it. It seemed out of place because she was told that the ocean was so far away. She was rubbing the moss away from the writing, trying to see the date, when she heard her name. She nearly jumped out of her skin. She told Nurse that she thought she was a ghost. Nurse asked what on earth she was doing way down here, she should be in the fields and not over the fence. Marjorie explained that she was exploring things, but Nurse told her to get up and come along with her as she needed her to go in, get washed up, and put on her school clothes to look presentable. Marjorie protested that it was not a school day, and reminded Nurse that they were on their summer break. The ease of her protest showed how much more comfortable Marjorie had become at the home.

"Marjorie, enough cheekiness. Just do as you are told. We have some special guests here today and they want to talk to you. Get down to the headmaster's office as soon as you are changed."

Joyce looked out her window. She could see Marjorie walking up the path with the Nurse. What was going on today? Every quarter of an hour or so, the Nurse would come out to the playing field and call in two or three of the children.

A short while later, Marjorie gingerly walked down the hall, towards the dreaded office. Most of the children tried their best to avoid this room. If they sent a child there, he or she usually came out crying. When children needed to pass by the room, they usually tiptoed to avoid disturbing the headmaster.

When Marjorie reached the room, a line of children already stood along the wall. One of the older girls told her to stand at the end of the line and wait until she was called. Marjorie stood for ages. She wanted to get back outside, her playtime was disappearing. Finally, it was her turn. As Marjorie walked in, she heard Joyce's name being spoken.

"No, it says here that she is already thirteen. I don't even want to see her." A man's voice answered. Marjorie wondered what Joyce's age had to do with anything, and besides, her sister was not thirteen, she was twelve. Marjorie was surprised to find two strange men in the headmaster's office, but no headmaster. She was about to tell the man in the white doctor's coat about the mistake in Joyce's birthday, but he immediately called her over to him, and as she did so, he asked if she was indeed Marjorie Arnison.

She whispered, "Yes, sir." Her voice always seemed to stick when she had to talk to people like this. His voice boomed out, showing Marjorie what he expected of her, and asked her to speak up. He told her that he needed to hear her clearly.

"Yes, sir, I am Marjorie," she yelled out, immediately putting her hand to her mouth, surprised at the loudness of her voice. He said the records show that she was eleven years old. He peered over his glasses and told her that she was pretty small.

"Sir, I am ten, sir." Marjorie whispered. Her age had become a bothersome topic. She didn't know how to get the adults to listen to her.

"What? Speak up."

"Ten, sir." It still came out as a whisper.

"What? Never mind." He asked her to come closer as he had to weigh her, measure her height, and look down her throat, all the while assuring her that it would not hurt at all.

The other man, who had been sitting quietly going over a stack of papers, called Marjorie over to him when the doctor was finished. He told her he had to give her a couple of tests, pointed to a desk beside him, and told her to sit. Next he handed her a paper. When she was done, he gave her another paper; this time it had a maze on it. He told her to trace her way through to the end. He didn't hurry her so she took her time.

Marjorie looked at the maze. She liked mazes. Before she put her pencil on the paper, she looked through to find the end, searching out the blind alleys. She hated having to trace back from them. She found it was best to spot the dead ends first. When she was done, she picked up her paper and handed it back and said she was finished and asked if she could go.

She sat back down when he said no. There was one last test to do. He handed her another group of papers and she started the test. Frustration filled her, but over the months she had learned that it was easier to do what they asked without questioning or complaining. It was the summer holidays and she resented having to do these tests, but kept her feelings to herself. When she was done she stood up and looked at him. He nodded his head and told her to go. "Send in the next one in line."

Founder :
KINGSLEY FAIRBRIDGE
RHODES SCHOLAR, OXFORD
Chairman Executive Committee :
C. J. HAMBRO, Esq., M.C.
Hon. Treasurer :
SIR PATRICK FAGAN
K.C.I.E., C.S.I.

Telephone :
TEMPLE BAR 6706
Cable Address
KALEGEFURA, LONDON
Secretary :
GORDON GREEN

FAIRBRIDGE FARM SCHOOLS INCORPORATED

Head Office : SAVOY HOUSE, 115 STRAND, LONDON, W.C. 2

All Orders, Cheques, etc., should be made payable to Fairbridge Farm Schools (Inc.), and crossed Westminster Bank Ltd.
All communications to be addressed to the Secretary

The Superintendent,   20th
Middlemore Emigration Homes,   August,
Selly Oak, Birmingham.   1937.

Dear Mr.Plenderleith,

      MARJORIE and KENNETH ARNISON.

     I have to confirm that subject to satisfactory psychological examination, Marjorie and Kenneth will be included in the party of children due to sail for the Prince of Wales Fairbridge Farm School, British Columbia, on the 10th September.

          Yours sincerely,

          E.Hart

        ACTING SECRETARY.

A formal letter under the Fairbridge letterhead, dated August 20, 1937. The Fairbridge Society, the Middlemore Emigration Homes, the Canadian officials at Canada House in London, and Department of Immigration and Colonization in Ottawa, Ontario, sent and received many pieces of correspondence with regard to Marjorie and her siblings' inclusion for the Fairbridge farm scheme in Canada.

Marjorie was about to ask the doctor what this was all about, but he was writing in a notebook. When he did not hear her leave, he looked up and shooed her away and told her to be quick about it, as he did not have all day.

She walked out and the next girl went in. Kenny was standing at the end of the line. He grabbed his big sister as she walked by and in a whisper asked her what was going on. She told him that that the doctor checks you and the other man just asks a bunch of silly questions and gives some tests, but she assured him that it did not hurt a bit. She told him that she would see him later and she skipped off towards the door. Before she could open it, Nurse shouted at her, "Where do you think you are going? Go up and change into your play clothes first."

Joyce watched Marjorie skip along the path from her kitchen window. As she scrubbed her dishes, she thought of asking Cook what was going on. However, she did not, as it would be easier to ask Marjorie later. Adults did not like the children to ask too many questions, and, besides, you could never be sure if they were telling you the truth. As she washed dishes, she thought about her mum and Phyllis and the babies. She missed them. Did they miss her? They had been at Middlemore Homes for several months now, and her mum had not sent a single letter to them. Never mind that, she told herself, she was twelve and a half now and she would soon be old enough to be on her own. They insisted that she was already thirteen. Maybe she should stop telling them they were wrong. It might mean that she would get out of here sooner. The first thing she would do would be to find her way back to Whitley Bay, and she would take Marjorie, Audrey, and Kenny with her.

What would she find in Whitley Bay? Would they still be living in the same flat on Whitley Road? Would her mum take her back? She would miss the nice clothes, the food, and the sweets, but she definitely would not miss the mountains of dishes and potatoes to peel. She scrubbed furiously at the big pan. She wanted her mother, but she also wanted the nice things too. Nothing was easy to figure out anymore. She looked up; Kenny was skipping down to see Marjorie. One thing for sure she would do anything for her little sisters and her brother. Cook had left the room for the moment. She quickly grabbed the cookie jar and snuck a handful into her apron pocket. During her break, she would run out to the field and ask Marjorie what was going on.

CABLE AND TELEGRAPHIC ADDRESS:
"TOROSUS, LESQUARE, LONDON."
TELEPHONE:
WHITEHALL 7787.

IMMIGRATION BRANCH

CANADA

DEPARTMENT
OF
MINES AND RESOURCES

WHEN REPLYING PLEASE REFER TO FILE 18.A.2064.

Oceanic House,
CANADA HOUSE,
1A, Cockspur Street,
TRAFALGAR SQUARE,
LONDON, S.W.1.

9th August, 1937.

Dear Sir,

I beg to advise you that the application submitted on behalf of Marjorie Arnison of 106 Whitley Road, Whitley Bay, has been approved.

Yours faithfully,

Commissioner.

The Secretary,
Fairbridge Farm Schools,
Savoy House,
115, Strand, W.C.2.

The approval for Marjorie's emigration.

Seven

Off to London

Marjorie's world is falling down,
Falling down, falling down,
Marjorie's world is falling down,
But no one cares.

SEPTEMBER 8, 1937

Marjorie quickly ran a brush through her short, straight brown hair. They had orders to make haste and not to bring anything with them. It was all so puzzling, but still it was exciting. She bent over to put on her shoes. The morning's oatmeal felt heavy on her stomach. A worried feeling ran alongside her excitement. Adults who talked in a high hurried voice like the one Nurse used this morning were normally to be mistrusted. However, she was going on an adventure! No school today!

"I am so excited. I wonder where we are going." Marjorie exclaimed.

"Me too. And anywhere but school and the kitchen will be good," a girl answered from across the locker room.

"I feel special. This is going to be a great day," a third girl piped in.

"Girls!" Nurse interrupted their happy chatter. "Put on your winter coats and your tams." This was odd too, because it was such a lovely warm September day, but they were well-trained children and rarely challenged orders now.

Nurse had approached the three girls just after breakfast and pulled them aside before they could get their coats and books and form the usual lineup for school. Olive would be waiting for Marjorie, but Nurse kept them shut away in a little office. Marjorie did not know what she did wrong. She worried about having to walk with a different partner and being late for day school. She trembled at the thought of being sent to the headmaster. It was generally not good news if the day began with anything out of the ordinary. When the Nurse came back the anxiety in the little room couldn't be contained. She told them not to fret since the school had already been informed of their absence. She clapped her hands and told them that today they were going on an exciting journey.

"Who wants to go on an adventure?" she asked. And naturally there was a chorus of "I do! I do! I do!" from the three excited girls, who had been standing patiently to hear what they had done wrong and what their punishment might be. They looked at each other and smiled their relief to one another. Nurse told them to not tell the others since they might feel bad because they were not invited to come with them. She bent down and whispered, "Okay, girls, this can be our little secret!" The girls nodded and quickly scampered off when Nurse said they had just ten minutes to get ready.

A twitter of excitement followed them down the hall. They did not have to worry about letting their secret out since the home was almost deserted. Most of the other children had already left for school and the younger ones were in the babies' room. That left just a handful of the older children at the home at this time of the morning and they were busy doing their chores. They ran up the centre stairs to the girls' locker room, chatting happily, without a care in the world.

The girls were ready in record time. The thought of doing something different was so exciting, and besides, they were the chosen ones that day. Marjorie quickly buttoned her coat, hoping there was time to slip into the kitchen to tell Joyce about her adventure. Joyce was good at keeping secrets, and she would tell her that she would come immediately to the kitchen when they returned instead of at their usual meeting place after day school. Marjorie smiled to herself; she loved their private spot down at the bottom of the field. Joyce would run up and laugh as she pulled the hidden treats out of her pocket. Sometimes Marjorie shared the treats with her best friend, Olive, but more often than not, she just popped the treats into her mouth, savouring the yummy taste.

Olive's friendship had become very important to Marjorie. She was there to whisper to at night and this was a great comfort as Joyce and Audrey's cots were too far away. It was difficult to make friends at the home because so many of the girls kept leaving. Marjorie felt special having such a good friend *plus* a big sister to look out for her. Joyce was the best big sister anyone could ask for. As she put on her tam, she thought that it was not so bad there really — at least they had each other. Not all of the kids were as lucky as she was; some of the girls had no family at the home, not even a brother.

Marjorie was ready first. This would be her only chance to run to the kitchen. As she charged out of the locker room, she ran smack into Nurse, who grabbed her and told her to slow down. She took Marjorie by the arm and led her right back into the room. Marjorie wiggled, trying to get loose, but Nurse held her tight as she told the other two girls to hold hands and follow. She looked at Marjorie, who was still wiggling trying to get away, and told her to stand still and that she could be her partner. She held Marjorie's hand tightly as they walked towards the stairway at the end of the hall. These stairs led to the side door. Marjorie wanted to go down the middle staircase. She could call Joyce from there. She wiggled again, then stammered, and told Nurse that she just wanted to see Joyce — just for one second. She promised to be really quick.

Nurse had expected Marjorie to try to run to the kitchen to see her sister. The two girls were extremely close. It was going to be difficult for them to be separated, but it was not in her hands, so what could she could do about it? Nothing. Absolutely nothing. It piqued her, but she had to accept it. She told Marjorie that there wasn't time and marched her ahead telling the other two to come along smartly, and no talking! Marjorie's delight began to fade. Something was not right. As they reached the bottom of the stairs, a group of ten boys walked out the door.

Marjorie groaned and asked why the boys had to come, but Nurse did not answer. As they followed the boys out the door and under the four big white pillars, she could see Kenny at the rear of the line. Marjorie tried to get his attention, but he was too busy marching like a soldier. The kitchen window came into view as they rounded the end of the building. She could see Joyce, but she was not looking her way. Marjorie squirmed, trying to get free. If only she could run to the window to get Joyce's attention, but Nurse held her even more securely. Marjorie yelled out as loudly as she could. It worked, and Joyce looked up. Marjorie waved frantically. Joyce saw her and waved back. Marjorie yelled even more loudly that she was going on an adventure and would see her later.

Nurse shook Marjorie and scolded her and said there would be no more talking. She warned her to look straight ahead and pulled her back into formation as they continued down the edge of the field. They walked past St. Mary's Church at the bottom of the field, and along the little side path that led to Bristol Road. Marjorie was not happy that the boys were coming on their adventure, but she was glad for Kenny. He looked behind and gave her a little wave.

After walking for a while, Marjorie looked up at Nurse and said that she was hot and thirsty. She asked, "Are we going to walk the whole way? How much farther?" She wanted to know where they were going. Marjorie pulled off her tam and tugged at her buttons. She wondered why they had to wear their winter coats. The three girls looked at Nurse, but all she said was for Marjorie to hush and to stop asking questions. She told her to put her tam back on, button her coat, and that she would see all in good time.

They carried on down Bristol Road and crossed over at the bottom where the road forked at Oak Tree Lane. They stayed on Bristol Road, and as they walked over a little bridge, Marjorie recognized where they were. She looked up — it was the train station. The very same station they arrived at when they came from Newcastle all those months before. She read the sign — Selly Oak Station. Memories of her mother, of her sisters and brothers, and of Whitley Bay flooded back. An image of Newcastle loomed in her mind and the terror was as fresh as ever. Suddenly everything was clear to her. They were sending them back to Newcastle. It was a trick! Fear wormed its way up Marjorie's spine. She dug in her heels, not wanting to get any closer. In a flash, she thought she could find her way back to the home if she broke free. She was a fast runner.

Nurse yanked at Marjorie's arm and told her to stop pulling. She looked down at Marjorie and could see the fear in her eyes and her heart softened as she asked, "What is wrong?" Marjorie choked back her tears, and asked if they were sending them back to Newcastle. Marjorie's comment puzzled Nurse — the children often came out with unreasonable and unexplainable fears. And, as it did now, it usually caught her off guard, but she knew it was important to put Marjorie's fears to rest or it could turn into quite a scene. In her kindest voice she asked, "Newcastle?"

"Please, I'll be good. Don't send me there."

"Marjorie, you are a silly girl at times. Whatever gave you that idea? We are not going to Newcastle."

It was little reassurance, and as she was about to ask where was it they were going, the excited voices of the boys up ahead distracted her. She could hear them yell out, "Look, the train station. Are we going on a train today? Sir, sir, do we get to go on a train?" It was hard for Marjorie to hear the master's reply, but there was a loud applause so she thought he must have said yes.

The children lined up along the platform while the master went to the ticket booth. It was difficult to stand still, for some because of the prospect of the exciting adventure before them, and for others because they were filled with uncertainty and dread. Trains were coming and going and people scurried in all directions. The master directed the children down the platform to wait for their train. They took the Selly Oak train to the Birmingham New Station, only to change trains there. As she boarded the next train, Marjorie wondered where they were going for their adventure and why it had to be a secret. Mistrust had piled up throughout the morning and now would not be shaken. The happy excited feeling from earlier in the day had all but disappeared.

Shortly after the train pulled away, Kenny ran up to Marjorie, a huge smile on his face, and announced, "Marjorie, Marjorie, we're going to London! I always wanted to go to London." Marjorie told her brother to be quiet and that they were not going to London. She turned to Nurse for confirmation, but she was busy and did not answer. A little girl sitting beside Marjorie whispered that she thought that he might be right. Kenny looked at his big sister and said that he told her so, and skipped back to his seat.

Fear and excitement mixed in Marjorie's stomach. She remembered London on the large map at school, and it was in a different direction from the Newcastle home, so maybe Nurse was telling her the truth about not going back to that horrid place. It would be exciting to go on an adventure to London, but it was too bad that Joyce had to work in the kitchen. She would love to go to London. Marjorie would have so much to tell her when she got back. It was puzzling though. It must take a long time to get to London. Would they travel that far for their adventure? It would be very late when they returned and Joyce might even be asleep when she got back. She might have to wait until tomorrow to talk to Joyce.

Marjorie sat quietly, afraid to speak as the train sped south, taking them away from Birmingham. Most of the children busied themselves looking out of the window. At noon, Nurse passed around some lunch. The children ate quietly. The excitement had kept them from realizing how hungry they were. Marjorie took advantage of the quiet moment to get Nurse's attention and told her that Kenny said they were going to London. She stood right in front of Nurse and said, "He's wrong, right?"

"Well, umm, yes Marjorie. We are going to London," said Nurse, lowering her eyes and her voice.

"Will we get back tonight? I promised Joyce ..." Marjorie was cut off by Nurse. She appeared flustered and told the girls to hush, after scolding them for all their questions. She looked over at the master and asked him to please explain. The children all stopped what they were doing and looked at him. He finished his mouthful slowly, aware that all eyes were on him. Clearing his throat, he started, "Well, children, let me explain." A sudden and total silence permeated the group.

He began by saying that he was certain that everyone had heard of Canada from their lessons at school. He looked around, "Put up your hand if you have heard of Canada." All the children raised their hands, including those who did not have any idea what or where Canada was. It would do them no good to admit that they had not paid attention to their lessons.

"Good," the master boomed out, "everyone knows where it is then." He went on, "Canada is a colony of this great country of ours — on the other side of the huge Atlantic Ocean." He told them that Canada was a very large country with not many people living in it. It needed good, smart, strong boys and girls like them to go over and help keep the country British.[1] He looked over his audience, and then continued. "Canada is a very beautiful country," he said. "However, because it is so large, many people from the other countries want to go there too. We need to make sure the colonies stay British rather than have foreigners of all sorts moving in and taking over. The King has chosen you to be his little soldiers." He told the children that each and every one of them had a very important job to do. He assured them that they would be very happy over in Canada, as this was a marvellous opportunity for all of them. He wiped his brow with his handkerchief and took another bite of his sandwich.

A stunned hush enveloped the car. This was no longer just a day trip. They would not be going back to the home. The questions started to fly. A boy challenged the master by asking if he had ever been to Canada.

He replied that he had not but he had heard a lot about it. He told them that there were cowboys and Indians in Canada and suggested that if were to look out of the train window when travelling across the country they might see some riding along on their horses. A wide-eyed youngster wanted to know if they were bad cowboys and Indians. The master replied, not reassuring anyone, "No, not at all." He told them there was no need to worry and that they might even see some buffalo on the prairies as well.

"Buffalo! What are buffalo? Are they dangerous? Where are you sending us?" One of the taller boys stood up, demanding answers.

The master coughed; the bread suddenly felt very dry in his mouth. He surveyed the group and took note of the looks on the children's faces. The expressions varied. He could see excitement, fear, and panic. He tried to answer only the questions from the children who appeared excited, but this quickly became impossible:

"How will we get there?"

"When will we be coming back?"

"How long will it take?"

"How long will we be gone?"

"But what about my sister? She is not here. I want her to come!"

"Hey, what about my little brother?"

"How will we get back?"

"What about my assignment at school? Do I have to finish that?"

"I am supposed to work in the kitchen on Saturday. Cook will be mad if I don't show up."

"Do we leave from London?"

"Is that why we are going to London?"

"My two sisters aren't here. Will they be coming to Canada too? Is Canada close to London? I really want to go to London." Kenny was going to get as many questions in as possible while he had the master's attention.

Marjorie heard Kenny shout out. He asked the one question that she was too afraid to voice. "What about Joyce and Audrey? Why did we leave them back at the home?"

"Well, Kenny," the master began, "we will be stopping at London. Who wants to see the lions at Trafalgar Square?"

Several children yelled out "I do! I do!" and drowned out the talk of brothers and sisters. Kenny kept asking about London. *Not London,* Marjorie screamed inside, *ask about Joyce and Audrey!*

Master told them that they would be stopping in London just for a night or two, and while there they would get to meet some real Canadian people at Canada House. "It's a lovely big building right beside the lions at Trafalgar Square." He warned them that they talk differently in Canada, so be prepared. He gave a little chuckle, but only Nurse laughed with him. Marjorie thought that was odd coming from him. She had had such a hard time at first understanding the Birmingham accents of everyone at the home. She could understand them perfectly now, as long as they talked slowly.

One girl asked if they were going to live at Canada House. Nervous laughter filled the car, but all faces turned to the master to see what he was going to say. He assured them that they would not be living there. He said, "From Canada House you will go over to Creagh House — a lovely old mansion in Kensington owned by the Fairbridge Society. They use it as a hostel. Then …" he began, but questions erupted again.

"What are we doing at Canada House?"

"Why are we going there?"

"My mum said she would come and get me from the home when she got better. Can she get me from Canada? I don't think I want to go."

"What if I don't want to go either?"

"Can we come back from Canada if we don't like it there?"

"Will I get to see my sister? I think she went to Canada."

"Does my mum and dad know you are sending us there?"

"Is it really cold in Canada?"

"Is that why we had to wear our winter coats?"

"Who is going to look after us?"

"Do buffalo have big horns? Can they get us?"

"How are we going to get there?"

"Nobody asked me if I wanted to go. What if I want to stay in England?"

The master found it difficult to tell who was yelling out with questions coming from all directions and all at once. He raised his voice and told them to stop. "Put up your hand and ask one question at a time if you want me to answer." He had fervently hoped that he and Nurse could keep the children occupied and their thoughts away from where they were going, then drop them off at Canada House and make their departure without this question period. He could see that he had better come up with some good answers, or they would have some very unhappy children on their hands. He surveyed the little group, assessing the impending mutiny. He asked them to be quiet and let him finish. He told them, speaking slowly, that from London they would travel to Liverpool. A lovely huge ocean liner, the *Duchess of Atholl*, would be waiting there to take them to Canada.

Marjorie asked if he and Nurse would be coming to Canada with them. But he shook his head, said "No," and told her that they would take the children as far as Canada House and then go back to Birmingham. He smiled and told the children that he and Nurse were not as lucky as them, since neither of them could go to Canada. Bending towards them, and with a very serious note to his voice, he said, "Now, children, listen carefully. You are going to Canada House so that some Canadian people can meet you. Canada will not let just any children into their country, only the very good boys and girls." He made them all promise him that they would be on their very best behaviour. "Promise me," he urged. "It is for your King and your country." The children had no choice but to promise. Master beamed his pride and said, "Good. Now, no more questions and finish your sandwiches."

"But, sir, can we see Canada from Liverpool?" asked a little boy.

"Of course you cannot see Canada from Liverpool. It is too far away. Now, I said no more questions!" The master put his sandwich down and pulled out some papers from the case he was carrying and pretended to be busy with his work. He didn't notice the look of alarm that spread over the children's faces. They had already travelled so far from their families that most of them knew they would never be able to find their way home. Now he was telling them they were going across the great big ocean. How could any of them ever hope to make it back to their families from there? Dreaming of a visit from their mums and dads had kept many children from losing hope and now this hope was gone.

Marjorie's appetite had vanished. She turned to Nurse and whispered. "If it is so far away, then we aren't coming back ever, are we?" She wanted to know about her sisters Joyce and Audrey and her best friend Olive. She begged Nurse to go get them. "They should be with us. Don't make me leave them," Marjorie pleaded. Marjorie felt Kenny squeeze in beside her and take her hand, but she did not take her eyes off Nurse.

Nurse reminded Marjorie that Audrey was in sick bay. She told her that if she gets better, she might come out to Canada at a later date. She looked away, and said that Joyce had to stay at the home — the home needed her. Although Nurse told Marjorie and Kenny this, she knew that the Fairbridge Society had rejected their big sister Joyce because they thought she was too old for their program.

"You need her?" Marjorie's tears flowed down her cheeks. "But I need her! She's my big sister!"

Kenny looked at Nurse with his big brown eyes, "I need her too."

Nurse had had enough and she told them so. "Some things are just the way they are." She assured them that when they grew up they would understand, but for now, they just had to realize that the home knew what was best. She noticed that many of the children were watching and listening. She turned and swept her arm to include them all, as she suggested that the children would simply have to learn to accept things. They all should be thankful that they were chosen to go to Canada, "It will be a wonderful new life, so don't be ungrateful for the chance you have been given." Refusing to answer any more questions, she got up and sat near the master.

Marjorie sat back in her seat. "Damn it!" she said under her breath. "Goddamn and hell!" That was why they did not let her run into the kitchen this morning. Kenny was watching her. He warned her that she shouldn't swear and that she would get into trouble. Then he asked her if he could finish her sandwich, as it didn't look like she wanted it. As Marjorie handed it over to Kenny, she asked him why she should care if they hear her swear. Then she whispered to Kenny that she was going to jump up and swear her head off and then maybe Canada would not want her because she was too bad and then she would get to go back to the home to be with Joyce, Audrey, and Olive.

She began to get up on her seat whispering to herself the horrid things she would say, but she stopped when she looked at Kenny. His eyes were wide, staring back at her in disbelief, his mouth open. He warned her not to do it. It was then that it occurred to her that she was all her little brother had now. If they sent her back, they would not send Kenny back with her. He would be all alone. How could she leave him? Joyce told her how their mum made her promise to look after the three younger ones. She guessed now it was her job to look out for Kenny.

Marjorie sat back in her seat and let misery creep in. There was no excitement left for the day — this was not a good adventure. She wanted to go back home. If only she liked working in the kitchen more, maybe Nurse would have needed her too. But she could not leave Kenny. Marjorie fought away her tears. There was no point in crying. She was afraid, but Kenny's worried face forced her to try to be brave for his sake.

An eerie quietness descended over the car. The children were lost in their own thoughts. Marjorie looked up as one of the girls walked up to Nurse and broke the silence. She wondered if she could ask just one more question, but carried on without waiting for a response and asked why she was told not to bring anything with her today, because if she is going to Canada, she should have brought her mother's picture and her letters that were under her cot in her treasure box and she couldn't get them now if she wasn't going back to the home. "Why?" she whispered. "Will you send them to me? Do they have a post in Canada? You won't make me just leave them will you? I have only one picture of me mum. I, I ..." Her voice trailed off towards the end and tears were streaking down her face.

Nurse could see the tears spreading to the other children. Even the tougher boys were struggling. There was no sign of the morning's jovial atmosphere. Not everyone agreed with the home's policy of sending children off without letting them know where they were going. She hated lying to them. She had worked so hard over the past few months to build up their trust, but all seemed shattered now. She wondered what it was like for these children not to take their few precious belongings, not to say goodbye to good friends, and especially not to say goodbye to siblings. She had tried to imagine what that was like on several occasions, but it was impossible.

The home had strict guidelines in place and she had to work within them. It was believed that toughening up these little children was crucial to their survival. They could not be sent half way around the world unprepared for the rigours they would face. The home looked down on any sign of weakness, especially from the staff. They felt it harmed the children's progress. The children needed to learn to be resilient. It would be a long, and perhaps rough, ocean passage, and then a long arduous train ride to the western shores of Canada. It would not be over then, because she knew that they needed to get on yet another boat before they reached their final destination. The Prince of Wales Fairbridge Farm School was on Vancouver Island, off the coast of British Columbia. It seemed so far away and so remote; the children could never imagine such great land spaces. That was probably one of the reasons they instructed her to tell them as little as possible.

"Let it sink in one step at a time," the headmaster had warned. "That way the children might be able to cope with it. Keep them excited about what might be around the corner, and do not let them dwell on what they are leaving. You don't want them crying all the way to Canada, do you?" The headmaster had growled as he dismissed her. But he had no advice about what to do when the children found that what was just around the corner too ominous to understand. Why had she been chosen to undertake this journey with the children? She had tried to get out of it, but to no avail.

Nurse hardly knew what to say to the girl. If she promised to send out something for one child, she would be making promises to them all, promises that she knew she could not keep. By now, the staff would have stripped their cots and all signs of these children would be gone from the dorm. They expected another group of children at the home any day now. It was even possible that by tonight a new group could fill the beds these children occupied this morning. The home tried to keep a steady stream coming and going. It was the policy.

It saddened her to think that they kept the children just long enough to fatten them up a bit. Most of the children would just start to settle in, find some security, and begin to trust her, and then they were gone. She wondered how these children really fared in their lives. Most of them came from backgrounds that left them unprepared for the harshness of emigration. The sending agencies expected these children not only to survive their ordeal but also to become perfect citizens in their new country. If they did not make it, they placed the blame on some weakness inherited from their poor parents. Everyone seemed to think it was the right and proper thing to do. It was cheaper than housing them in English institutions. They thought the best way to break the pattern of poverty and keep the children from following in their parents' footsteps was to remove them from their backgrounds. To her, that was the tragedy — these children would no longer have any sense of family.

Unfortunately, this was precisely what most of the sending agencies saw as positive about child emigration. Once the children were removed from their parents they could mould them into good, useful, and obedient citizens. Yet, what actual changes were the children offered? For the most part they only trained them to be domestic servants and farm hands. They were simply preparing them for the same roles but in a different country, and there they had no family support. The children supposedly had the support of the Fairbridge Society, and it was believed to be far better than anything their families could give them, but she was not convinced. Maybe it worked. She rarely heard of them sending children back. Nevertheless, she felt that they expected the little children to undertake a journey that they would never embark on themselves. She was certain, too, that they would never, in a million years, consider sending their own children away on such a journey. This seemed to be the plight of the children of the country's poorer classes. The poor had always been unwanted. She turned to the tear-stained child but could see that there was no need to respond. The little girl's face showed that she already knew the answer.

By the time they pulled into London's Euston Station, the mood had brightened a little. The children had heard of London, England's capital, but had never expected to see it for themselves. The master shouted out orders for the children to line up on the platform and told them that they needed to take the Underground to Charing Cross. They were to find a partner, pay attention, and not get lost. He told them he hoped he had made himself perfectly clear but did not wait for a response before warning them that he would personally punish any of the children who let go of their partners' hands. When he asked if everyone understood him, a chorus of "Yes, sir" rang out.

Getting everyone to the correct platform and on the Underground all in one group was a feat. Once they stepped inside the train, the children crowded around the door, making it impossible for others to get on. The master urged the children to keep going, to move ahead and find a seat. He counted them again, three girls and ten boys, and then breathed a sigh of relief — almost there and everyone was accounted for.

PHOTO BY JACK WEYLER.

One of the four lions at Trafalgar Square, London. The children would have walked across the square in September 1937 to get to Canada House.

Their stop came quickly. The master ordered them to take their partners' hands and follow him. "Be quick or the doors will shut and take you to the next stop." Someone saw the sign and yelled out that they were at Charing Cross. The group marched out of the station, their eyes widening as they walked along Craven Street and then down Strand. They had never seen such sights and sounds before.

"There's Trafalgar Square! Can we get over there?" A boy yelled out.

It was a feat getting all the children across the street. For the past several months, they had spent all their time at the home, except for their daily monitored excursions to the local day school. Nurse was thankful when all were in the square and safe for the moment. Her obligations were almost at an end. She pointed and said, "Look, children, there's Canada House."[2] If all went as planned, she and the master could catch the late afternoon train back to Birmingham.

Squeals of delight rang out as the children ran around the square. It would not be wise to take them over to Canada House until they ran off a little energy. Two of the boys were sitting by one of the lions and yelling for someone to notice them. Master waved to them and told them to be careful. A younger boy chased the pigeons, but just when he thought he had one, the bird flew away, leaving him staring at his empty hands. The three girls wandered off and were walking arm-in-arm, staring about and looking agog at all the sights. A small group of boys stood by the statue of Lord Nelson.

"Blimey, that statue is high! I wonder who he is."

Nurse was about to give a history lesson but was interrupted. It was unfortunate timing as it was one of those rare moments when the children seemed to have forgotten their plight and were living in the moment. The master's voice broke the spell as he ordered the children to form partners again and line up. A groan broke out, but they scurried to comply. He counted them first, then walked up and down the line, inspecting each one, pointing to the child as he barked out his orders:

"Button your coat."

"Put your hat on straight."

"Pull up your socks."

"Tuck in your shirt."

It was important for the children to look their best before going into Canada House. His job was to ensure that the Canadian officials had no immediate grounds to reject any of the children.

"Now, boys and girls, we will be leaving you soon. You must be on your very best behaviour. You are getting to go on a grand adventure, but you must prove that you are worthy of such an honour. The King and your country expect you to be brave. Do not disappoint us. Alright, my little soldiers, line up by twos and follow me."

Suddenly it hit Marjorie — it was important for her to make a good impression because if Canada did not want her, then who would?

The children marched to the far side of the square and waited for their chance to walk across the street. They clambered up the front stairs of Canada House.

"C-A-N-A-D-A. It spells Canada." The girl beside Marjorie pointed to the letters at the top of the wall high above the columns.

As she scrambled up the foreign stairs, Marjorie longed for the familiarity of the home. She pictured Joyce looking everywhere for her. What would she think when she found out she was gone? Forever and ever. She had wanted to get away from Middlemore, but not like this.

PHOTO BY PATRICIA SKIDMORE.

In 2001, Marjorie visited Canada House with her grandson Jack Weyler, sixty-four years after she had been taken there in preparation for her departure for Canada.

Eight

THE LAST TEA PARTY

Sent o'er vast shores
A pocket full of promises
Hush-a, hush-a,
We are Brits no more!

SEPTEMBER 8–9, 1937

The little Brits stepped over the grand entrance and into the Canada House foyer. Instinct made them look up. They were gobsmacked. The magnificent room was lined with several columns, large chandeliers with lights sparkling like diamonds hung from the high ceiling. Someone whispered that they must be in a palace. Another boy said that this must be the King's house. With his eyes on the splendour and not where he was going, he bumped into the boy in front of him, who shoved him back and told him not to be so daft, that the King's house was much bigger.

"Mind your manners. Stand quietly along the wall," growled the master as he walked over to talk to a man sitting behind a nearby desk.

The two men glanced over at the weary group as they talked. The children tried to stand quietly, but the day had been long and difficult. Two of the younger boys slid down the wall, landing on their bottoms with a plop. Nervous giggles filled the hall. Nurse quickly grabbed the little mutineers by their collars and yanked them up, warning them to stand still. Master walked over and told Nurse to make certain that the children behave and that he would be back shortly. The two men disappeared down the hallway.

Keeping order was almost impossible. The day had been such an ordeal, yet the next several days would test the children's endurance. That day's travel was nothing compared to the challenges they would face before they settled in their new home. As she waited, Nurse struggled with the pros and cons of child emigration. Not all accepted the country's policy of sending poor children off to the colonies, without their parents and sometimes *even* separating them from their siblings. Well — there were Marjorie and Kenny for example. It would be very difficult for their sister Joyce to cope with this loss. She had overheard a conversation between the headmaster and the doctor representing the Canadian Immigration Officials while she was standing in the hallway. The headmaster had argued fiercely against the rejection of so many children. She had not planned to eavesdrop, but it couldn't be avoided. The last word belonged to the doctor, so there was little anyone at the home could do about it.

"I'm sorry," the doctor's voice rose. "It is all I can do. I have my guidelines. This group will have to go through one more set of tests at Canada House when they get their inoculations. If I let any riff-raff through, that will be the end of my reputation with the Canadian Immigration Department. And bear in mind that the Fairbridge Society is very strict regarding the age limit of the children."

"Yes, but what about the children with younger brothers and sisters going? It is not fair to separate them," the nurse had burst in, unable to contain her frustration any longer.

The doctor had simply said that in a perfect world that wouldn't happen, but unfortunately, accommodating all the children and their needs just was not possible. To approve older children who would likely be rejected once they were in London would not be a feasible situation. He had promised the Canadian officials to send sound stock only, and that was what he planned to do. Sound stock and the right age group were his two main criteria. With British Columbia already having expressed fears of becoming a dumping ground for England's street urchins, it was important to keep the bigger picture in mind. The society had plans to open farm schools in every province of Canada, so making a good impression at that time was very important.[1] If the "material"[2] arrived in

London in anything less than a perfect state, the authorities at Canada House would simply reject the child then and there and send them back at the Fairbridge Society's expense. "My hands are tied. I don't make the rules. Now, please let me get on with my job, as I do not have all day." And he dismissed her.

Nurse looked over at Marjorie. She had not moved an inch. The child's eyes looked wary as she kept track of her younger brother. She looked up and down the line of children. They were all so young — some were really just babies.

The master marched back, with a third man leading the way. The man at the desk had busied himself with some papers. Nurse stared at them, looking for signs that all had gone as planned. It would not do to take any back to Birmingham. One nurse nearly lost her job over that. It was with a sigh of relief she heard the man say, "Everything is in order." The master spoke to the children and told them that the people at Canada House would take very good care of them. As he and the nurse were about to leave, he warned them to be good boys and girls, mind their manners, and, above all, mind their benefactors. He took the nurse's arm, moved towards the door, and said, "Goodbye, God speed, and good farming!" All eyes were on the door. A few children murmured half-hearted goodbyes and big fat tears streamed the cheeks of some of the younger children.

"Please, take me back with you. I have to see Joyce and Audrey," Marjorie wailed at the closing door. "They will be wondering where I am." She swallowed the escaping sob as the door slammed shut.

Their new Canadian host surveyed his charges. He thought it was a pitiful looking group, but that had become routine behaviour for him. He needed to act quickly to stop the impending mutiny. "Well, well, well! What have we here! Welcome to Canada House! Why are you just standing there? Come along with me. Are you hungry? Yes! Well, I am sure you are. We have a special tea all arranged for you. Just one last short journey for today."

He turned and headed down the hallway. After a few steps, he stopped and looked back. Not one child followed him. They stood, glued to the floor, their eyes still locked on the closed door. He urged them to come along and assured them that there was nothing to be worried about. A few of the braver boys stepped forward and the others soon followed. Instinct told them it was very important to stay together.

As he walked down the long hallway, the man spoke in a soft voice telling them about the wonderful hostel that had been set up in a beautiful old mansion called Creagh House on Holland Villas Road. They would all be very comfortable while getting ready for their big trip. The house could put up as many as fifty children while they waited for their boat to be ready to take them to Canada or to Australia, and it had a beautiful large playroom with a shiny polished floor and lots of toys and books for them to play with. The children were to spend a night or two at Creagh House before going back to Canada House to prepare for their departure to Liverpool.

"All right now." His voice suddenly became booming and cheerful. "Here are the ladies who will take you on your bus ride. Okay, boys and girls, have a good trip and good luck with your new life."

He wiped his brow as he shut the door after them. England and the colonies were doing the right thing, blast it! Even the Prince of Wales was behind this scheme. He had attended a meeting a couple of years ago at Grocer's Hall, where he listened to the prince himself state that child emigration was the only "completely successful form of migration"[3] during those present difficult economic times. England had a surplus of

A copy of the Prince of Wales' Cheque - printed in the London Times, June 21, 1934, for the article: 'Farm Schools for the Empire'

The Prince of Wales donated his own money to assist the fundraising goals of the Child Emigration Society, to help establish three more farm schools based on the 1912 Fairbridge model in Western Australia. The Prince of Wales Fairbridge Farm School was the first of this next group of farm schools.

slum children and Canada had a surplus of space just waiting for them. The Prince of Wales himself put down the first £1,000 to get the Canadian farm school going. Everyone knew how important it was to maintain the supply of good British stock going into Canada to keep it within the British Empire. Someone else would fill Canada's empty spaces if the British failed to fill them first.

The meeting stressed that child emigration was not a charity, but an *Imperial investment.* As a reminder, he had kept the article written about the meeting from the *London Times*: "Farm Schools for the Empire."[4] He had read it several times and could see no flaw in the argument. There had been many heated discussions with his colleagues as to whether a country's needs were more important than the children's needs, but really he was certain they were doing the right thing. Child emigration was a sound scheme. The fact was indisputable that the poor and unemployed simply overcrowded England. Someone had to do something. The country could not just sit back and ignore this situation. Yes, they were doing the right thing, he assured himself. Still, the lost and frightened looks on many of the children's faces haunted his sleep.

———————————

Marjorie sat on the edge of her seat on the bus. She did not want a new life! She wanted to get away. Oh, where was her mum? Her father might be in London. Could she find him? She would run up to him and beg him to take her home. Back home with her mum, not back to the Middlemore Home. She looked at the faces of all the men as they walked along the sidewalks. She looked at each man who boarded the bus. Her search was hopeless. How could she find her father in London when she could not even remember what he looked like?

After a short ride the children got off the bus and walked up the stairs of Creagh House. An assortment of strangers greeted them, including another group of fifteen children who would be travelling with them to Canada. One of the women introduced the children to a man who was the acting agent-general for British Columbia and told them that he was a very important man.

William McAdam turned to the children, "How do you do? My, my! What a fine looking bunch of children you are! I am so sure that you will all be happy in your new home. When you get there, you will see how very lucky you are because the Fairbridge people have found one of the most beautiful little valleys in the world for your farm school. I am sure you will all grow up to reflect credit on Fairbridge and become good citizens of British Columbia."[5] The adults all cheered, but suspicion crossed over the children's faces. A few, however, thought that this might be their opportunity to get some answers.

A bold boy piped up, "Can you tell us about Canada and about the Fairbridge farm school? Where is the school and when are we going?"

A chorus of questions followed:

"Are there really cowboys and Indians?"

"Is it a long way?"

"Is it across the ocean?"

"Why are we being sent away?"

"Where is Liverpool?"

"When do we go?"

"Is Canada a really big country?"

"Children! Children! Not so noisy! One question at a time," one of the men responded. "What an inquisitive group you are! That is a very good sign. I like to see that in children. Well, sit down and I will tell you about the Fairbridge farm school in Canada. First, I must tell that we have a marvellous telegram sent especially for you lot. It is from Prince Henry, the Duke of Gloucester. He is the president of the Fairbridge Society. He wants all of you to know that he is glad you are getting a special farewell party and he sends his very "best wishes for a good journey and all possible success in the future."[6] It is quite wonderful of him to take time out from his busy schedule to send a telegram. Now, I will tell you about another very special man named Kingsley Fairbridge. He had a great vision when he was a young man." He sat back and grinned at the children.

"Are we going to meet Kingsley Fairbridge?" Marjorie asked.

"No, my dear, unfortunately he died a few years back, but his name lives on in the farm school scheme that he founded." He smiled broadly at the children before continuing. He told them that Kingsley Fairbridge had the great vision to take poor little children out of the crowded cities of England and set them up on beautiful farm schools where they could learn the skills to live a happy life in the colonies. He opened his first farm school almost twenty-five years ago in 1912 near Perth, in Western Australia, and it has been so successful that the Fairbridge Society now wants to set up farm schools in every man-hungry corner of the Empire.[7] He sat back in his chair and beamed at the children. Puzzled stares looked back at him.

One of the boys stood up, "What do you mean hungry men? We don't want to go to Canada if there's no food." He held a deep mistrust of these adults. Were these Fairbridge people going to send him across the ocean to starve?

"My son, I said 'man-hungry.' What I meant by that is that Britain's colonies are vast, and there is so much land that it needs many men to fill them up. I meant that the land is hungry to have you bright little British boys, and you girls too, over there to take advantage of all that it can offer. Both Australia and Canada have a bounty of beautiful farmland just waiting to be cultivated. And at your Canadian farm school, you will be taught all you need to know to survive in your new homeland." The man sat back and smiled again at the children. The children stared back, quiet, for a moment.

He continued, telling the children that the first group of children had been sent over to the Canadian farm school two years ago, in September 1935. "You are the fourth group of fortunate children to go to this wonderful Fairbridge farm school. There are ninety-eight children there now, and, with your group, that will make a total of 126 children."

He smiled again and told them that he wished that he could have been so lucky. "Your new home is on a beautiful island on the very west coast of Canada. That part of Canada will remind you of England and you will not be homesick at all. There are several attractive cottages set up for you to live in and each cottage houses twelve to fourteen children. There are separate cottages for the boys and for the girls, and in each cottage you have your very own special cottage mother to look after you. Kingsley Fairbridge wanted the farm schools set up as cottages because he thought it would be more like a real home, rather than everyone staying in a huge dormitory such as the one at the Middlemore Home. The Prince of Wales thinks your farm school is a grand idea too, so he gave some of his very own money and encouraged others to give as well to ensure your school had enough money to get started. Your new farm school's official name is the Prince of

Wales Fairbridge Farm School, therefore you can see it is a special place." He finished his speech by telling the children that they will be doing their duty to their country and their King.

The children struggled to understand all that they had been told. Marjorie puzzled over what had been said about the Fairbridge man taking children from the crowded cites of England. London seemed crowded, as did Birmingham, and even Newcastle, but her Whitley Bay was not crowded, except maybe on a beautiful sunny day when everyone headed down to the beach. Why did they have to take her and Kenny away? Marjorie wanted to say that if everything was so beautiful in Canada, then you big people should go and live there. Why did she have to go? She was just a kid. She would rather stay with her mum. She tried to tell them, but her voice was stuck.

"Why couldn't we bring my sisters?" asked Kenny.

"If Canada has so much space, why don't you move there? And why couldn't we bring my whole family? I already have a mum, and I don't want a new mum." Marjorie surprised herself with this outburst, tears were close, but the talk of new mums upset her, especially since she had a perfectly good one already.

"Now that's a good question. But, you see, your farm school is designed just for children." He cleared his throat as he answered, and, turning to the whole group, told them that Kingsley Fairbridge was a visionary, a man who saw that the colonies needed farmers. "You cannot be farmers without training and Fairbridge felt that properly trained children would make the best farmers. Fairbridge knew that full-grown unemployed men and women failed when taken out as labour to the colonies."[8] He finished by saying that Kingsley Fairbridge set up the farm school system for lucky boys and girls just like you.

"Well, I want to be a nurse when I grow up, not a farmer!" a little girl shouted out.

Someone chuckled, then turned to the little girl and told her that she would likely be a farmer's wife when she grows up. "You will see, once you get there, you will become used to the farming life and because you will grow up farming, you will understand it and come to love it. I bet each young girl here will find herself a handsome farmer to marry when she gets older, how would you like that?"

UNIVERSITY OF LIVERPOOL ARCHIVES, SPECIAL COLLECTIONS BRANCH, FAIRBRIDGE ARCHIVES, D296.F4.

The September 1937 group of children were photographed at a final farewell tea party given for the children at the Fairbridge Hostel in Kensington, London, on September 9, 1937. Kenny is sitting on the floor in the front row, second boy from right, with Marjorie behind him to the left, her hand on his shoulder.

Displeasure quickly filtered through the girls, and Marjorie was about to complain when a bell rang, announcing tea time. With no more time for questions, it was suggested that they should just enjoy their meal, and, since every little detail of their journey had been arranged, they need not worry about a thing. The children stood up, but were first directed over to a spot for a group photograph, before being taken to the other room for tea. The man with the camera took a few more photos while they ate. It was all a little overwhelming: the special tea, the flashes from the camera, the happy adults. The children had no choice but to do as they were told.

The next morning the children were hurried through breakfast. There was much to do before leaving for Liverpool. First on the list was for everyone to pack a suitcase,[9] according to a checklist set up to make sure that each child had all the necessary items for the journey (see Appendix A). Then they needed to take the bus back to Canada House and have a final visit with a Canadian doctor.

"Okay, now. What is your name?" Marjorie did not realize at first that she was being addressed. "Child, your name please," she repeated.

Marjorie pointed to herself, "Me?" she asked as she choked out a whisper. The woman nodded. "My name is Marjorie."

"Well, Marjorie. Come along with me. Let's get your suitcase packed."

"My very own suitcase?"

"Yes, now, let me see. What size would you be? Stand up here and let me take some measurements." Marjorie relaxed with her soothing gentle voice. Soon the suitcase snapped shut. She told Marjorie that she was all set and she should take her case and line it up with all the rest. Marjorie looked down at the case. Her case! It had her name on it and everything. She wondered, would she get to keep this suitcase for her very own or would she have to give it back after she got to Canada?

The twenty-eight children were marched out to board the bus back to Canada House. One by one they went in for their final shots and inspections. The first boy walked in boldly enough, but soon his howls created a panic. He came out a short while later, red-faced.

The suitcase belonging to Kenny, Marjorie's brother, was stored in the attic at a former Fairbridge house until 2006. The tattered labels show the departure port of Canadian Pier Head, Liverpool; the steamship, *Duchess of Atholl*, date of departure, September 10, 1937, landing port, Montreal; and the final destination, Cowichan, British Columbia.

PHOTO BY PATRICIA SKIDMORE.

"Gor' blimey, they jabbed me full of needles. Look at this, will ya!" he pulled up his sleeve to show his arm. As he saw the look on the other kid's faces, his distress turned to a sense of pride and he quickly displayed his poke holes. "Just wait until they get you in there. The needles are gigantic. Ow, that's me sore arm," he cried out as a nurse whisked him away before he totally frightened the rest of the children.

Marjorie was the second to last to go in. The waiting made her so tense that her breakfast was in danger of coming back up. Why were they doing this? She nearly fainted as the nurse jabbed and stuck her with the needles, but her tears stayed stuck behind her eyes. The doctor prodded, poked, and looked down her throat and then in her ears, asking questions all the while, and then the ordeal was over. The last girl in line looked at Marjorie's face as she came out, "Oh, Marjorie, was it really awful?" Marjorie was unable to answer and she simply nodded her head.

Restlessness was in the air as the morning dragged on. It was hard for the children to sit patiently and wait. Marjorie saw Kenny slumped in a corner. He looked sad and it was obvious that he was trying not to cry.

"Leave him alone," she warned a group of boys who had been bullying him. But they asked her what was she going to do about it. Marjorie felt powerless as she stuck out her tongue at them. She knew that Kenny would have to put up with the bullying. It was impossible for her to protect him. How had Joyce managed so easily? She worried that she would not be as good as her big sister at looking out for Kenny, but she would try to do her best.

A nurse walked into the waiting room and clapped her hands. She announced that everyone should be all set to go now. They would be leaving shortly but first they would have an early lunch, and she passed around sandwiches and a bottle of milk for each one.

Four adults were to travel with the children. Mr. E.S. Healy, headmaster of the Fairbridge farm school in Western Australia, and Mrs. Healy, who were returning to Australia via Canada, would accompany the children to Vancouver, British Columbia. Two other specially trained women would also travel as chaperones for the children until they reached Montreal. Once they landed in Montreal, two new chaperones would travel with them across Canada to their final destination.

As they left Canada House, the children could once more see the tall statue at Trafalgar Square. A coolness in the air made them shiver and droplets of rain formed little dark spots on their cases. The walk back across Trafalgar Square differed from the previous walk such a short time ago. Now, at twenty-eight children, their numbers had more than doubled from the thirteen sent down from the Middlemore Home. Each child carried a suitcase. Twenty-eight arms ached from their jabs. No one climbed on the lions today. There was no happy chatter. The "little soldiers" solemnly marched across the square and headed for the Underground. This train would take them to Euston Station, where they would catch the train to Liverpool. A few appeared eager for the journey, but Marjorie was not one of them. She longed to be with her sisters. No one asked her if she wanted to go away. She felt afraid. She wanted Joyce.

Getting the twenty-eight children on and off the Underground without losing anyone was a feat. Once at Euston Station, they quickly found their way up to the top platform area and located where they should be for the Liverpool train. They were lined up along the platform by their car, and, with a few of the boys already inside, looking out of the windows, some

The Fairbridge children are likely at the Euston Station in central London where they boarded the train for Liverpool. They were photographed waving goodbye to the country of their birth. Marjorie is second from the left in the first row and Kenny is top left, inside the train.

UNIVERSITY OF LIVERPOOL ARCHIVES, SPECIAL COLLECTIONS BRANCH, FAIRBRIDGE ARCHIVES, D296.F4.

final photographs were taken, including one where they asked the children to smile and wave goodbye.

Marjorie followed along, keeping an eye out for Kenny to make certain he didn't get lost, but it wasn't easy, as she didn't really understand what to expect from one moment to the next. She needed to keep her tears away for Kenny's sake. The train ride from Euston Station up to Liverpool was quiet and uneventful.

By the time the train pulled into Liverpool, many of the children were cranky. The chaperones could see that the journey ahead would likely be very taxing for both the children and themselves. It was hoped the crossing would not be too rough. The thought of looking after twenty-eight home-sick and seasick children for several days while crossing the Atlantic Ocean made them shudder. One of the women found herself quietly singing a little tune. Funny, though, she could not remember where she learned it, but it seemed appropriate, somehow:

> Don't forget the Orphan Homes of Scotland,
> Don't forget the dear friends here;
> Don't forget that Jesus Christ, your Saviour
> Goes with thee to Canada.
>
> And remember we are still a-praying
> That your life will be good and true,
> And that you may find a blessing
> In the land you are going to.[10]

The busyness of Liverpool's harbour overwhelmed Marjorie. The *Duchess of Atholl* was at her berth on the River Mersey, ready to take her out to sea and across the ocean. All the way to Canada. She simply could not understand why they were taking her to Canada. The sense of independence she experienced in Whitley Bay had almost disappeared, and she stood on the platform, feeling terrified, and waiting for the order to tell her which way to go. She was tired of everything. Tired of feeling afraid. Tired of feeling alone. Tired of not knowing what they were going to demand of her next.

$\mathcal{N}ine$

Joyce's Sorrow

The loneliness ravaged her,
She swooned.
Why did they leave her
On this lonely verge?

SEPTEMBER 8, 1937

"Peel this pile, clean that mess." Joyce[1] whispered under her breath as she plugged away in her usual spot in the kitchen. The mound of vegetables never seemed to get smaller. Her eyes drifted over the playing fields. The church spire cut into the clear blue sky; today was going to be just like a summer day. She felt in her pocket where she had several cookies tucked away — Marjorie's favourite kind. Her other pocket held a special treat. Cook had given her four sweets.

Joyce thought something was wrong with Cook this morning. Her face looked odd — sad or something. Usually she was such a tease. When Joyce felt her slip something in her hand, she looked up, and Cook winked at her. Her familiar smile was back. Four sweets and it was not even Sunday!

Joyce popped one into her mouth right away. That left three. She worked hard to finish her kitchen chores early so she and Marjorie could go down to their favourite spot near the church. Maybe they could get Kenny's attention and the three of them could share the sweets and cookies. They had quarantined Audrey because she had a miserable disease[2] or something and the sisters could not visit her in the sick bay. She didn't have to save a sweet for her.

Joyce grabbed a handful of carrots and worked steadily without looking up. Peelings flew everywhere, and, finally, the last carrot landed in the pot. As she set to cleaning, she thought she heard someone call her name. Cook was across the room.

"Cook, did you call me?"

"No, dearie, I didn't."

Joyce looked out the window. The headmaster was there with a group of boys and following them was Nurse with three girls. The girl walking beside Nurse squirmed and tried to get away. *That girl better watch it,* Joyce thought, *or it will be kitchen duty for her if she does not behave.*

The children looked alike in their Middlemore clothes: the boys in their suits and caps and the girls in their long stockings, and matching coats and tams. Joyce sometimes found it hard to tell them apart from her window. She watched the little girl turn back towards the school. The nurse held onto her, but she turned back and looked up at the kitchen, madly waving. Oh, it was Marjorie! Joyce waved back. She waved until they reached the end of the pathway even though Marjorie did not look back again. She watched until they went out of sight. She thought she could pick

Joyce and Audrey visiting the former Middlemore Emigration Home in Birmingham in the summer of 2001. The window from which Joyce watched Marjorie and Kenny leave in 1937 is on the second floor in the centre of the building.

PHOTO BY PATRICIA SKIDMORE.

out Kenny at the back of the line of boys, marching along. He was always too busy to look up at the window. Joyce was used to that. It pleased her though, that Marjorie never failed to wave to her as she ran past on her way to play in the field.

But something was puzzling! Day school started ages ago and they were heading the wrong way for school. Whatever were they doing? They must be going on a special outing. Nurse held a basket. Probably they are going on a picnic. It was too bad Audrey was still in sick bay — she loved picnics.

Cook, fully aware of what was going on, walked by and gently reminded Joyce to get on with her job. Joyce quickly scooped up the rest of her peelings, expecting a smack at any moment. Once she had lost her Sunday treats for not paying attention. She went back to work with a growing feeling of jealousy. Those lucky sods were out for a bit of fun on this beautiful day and she was stuck in the kitchen.

Later that afternoon, Joyce found time to look for her sister. It was strange that Marjorie had not come to find her, usually she ran to the kitchen right after school. She headed upstairs to the dorm, checking her pocket to make sure the treats were still there. She smiled to herself. Marjorie would be pleased — cookies and a sweet. It had been difficult to resist eating another sweet. At one point, she told herself that it might be hard to get Kenny away from his games with the other boys, so she should just eat his sweet. However, the thought of seeing that big grin of his stopped her.

No Marjorie in the dining room. None of her friends had seen her. It was odd. If she were back from her picnic, Marjorie would come looking for her. She always came looking for her. She always ran up to her pulling at her pockets, laughing, checking for treats.

Where was she now? Joyce ran upstairs again and looked in all the usual places. Not in the dorm. Something about the dorm was different, but she was too preoccupied with finding her sister to pay much attention to it. She ran over to the locker room. Not there either. She was about to explore further when she was called to her afternoon chores. Oh well, she shrugged, as she popped the second sweet into her mouth, they were probably still at their picnic. She would look for her just before tea.

At teatime there was still no sign of Marjorie. They should have been back long ago. A girl said that maybe they left for "Cannon" or something.

"What do you mean, Cannon?" Joyce asked.

"I dunno, that's what I heard," she replied as she skipped away.

"Where is that?" Joyce yelled after her. "It must be a good distance away or else they would be back. Wait, don't go."

"Nurse! Nurse!" Just before bedtime, Joyce finally caught up with her. "Thank goodness, you are back! I can't find Marjorie anywhere. Do you know where she is?" Joyce's voice cracked as her panic leaked through. "Where did you go for your picnic? Where is Cannon?"

"Joyce, settle down. You are not listening properly. Canada," Nurse repeated it slowly, then spelled it out for her, "C-A-N-A-D-A. Canada"

"Well," Joyce persisted, "when will she be back? I have to look after her. I promised me mum."

Nurse drew in her breath, the exhaustion of the long day threatened to overtake her. Why had no one told this child yet? She did not know whether she could put up with any more stress. "Back? Oh, my dear, no one told you? They have gone to Canada. It is a long, long way to Canada. They will not

Letter from Marjorie's sister, Joyce (Arnison) Earl, to Pat Skidmore, dated February 13, 1995. Aunt Joyce wrote: "the last I saw of Ken, and your Mum [Marjorie] … I was looking out the window seeing them go down the garden path with all the other children off to Canada, but at the time I did not know where they were going, that was the last time I saw them. I was ill in Sick Bay a long time; they said I was ill with a broken heart because they had taken them away and left me."

be coming back. They are going to find a lovely new life. They are good little soldiers and they are helping out England and the King by going to live in the colonies."

Joyce's knees buckled. She refused to believe Nurse. There was no understanding it — she did not want to. In her fear and anger she lashed out, "What have you done to them? Where are they?" She ran off, stumbling, blinded by her tears.

It was futile to demand answers. Other children walked down that pathway before and never returned. She had never fully understood what had happened to them until now. Where were Marjorie and Kenny? Why did they leave her behind? Suddenly she knew what she would not allow herself to see before. They had stripped Marjorie's cot and it was not even washday. She tore into the dorm, and, sure enough, there was no trace of Marjorie around her cot. There was just a plain mattress with the grey blanket folded at the end. She ran into the locker room and opened Marjorie's door. Empty! Empty, exactly as she was beginning to feel. She ran to her cot and hid under her covers. A few of the girls tried to talk to her.

"Leave her alone for now, she'll be all right in the morning," Nurse assured them.

"I will not be all right!" Joyce bawled from under her covers. "I will never be all right. I hate this place! Are they really never coming back?" Joyce's sobs wracked her slight frame. She pulled the covers tighter over her head and lost herself in her heartache.

Late the following morning, Nurse lifted Joyce out of her cot and carried her to the sick bay. She was listless and running a fever. Nurse gently removed her work clothes and put a clean nightdress on her. A little pile of crumbs rolled out of the apron pocket onto the floor. She washed her tear-stained face and then her arms. She became aware of Joyce's clenched fist for the first time. Gently prying her fingers open, she found and removed two very sticky sweets.

═══════════════

Many days passed before Joyce was well enough to get up. As she lay in sick bay, she overheard the doctor tell the nurse that she was ill with a broken heart. She didn't know a heart could hurt this much, but she had no desire to get better. What did it matter now?

The weeks dragged slowly by. Time no longer held any meaning. They should have let her say goodbye. She missed Marjorie and Kenny so much but hated them for leaving her. She barely remembered that Audrey was still in the quarantined section of the sick bay. They told her that as soon as Audrey was better she too would leave for Canada. What was the point of caring about anybody now? Audrey would go too. Did Audrey even know that Marjorie and Kenny were gone?

Joyce missed the little routines with her sisters. They had made her feel important, and now all was gone. Gone. Gone. Gone. Everything important was gone. She felt torn and sick with guilt — guilt because she had promised her mum that she would look after them and guilt because she hated them for leaving her behind. How could she hate them? But, she did. She had been a good girl. She had worked hard in the kitchen. What was wrong with her? Why did they leave her behind?[3]

Early one morning Joyce woke up with only one thought — to get away. She was not sure which way to go or how she would get there, but she left, determined to try to find her mum. Thoughts and images of seeing her mum again played in the back of her mind. She even dared to hope that maybe the others had not really gone to Canada, just maybe they had been sent home instead. When she found them, they would all be together again. They would be a family again! She had learned many things at the home. She could be a better help to her mother now.

Joyce made her way as far as the Selly Oak train station. There were so many trains coming and going. Panic set in as she wondered which way was home. In her distress it had never occurred to her that she had no money to get on the train. She was lost and terror grew at the thought of being even more lost. Defeated, she plunked down on a bench and cried. All the months of choked-back tears flooded out. Nothing could stop them.

People walked by her. Some wanted to help. They reached out, but Joyce did not respond. One woman informed the ticket man that there was a very upset young girl crying on the bench.

"I have contacted the home," he assured her, "and they will be down shortly to pick her up. This has happened before, you know. I am against having a large orphanage in this area. It only brings trouble."

Puzzled, the woman asked, "There's an orphanage in this area?"

"Oh, yes, just down on Weoly Park Road. It is an emigration home for slum children. The sooner they ship these street urchins out of the country, the better we will all be."

Mystified by his comment, the woman frowned at the man. "Well, I don't think she looks like a street urchin. She is clean and nicely dressed. She just looks very unhappy. I think I'll try talking to her."

"She is wearing the Middlemore dress; all the girls dress the same. Well, I wouldn't bother...." he began, but she had already walked away.

As she approached the bench, the look of despair on the girl's face stopped her in her tracks. She took a step forward, and then hesitated again and thought, maybe the ticket man is right, I had better mind my own business.

A short while later a nurse from the home came for Joyce. The little figure presented a sad sight, curled up on the bench, and staring forward with unseeing eyes. There was little resistance or response when the nurse took her arm. Joyce got up and started walking. She went back to the home without a struggle, without a tear, and without a word.

Nurse thought that Joyce's spirit seemed to be broken, and her heart went out to this child. The Fairbridge farm school officials stated that it was their policy to keep children in the same family together whenever possible, but time and again they left children behind, while their siblings were sent overseas. Sometimes it was because a child could not see properly or perhaps they were nervous or could not do their school work quickly enough. Moreover, they rarely bent the strict rules about taking children over twelve, especially if they were girls. Joyce's papers showed that she was going to be fourteen in a few months, so she was likely rejected because of her age. It was funny, though, how Joyce was adamant that she was only twelve, and not thirteen. When she thought about it, she had heard many of the children argue about their ages. Marjorie was also one of them. Joyce had backed her up when Marjorie told Nurse that she was ten, not eleven. At any rate, you would think they would make an exception in this case. Joyce was such a good worker; she could not understand why they did not jump at the chance to take her. Well, what could she do about it? They would have to watch her though, to ensure she moved past this difficult time, or she wouldn't be any good to anyone.

Joyce relived that awful morning over and over again — waving to Marjorie and watching her little brother march down the path. It was the absolute worst day of her life. At the time, she had no idea that they were walking away forever. What made her think they were just going on a picnic? Was it the basket the nurse was carrying? If she had only known, she would have run out and grabbed Marjorie. She would have hung on to her and never let her go, no matter what. They would have to take her too. She would have begged them to take her.

"Oh, Mum, how could you make me promise? I tried," Joyce yelled at the ceiling as she wept. Where were they now? Did they still remember her? Did anyone miss her? Nurse heard Joyce's cries. She peeked in the dorm and saw that she was alone in the room, lying on her cot. She decided that it was best to leave her alone. She would eventually get over it and be tougher for the experience.

Chapter 10

LEAVING LIVERPOOL

Come cheer up, my lads, the way groweth clear
To migrate some more in this glorious year
To the Empire we call you, free men, not slaves,
You will enjoy the life o'er the waves.[1]

SEPTEMBER 10, 1937

Marjorie stopped halfway up the gangplank, put her suitcase down, and looked up towards the deck. A puzzled expression crossed her brow. She glanced back down at the dock but saw nothing to explain what caught her attention, so she hurried to catch up with Kenny. They both marvelled at the size of the ship. Being this close filled them with awe.

Kenny's excitement left him almost speechless as he pointed out to Marjorie the flags flying at the bow and the stern of the ship and the two large smokestacks. He told her that he saw the name — *Duchess of Atholl*. He wondered if they would allow him to explore all over the ship, especially the engine room. He hurried his sister, wanting to get up on deck as quickly as possible.

Marjorie was about to ask him how he could get so excited about exploring the ship's engine, when the strange sound caught her attention again. Kenny kept going, his suitcase weighing him down, but she stopped to look around and tracked the sound to a group of people huddled on the deck of the ship near the top of the gangplank. A little girl was crying.

Crying was a normal sound, but the sound that she heard was different — all mixed up with the regular cry. Something was seriously wrong.

As she neared the top, she could see that part of the commotion was coming from a very distressed woman, who was pulling at a little girl.[2] Marjorie recognized the girl as one who had come from the Middlemore Home with her. The two younger chaperones were trying to bring the situation under control. Marjorie watched, horrified as one of them held the girl while the other pried the woman's fingers from the little girl's arm. When the woman fell backwards onto the railing, one of the chaperones quickly headed for the cabin with the child, while the other stayed behind. The sobbing woman stood motionless for a long moment, then screamed that she wanted her daughter, and begged them not to take her away to Canada. The chaperone reminded her that the Fairbridge Society now had guardianship over the girl and that nothing could be done about it. As she walked away from the distraught mother, she told her it was time to leave the ship. Marjorie jumped aside as the mother stumbled past her, her wails growing louder as she neared the bottom of the gangplank.

CANADIAN PACIFIC S S. "DUCHESS OF ATHOLL".   Gross Tonnage 20,119.

SKIDMORE FAMILY COLLECTION.

Marjorie's group travelled across the Atlantic on the Canadian Pacific steamship *Duchess of Atholl*. The first ten parties of Fairbridge children travelled across the Atlantic on one of the CPR Duchess series of ships: *Atholl, Bedford, Richmond,* and *York*. The *Duchess of Atholl* was sunk off the coast of Africa in October 1942, by a German U-boat when the liner was serving as a troop ship for Allied Forces.

Telegram from London to the Immigration Branch in Ottawa, announcing that the Fairbridge party had sailed for Canada on September 10, 1937. Documents such as this were a valuable source of information for enabling verification Marjorie's dates of travel.

The skyline of Liverpool has undergone little change since Marjorie sailed from this port on the Mersey River.

Marjorie reached the boat deck, but, instead of finding her group, walked towards the bow, put her suitcase down, and stood as if glued at the railing. The little girl's mother yelled out her daughter's name one last time, then a strange quietness enveloped her. Marjorie kept her eyes on the dock, fascinated by the slumped figure. There were people everywhere, waving on the docks, climbing the plank, pushing carts, but to Marjorie there were only two — herself and the woman whose grief seemed to match her own.

Marjorie sat on her suitcase, and stayed by the railing for a long time, just watching. The last of the travellers arrived and seamen hauled the gangplank aboard, but the mother didn't move. Men on the dock untied the huge lines, while others pulled the ropes aboard, dripping with water, and coiled them neatly on the deck. Marjorie stayed, spellbound by the mother's misery.

Did her own mum miss her? She had not seen or heard from her since she left Whitley Bay. Did her mum know what was happening? No! How could she know? She would not have sent them away if she knew they were going to take them to Canada. Still, it was Joyce and Audrey that she needed the most right now. She was used to being away from her mum. It was not fair that they allowed Joyce to stay to stay in England. But they said that Audrey would come to Canada one day. Joyce would probably get to go back home. As quickly as they surfaced, she forced her memories out of her mind. She had to. It was fast becoming her survival mechanism. She had to forget. Remembering hurt too much. Marjorie stood up and leaned over the railing and imagined her tears dripping into the water. Maybe they would reach the beach at Whitley Bay.

She jumped when she saw a smaller boat travelling alongside her big boat. She jumped again when the ship's horn blew. A nervous giggle escaped followed by a little sob. Still she clung to the railing as Liverpool grew smaller and smaller. Would this be the last time she saw England? Why did her mum send her away? For the millionth time she tried to make sense of what was happening to her.

It took ages to settle the children. The mother's cries had caused so much distress that it was some time before the chaperones could finally take stock of their charges. Panic ensued when they realized that they were one short; "We should have counted them before the boat pulled away!"

"Who is missing?" A chaperone demanded of the children as she hurriedly pulled out her list of names.

"I think Marjorie is still outside on the deck. She's my sister," Kenny told them.

Marjorie had not moved from her railing. Tiredness rooted her to the spot. Seagulls flew alongside. Did their wings ever get tired? She wondered. The chaperone pulled her arm and asked her what she was doing on her own. The relief in her voice was audible as she told Marjorie that she had given them all quite a fright. Marjorie clung to the railing, ignoring instructions to come in out of the cold and find her sleeping berth before tea time. As she watched the shoreline fade away, the twinkling of the city lights was all she could see.

Marjorie's distress was threatening to swallow her whole. The feeling was so overpowering that she wrapped herself in an imaginary cloak in an attempt to block out the family she missed, the land she loved, and all the things she couldn't understand. Although only ten years old, she instinctively knew that to survive she had to forget. Marjorie looked away from Liverpool and whispered, "I'm never going to see my mum again, am I?"

The chaperone replied, her voice cheerful, "Now what do you think we'll have for our tea? I'm really hungry, how about you?"

Marjorie followed her, and as the door was closing, she grabbed one last look at Britain's shoreline. "Do you think the seagulls ever get tired?"

Impatiently, the young woman pulled Marjorie into the room and told her to stop asking foolish questions. Once they were below deck where the girls would be sleeping, she warned Marjorie not to go off again and to stay with the other girls at all times. The girls had five minutes to stow away their suitcases in their small sleeping quarters and then it would be tea time.

Afterwards everyone readied for bed. No one complained; it had been a very long day. Marjorie shared a tiny, windowless below-deck cabin with three other girls. As the girls settled into their beds, they became more aware of the boat's movement — up and down, and side to side as the ship wallowed in the ocean swells. A few moans and complaints of upset stomachs started the first night and became the trend that followed them all across the Atlantic. Many rarely left their bunks during the entire crossing.

Whenever they did venture out, they immediately felt queasy and the little food they were able to swallow came right back up. Marjorie had no idea that she would get used to the stench before the boat docked in Canada.

She was lying in her bunk, wishing she could just die. The motion of the boat, the smell of the little room, and thoughts of where she was going and what she was leaving behind all came together and put her in her own little world of chaos. She did not want a new life. She just wanted to be with her family. She did not want to be brave and go to a beautiful country. She did not want to be a farmer's wife. She tossed and turned in her bunk those first couple of days, lost in a nightmare that knew no boundaries between night and day or between being asleep or awake.

On the third day, Marjorie ventured out on deck. She took a few big gulps of fresh air and felt even better. One of the sailors welcomed her and told her that he was happy to see that she finally found her "sea legs." She told him that she still felt horrid, though it was lovely being away from the smelly cabin. Just then Kenny came into view and Marjorie caught his attention. The sailor laughed and said that the young man hadn't had any seasickness at all and had explored every inch of the vessel — a true sailor in the making.

"I hear you didn't get seasick at all, you lucky sod," Marjorie said as she ran up to him.

"Marjorie, they let me see the engines and I've been all over the ship," Kenny exclaimed. He told her that the sailors had rigged up a jumping platform in one of the holds by stretching a heavy piece of canvas and tying it tight to the beams on the boat, and offered to show it to her. As they got closer, they could hear squeals of delight. A sailor welcomed Marjorie and helped her on when it was her turn. The jumping tarp proved to be one of the highlights of the trip, at least for those children who managed to shake off their seasickness.[3]

The sailors were the best. They thought of ways to amuse the adventurous children and were very kind to those cooped up below deck. They made a point of visiting them, taking words of encouragement along with some oranges and sweets. And best of all, they made sock dolls and gave one to each girl. Most of the girls did not have the stomach to eat the treats, but they hugged their little dolls.

In spite of the cramped quarters, the sour smells, the constant movement of the ship, the stormy weather, and the seasickness, Marjorie felt apprehensive about the prospect of having to leave the boat. As they travelled up the St. Lawrence, a light rain drizzled over the deck, and the air chilled her to the bone. She tried to make sense of all the stories she heard about Canada. Were they all true? Was Canada really a land of ice and snow? If this was Canada she was looking at right now, it was just wet.

Were they telling the truth when they told them that Canada was full of cowboys and Indians? If they were anything like the pictures shows, then this could be a serious problem. One of the girls in her group had seen a movie about such things. She talked of tomahawks and bows and arrows and scalping and sneaking up and getting you in your sleep *and* attacking trains — all the things nightmares were made of. Some of the children said that Canada also had mounted police and they would take care of the bad people. But adults couldn't be trusted to recognize bad people. The people who were sending her away were bad, but all the other adults seemed to think that these were really good people.

When it was almost time to leave the boat, they were told to get their suitcases ready. Marjorie had no desire to cross the ocean again, but at the same time she was afraid to go ashore. Were the great empty needy lands of Canada really waiting for her? They told her it would take four days to cross Canada, and she thought that gave the cowboys and Indians a lot of opportunity to attack their train. She considered finding a good hiding place until the boat headed back to Liverpool. Being seasick was awful, but it was preferable to being attacked. When the boat got back to Liverpool, she could get off and find her way back to Whitley Bay. That would mean leaving Kenny, unless she could somehow find him and tell him about her plans. She would do that as soon as she found a good hiding place. Yes, then she could take him too; he would love to stay on the boat.

Marjorie found what seemed like a good spot, but when she tried it out, it was dark and scary. The experience jolted her, and, once again she instinctively knew she could not trust herself to make the right decisions, now that she was in this foreign land that had been thrust upon her. Suddenly, it seemed important to stick together with all the others.

SEPTEMBER 18, 1937

The boat docked first in Quebec City. Marjorie looked at the unfamiliar land. She wiped the drizzle from her face and was glad to be wearing her heavy coat. There was no September warmth to greet them on this new shore. What a busy port! So many boats, some coming in, some going out, and some with huge fumes of black smoke billowing above their smokestacks. She wondered what would happen next, but part of her did not care anymore.

Once the boat docked, the Fairbridge children were escorted into a separate room on the ship to be examined apart from the other passengers. A chaperone handed a uniformed man a large envelope full of papers. It seemed to take him forever to go through all the papers, all the while looking up and down the line of bewildered children.

Finally he spoke, and, in a gruff voice, warned that they had better be in good health and have had all their shots. They were told to take off their coats and pull up their sleeves. With memories of the shots at Canada House still fresh in their minds, the travel-weary children reacted with alarm and tears began to flow. Each had four scabby red welts, the size of a farthing on the top of an arm.

(THIRD CLASS)

IMMIGRATION IDENTIFICATION CARD

THIS CARD MUST BE SHOWN TO THE EXAMINING OFFICER AT PORT OF ARRIVAL

Name of passenger _Marjorie Arnison_

Name of ship _33_ DUCHESS OF ATHOLL _2_

Name appears on Return sheet _33_   line _2_

Medical Examination Stamp | Civil Examination Stamp

(See back)

Marjorie was surprised to discover her original immigration card, along with a birth certificate sent out by her mother in 1947, were placed in her personal file in the British Columbia Archives, Victoria. Many child migrants found it difficult to gain access to their records until the Child Migrants Trust was established in 1987 by Margaret Humphreys.

"Do we have to have more jabs?" The chaperone assured them that all they needed to do was to show that they had all their shots before leaving England. The relief was audible. Eventually they all cleared customs and marched to a holding room where they were told to put their cases along the wall since they would be staying aboard until the ship reached Montreal. There, they would meet their new escorts and join the train that would take them across Canada.

The children busied themselves as best as they could. It was cool on the deck, but most of the children preferred to be out there, taking in the sights and sounds of what was to be their new homeland. Finally, they were told to get ready to disembark, and to make sure they had all of their belongings. Mr. Healy told them to line up with their partners, boys first, then the girls.

The latest batch of new little Canadians bustled down the gangplank. Many were eager to set foot on the new homeland that they were going to help settle, others followed because there was little else that they could do. They walked to the terminal and stood along the platform, waiting to board their train.

In the busy Montreal station, the children clung tightly to their partners, trying not to get lost. Mr. and Mrs. Healy had walked ahead and were talking to a young man and woman. The young chaperones approached the two newcomers and were visibly relieved to find they were representatives of the Prince of Wales Fairbridge Farm School in British Columbia. The six adults talked briefly, exchanging papers and information, then the chaperones from the ship turned to the children and said goodbye. Mr. and Mrs. Healy, and the two new chaperones, Ivy Whitman, and George Nairns turned their attention back to their wards.[4]

Mr. Healy counted heads as they boarded their train. Mrs. Healy and Mr. Nairns led the way, and the girls followed, "… 7, 8, 9. Good! Now boys, do not push. Up you go … 15, 16, 17, 18 … Oh no! Did I count correctly? Who is missing? Miss Whitman, we have one boy missing. You look this way and I'll look down here."

Miss Whitman looked behind her, and then down the platform. There were so many people it was difficult to see past them. She could see a youngster way down the platform, but from this distance it was impossible to tell if he was one of theirs. She ran up to him. Yes indeed, she recognized his Fairbridge coat and hat.

"Goodness, what are you doing?"

"I got lost. Everyone was gone." A relieved sob shook his little body.

She grabbed the youngster by the arm and headed back to their train car and helped him up the stairs. They seated the children and did another head count just to make sure. With a sigh of relief, they counted twenty-eight children: nineteen boys and nine girls. The children were to be on the train for four days. They would have use of the dining car they were sitting in and the one sleeping car just behind it.

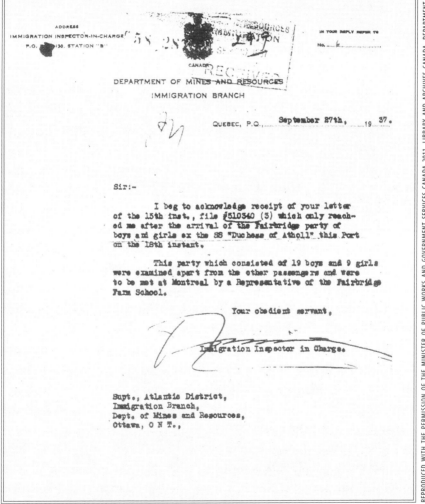

The formal letter from the Immigration Branch regarding the arrival and successful entry to Canada of the September 1937 Fairbridge party of home children.

"No running around the train." Mr. Healy pointed to a large box and told the children that the YMCA in Montreal had provided them with puzzles, crayons, books to colour, and books to read. They were to help themselves and share with one another. He finished by telling them it was expected that they would all be on their very best behaviour — at all times. He asked if anyone had any questions.

Someone read out "CPR" and said that was just like the ship they were on — the *Duchess of Atholl* said CPR too. He wondered what it meant but did not get an answer, his voice drowned out by others who were suddenly concerned about the cowboys and Indians and buffalo. Excitedly, they jostled and pushed each other as they scrambled to look out the window. An older boy told them they were silly fools, since they had not left the station yet.

Marjorie wished that the talk would keep away from cowboys and Indians. She had too many things to worry about already. She went towards one of the empty window spots on the platform side. Some people were saying goodbye, some were saying hello, and others were running this way and that way. She watched a small group on the platform below her. The mother had three small children with her. The father was kissing and hugging them. A jealousy crept in almost choking her — her own father had never given her kisses or hugs, at least none that she could remember. The train's whistle blew, and the father jumped on board the train. The children clung to their mother. Marjorie could hear the children call out, "Bye-bye Papa, come back soon. Bring me a present when you come back."

"Indeed I will!" he yelled back. "Bye now, and be good for your mother."

The family seemed so happy with each other. Marjorie wondered why her family was different. She hardly knew her own father. He never ever brought her a present. She looked closer and could see the mother and her children standing there and waving as the train pulled out. Marjorie, frightened by her tears, brushed them away. She missed her mum. She missed Joyce and Audrey. She noticed Kenny looking at her. It was no good crying. She put on her brave face.

In the evening the porter made up their beds. Marjorie was surprised to see that the dining-car tables folded down to make bunks. She shared hers with another girl. She made sure she slept on the outside, curling up as close to the edge as possible. That way, if the Indians attacked the train at night they would probably reach into the middle of the bed, get the other girl, and miss her. She was glad that there was nowhere for the bad people to hide under the bed. There was so much to be afraid of in her new world. She had always felt safe when she was with her mum. Besides, the mattress at home was on the floor.

It was a different experience sleeping on a train. Marjorie found the constant movement and swaying of the train easier when she was lying down. The *clickety-clack* of the wheels soothed her and helped to get the scary thoughts out of her mind. Nevertheless, that first night she awoke abruptly, caught up in a nightmare. She tumbled out of her bunk, a mass of tangled bedclothes, and landed with a loud thud on the floor. Someone scolded her for making noise. She quickly scrambled back and tried to make herself safe under her blankets. The other little girl she was sleeping with didn't even wake up.

In the morning, the porter put the beds away for the day and quickly transformed the area back into a dining room. Soon the children were hungrily slurping down bowls of shredded wheat. For most, their appetites had returned after not being able to eat much aboard the *Duchess of Atholl*. On the afternoon of the second day, Marjorie found the nerve to look out of the window. She was relieved to see no sign of cowboys, Indians, or buffalo. She saw land, flat and golden and she could see forever. That was all. Great empty spaces. Where were they taking her? Four days to get to the other side — how the train could be going this speed for another two days and not reach the other side before then baffled her. But then, everything baffled her.

Tomorrow would be her birthday. She would be eleven years old. Her last birthday seemed centuries ago. Was her mum still living on Whitley Road? They had moved so many times that she doubted they would still be there. Would she remember that it was her birthday? She hoped so. She was going to be eleven years old — and it did not seem real that she was riding on this never-ending train. She was now in a foreign land. People here spoke English, but they didn't sound English.

Marjorie had been struggling with a nauseous feeling ever since she climbed on the train. Her tummy felt best when she was lying in her bunk. But even that was turning out to be a bad place. At night, it was impossible to ignore the worry that spun around in her mind. As she lay, she thought and thought and thought about things. She wanted to cry, but fear held the upper hand. How on earth would she ever find her mum and Joyce again? She worked at pushing these thoughts away and tried to think about where she was going. When at last she fell asleep, another bad dream was waiting for her.

Eleven

PIER D, PORT OF VANCOUVER

Here I stand,
Tears denied, dry-eyed.
Peering over this strange land
How I long for my Whitley Bay sand.

SEPTEMBER 22, 1937

The children were excited as the train wheels screeched to a halt at the CPR station in Vancouver. They tussled with each other, pushing open the train windows, trying to get their first glimpse of the city. People standing on the platform stared back at them. The Fairbridge farm school officials waiting for the train headed over to gather up their new charges.

Reporters from the *Vancouver Sun* and the *Daily Province* (Vancouver) were also waiting. They paced the platform, impatient for a story. As the train stopped, one of them commented that the train was sharp on time. "Now, let's see what these little Brits have to say for themselves." The other reporter pointed to the man leading the Fairbridge group and said that he recognized that fellow from the last group of child migrants. They started to make notes as the children yelled from their train window.

"Hooray, hooray, hooray! We're finally here!" A chorus of happy cheers rang out over the platform as the young travellers clambered off the train — the boys wearing caps, short brown wool pants, long socks, and long brown coats with the Fairbridge orange and brown striped ties decorating their necks, and the girls in blue coats with matching tams. The escorts followed, equally happy to be disembarking. Vancouver's wonderful September sunshine greeted them. It was a welcome sight after the long ocean crossing and four days confined to the train. The children looked around, suddenly subdued they blinked in the morning sunshine and cautiously surveyed the new country they were to call home.

Marjorie looked wary. A deep tiredness had invaded her. She held onto a small white box, her hands almost crushing the paper. She didn't want to lose it. The porter had taken her suitcase, so the only thing she had to look after was the little box and her little brother. She noticed her escorts greeting a new group of people and imagined that they would be their next escorts. She just barely got used to one set of people when everything changed again. The Vancouver station was busy. She stuck close to her group, not wanting to find herself alone but also kept her eye on Kenny, to make certain that he didn't wander off.

THE VANCOUVER SUN, SEPTEMBER 22, 1937.

The Vancouver Sun on Wednesday, September 22, 1937, carried a story and photograph of the arrival of Marjorie's group. Marjorie is the girl, bottom centre, with the white box in her right hand and waving with her left hand. Kenny is the boy hunched over in the top centre hunched over.

"Colonel Logan, how nice to see you!" The escorts shouted in unison to the principal of the Prince of Wales Fairbridge Farm School.

The cook and the head chef strolled off the train next. A huge cheer interrupted the morning as the children yelled out: "Hooray for the cooks!" The head chef smiled and said they could report that they fed this lot six hundred meals in four days in the special colonist car. "Nothing wrong with their appetites. They're the best bunch yet."[1]

Seizing the moment, the reporters hurried over to the children. "Welcome to Vancouver. So, you are happy to be here in Canada, are you?"

"Oh, yes indeed!" one of the boys shouted out.

"We hear you are bound for the Fairbridge farm school? What was your trip like?"

"We were seasick on the big boat," began one youngster. "It was horrid!" he added, making a face to show just how bad it really was.

The action of a little boy, carrying a small toy gun that was cocked and ready to fire, caught one reporter's attention. The boy looked wary. "Why the gun, laddie?"[2] the reporter asked.

With a charming smile the little boy whispered, "It's for the Indians and the bad men." The reporter laughed as he replied that there were not many Indians and only a few bad men. The boy smiled again but kept the gun cocked.[3] A bystander, listening to the conversation, warned the children to watch out for the Indians on Vancouver Island. The children stopped, the grins quickly disappearing from their faces. They had been told that the farm school they were going to was on Vancouver Island. A young fellow with a strong Irish accent asked if there really were Indians there. The man chuckled and said there were and told the lad that he would have to be awfully careful, as the Indians over on Vancouver Island just love Irish stew.[4]

The reporter, seeing the concern in the children's faces, thought it best to change the subject. "Hey, let's take your picture," he suggested. "Here, some of you stand on this baggage cart and then we can get you all in." The children scrambled and jostled to get into position. Most stood, but it quickly became crowded so some stood on the ground in front. Marjorie sat on the edge of the cart, and, when they told her to wave for the camera, she held her little white box tightly with one hand, hoping she wouldn't drop it. A few of the boys waved their hats and cheered.

The reporters had more questions for the youngsters. They had a curious public who wanted to know all about these little immigrants and their Prince of Wales Fairbridge Farm School. Some of the children were shy, but others in the group looked boldly about them. A reporter turned to a boy who looked eager to talk and asked him what he thought of this great country of Canada.

"Well," he began, "it's a whacking big country.[5] But mister, we were told that English money is no good here and that you have to use cents and dollars.[6] Is that true?"

"Oh, yes indeed. Canadian money is different from English money."

Another lad boldly walked forward and told the reporter, "I think Canada needs people to cultivate it and we're the people to do it."[7]

"How is that?" a voice behind the lad asked.

He turned to the other reporter "We saw so much vacant land. Fairbridge is going to teach us how to farm and that will give England a good name and Fairbridge a good name. We are here to help make the country British."[8] The reporters would have pressed for more, but the children were soon whisked away.

A matronly woman addressed the children. "I want to tell you about your new home," she began, and described the farm school valley with its meadows and rivers and beautiful forests. One young boy, who looked puzzled, as if he was trying to picture this new home in his mind, asked if there weren't any sidewalks where could they play. She assured him that they would have beautiful meadows and fields in which to play that were so much nicer than the dirty old streets.[9] The boy, however, looked unsatisfied with her answer.

Colonel Logan turned to face his charges and asked for everyone's attention. He introduced himself as the principal of their new home, the Prince of Wales Fairbridge Farm School. He said that he and Mrs. Logan would be making sure that they all arrived at the Fairbridge farm school safe and sound later today. It was now time to carry on with their morning tour and he asked them to follow him as he walked over towards a waiting bus.

The young travellers scrambled up the bus steps and found a seat. Marjorie sat, watching and wondering what would happen next, her little white box safely on her lap. They were told that the bus driver would be taking them on a tour of Vancouver, first through the downtown section and then around a huge lovely park called Stanley Park. The driver was to have them back in time to catch the eleven o'clock sailing on the ferryboat, the *Princess Elaine*,[10] for their trip to Nanaimo.

Someone shouted, "Is the Fairbridge farm school at Nanaimo?"

"Sir, how much longer? Will we ever get there?" a little lad piped up.

"Not another boat ride!" a girl cried out.

A growing fear of yet another unknown and the fresh memories of seasickness flooded their minds and a wave of panic threatened to erupt. One young child burst into tears, worried that they were going out to sea again. Colonel Logan quickly responded in a calm but firm voice, ordering them to settle down while assuring them that they had nothing to fear. He told them that the ferry trip was not a long one, and, since there was little wind, it would be a smooth crossing. There was nothing to fear. Once the ferry docked at Nanaimo on Vancouver Island there would be another bus waiting for them. It would only take a couple of hours to get to the farm school, and they would be there in time for tea.

"Then, no more travelling. You will finally be home." Mrs. Logan smiled at the children.

Hearing this, one of the younger children wailed that he wanted to go to *his* home because he missed his mum. A quick retort came from one of

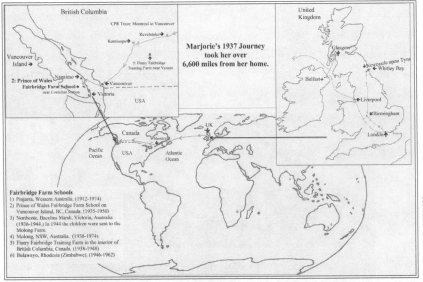

A map of Marjorie's journey from Whitley Bay to the Fairbridge farm school on Vancouver Island.

the older boys telling him not to be a silly sod as it was way, way too far away. Marjorie looked at her little brother, her heart going out to him. It would not take long before Kenny stopped asking for his mum. The bigger kids bullied the crybabies. Her short experience as a new "orphan" had taught her that complaining or crying was a waste of time. All it brought was trouble. It was important not to make too much noise, not to ask certain questions, and not to expect answers to the few questions she did dare to ask. She knew that she had to accept what was happening without complaint or tears. To do anything else just brought punishment or teasing.

Tiredness clung like a shroud around many of them as they were bussed around Vancouver. They had travelled over 6,000 miles in the last two weeks and the hustle and bustle had taken its toll. Few even noticed the scenery during their trip through the city of Vancouver or its beautiful Stanley Park. They looked out the windows but could not absorb any more information in their weary minds.

A group of children stood by the railing with Colonel Logan as the *Princess Elaine* ploughed her way across the Strait of Georgia, gently riding the swells. Soon the coastline of Vancouver Island was taking shape.

The CPR ferry that took the children to Vancouver Island, the *Princess Elaine*, entered service on the Vancouver to Nanaimo run in May 1928. The children had travelled the entire way from Liverpool to Vancouver Island via CPR.

They were getting close. One of the escorts caught the children's attention and pointed to an island, which formed part of the entrance to the harbour. He told them that it was called Newcastle and that just beyond the island was Nanaimo where the ferry would dock.

Marjorie looked at him as if he was daft. She dropped her box on the deck and quickly picked it up as she responded with "Newcastle, sir? Surely it's not our Newcastle?" A funny feeling spread through her, could it be that they were still in England and Newcastle was not far from Whitley Bay. He took a moment to realize what she meant. He assured her that this was a different Newcastle, that this Newcastle was a little island off the town of Nanaimo.

Soon the whistle blasted, signalling that the boat was getting ready to dock. The escorts counted their children and prepared everyone to disembark and make their way to the bus waiting for them on the platform, ready to take them home. It sounded strange to hear the man to say "home" when everything felt so unfamiliar to the children as they walked off the ferry. Vancouver Island, Nanaimo, Duncan, Cowichan Station — the names in this country sounded so alien. Home should be something familiar and comforting. For Marjorie the seagulls were the only familiar things here. They reminded her of Whitley Bay and a chilly sadness poured through her as she thought of how far away she was from her real home. She hated hearing them say "home." This was not her home. How could it ever be?

A Vancouver Island Coach Lines bus, hired to pick up the arriving group of children once their ferry docked, sitting on the Nanaimo dock. The suitcases are stowed on top and the children are aboard, ready to go the last thirty-five miles of their journey to Cowichan Station and their new home.

When the bus pulled away from the ferry landing, restlessness and anxiety settled over Marjorie. She had no choice but to hang on for the ride. She dropped her little white box again as the bus lurched, and nearly lost it as it slid under her seat and ended up somewhere behind her. Luckily Kenny grabbed it and passed it back to her before one of the older boys claimed it. They soon left Nanaimo behind. The scant buildings became fewer and fewer and the forests thicker. She thought of stories of children being taken deep into the forest and left there to perish. How could she be so certain that they would not be doing that with them? This new country seemed so very isolated and lonely. Where were towns and cities? They were told that they were travelling south to the farm school and that it wasn't far now. For Marjorie, they were just travelling away, far away from everything she was accustomed to and heading to she knew not where.

Twelve

PRINCE OF WALES FAIRBRIDGE FARM SCHOOL

The old bus drove through
Town after town
Taking the children
To the end end end
Of the road.

SEPTEMBER 22, 1937

Travelling, travelling, travelling. The road seemed endless. Sometimes Marjorie could see glimpses of water from the twisty road. Was it the ocean? Huge trees towered over them. At times she could see seagulls flying overhead and also some huge white-headed black birds sitting in the treetops. Colonel Logan said they were bald eagles. Marjorie wondered why they were bald.

Some of the mountains had snow on them, but not like the Rocky Mountains though. The Rocky Mountains were a sight to see after the flat land. The chef on the train told them about how the mountains went for miles, all the way down the United States. The chef also told them that the United States was very close. Imagine — she was in Canada, and really close to the United States! She never dreamed that she would ever see such places.

Marjorie watched Kenny out of the corner of her eye. He was trying to be brave. Why did they keep telling them how wonderful their new lives would be? No one seemed to care or to understand that she was happy with her old life. She never asked for a new life. She did not want a new family and a new country. Marjorie let out a sigh. Kenny turned to her and she forced a smile at him.

Colonel Logan's experience with children on long bus rides had taught him to keep them busy and occupied so they would have little time to worry about what was going to happen next. He was aware of the restlessness settling in and felt it was time for some singing — always a good diversion. The Fairbridge songs would be perfect and they could drive through the Fairbridge gates with a sense of pride and belonging. He stood up and told the children that if they were very good, he would teach them some new songs.

"Would you like that? Let me see your hands." All the children put up their hands. He told them that he would sing the song first, and then they could try it with him. The first song was about the founder of their new farm school.

"Who knows the founder's name?" Several of the children blurted out in unison: "The Prince!" An older boy sneered, showing his scorn told the "dolts" that they didn't know anything and that Fairbridge was the founder. He looked ahead, seeking approval.

"Yes, that's right, it was Kingsley Fairbridge and the song, 'Fairbridge the Founder' goes like this:

> We are Fairbridge folk, all as good as e'er,
> English, Welsh and Scottish, we have come from everywhere;
> Boys to be farmers and girls for farmers wives,
> We follow Fairbridge, the Founder.[1]

Now, repeat after me: 'We are Fairbridge folk, all as good as e'er....'"
The children's voices echoed around the bus. After they sang "Follow the Founder" several times, Colonel Logan told them they were such very good singers that he would teach them the "Fairbridge March." He stood up and pretended to be marching in the aisles of the bus.

> Cheerio!
> Here we are
> Working hard

On the land

On our Fairbridge Farm....[2]

The principal's voice boomed down the aisle of the bus. Most tried to keep up with him and did their best not to jumble the words. Marjorie, however, would not sing. She did not want God to bless her home in Canada. She did not want to be in Canada. And they can't make her be a farmer's wife! The swaying of the bus was making her feel nauseous. She sat and looked out of the window, but all she could see was the forest. She tried her best to not think of the stories where children were taken deep into the forest and left there.

Marjorie worried about everything and now she was especially worried about Kenny. There were only fleeting moments when they could talk about things. Kenny's urgent voice had startled her when he cornered her on the ferry. He had begged her to promise not to tell anyone and he hadn't even told her anything yet. He whispered that he would really get it from them if she told. Marjorie assured him that she wouldn't say anything to anybody. He looked over his shoulder first, and, in a very low voice, told her that he had trouble going to sleep at night because of bad dreams. Marjorie hesitated and then confidentially told him that night time was also her worst time.

Kenny seemed relieved that he was not the only one afraid at night. He told his big sister that one night at Middlemore he pushed his blanket in his mouth so that no one could hear him cry, but a bully caught him and it was awful. He kept poking him and calling him a cry-baby and said that he needed a suckie blankie. Then he pushed the blanket into Kenny's mouth, really far until it choked him. Kenny was able to pull it out and yell until someone came and stopped the boy. The bully was punished but he really got Kenny after that and now keeps on picking on him. Marjorie looked at her little brother. He was only eight years old. How could she protect him?

He looked at his sister and asked what she had asked herself over and over. Why? Why did they send us away? He told her he missed their mum and wanted to go home. Kenny sighed. Marjorie could see that he was trying his best to be brave. He whispered to his sister that he hated it when the big boys called him a cry baby. As he turned back to stare out of the window, Marjorie could see a tear sliding down his cheek. He wiped furiously at it. Marjorie wanted to comfort him, but her own fears were too raw. Kenny's brown cap had slid over on a funny angle and she could see his shoulders shudder.

The bus lurched as it went through a tight corner. Huge trees lined the roadway, their tops now impossible to see from Marjorie's seat. As she looked ahead, the trees seemed to form a tunnel. She bounced along in silence, listening to the singing, and watching the trees go by. It had been over a fortnight since they left Middlemore and it seemed that they had not stopped moving in all that time.

Marjorie opened the lid of the little box she was carrying. Her little piece of birthday cake was not travelling well. It had broken apart and squished to one side, and some of the icing had stuck to the lid. She scraped her finger through it and popped some into her mouth. It had dried out a bit on the surface but was still creamy underneath. The taste held hope for her. Marjorie had survived the passage over the Atlantic Ocean and nothing had attacked them crossing Canada, but would she survive what lay ahead? The little piece of cake was something to carry to her new home.

UNIVERSITY OF LIVERPOOL ARCHIVES, SPECIAL COLLECTIONS BRANCH, FAIRBRIDGE ARCHIVES, D296.F4.

The bus carrying a new group of children nears at the remote Prince of Wales Fairbridge Farm School near Cowichan Station. The last leg of the children's over six thousand-mile journey is almost at an end.

Marjorie took another taste of the icing and closed the lid. She liked the chef on the train because he was good to all the children, and he was such a nice man to give her this piece of cake yesterday. It hadn't been a happy birthday for her, but the cake was a nice surprise. She longed to eat it, yet she couldn't. She couldn't really name the reason why not, but she sensed that to eat this foreign birthday cake might symbolize an acceptance of her new life and having birthdays without her family. She had been so happy at turning ten on her last birthday. Maybe they sent her away because she skipped school and snuck down to the Whitley Bay sands to play. Maybe it was because she was bad and always asked for things. Maybe that is why her mum sent her away. No! She was not always bad and her mum loved her! That was the one thing she was certain of, and the reason why it was so difficult to understand why she put them on the train and sent them away.

Colonel Logan stopped singing to announce that they were almost at the end of their journey. He turned to look at the busload of children. Twenty-eight pairs of young eyes looked back at him. The bus swayed a little and he had to hang on to the top of two seats to keep his balance. One more corner and they would be home. Moments later, the bus passed through a set of gates. Colonel Logan called them the "Pearly Gates" and said that they were the entrance to the Prince of Wales Fairbridge Farm School. He said that everyone at the farm school was expecting them and looking forward to meeting the newcomers. He reminded them that some had a brother or a sister already at the school, and they were very happy that their brothers and sisters were coming to join them.

As they drove past the farm gates, the remoteness astounded Marjorie. They had travelled through miles and miles of trees to get here. The farm school was in the middle of a great forest. Children lined the road and ran alongside the bus yelling, "The bus is here. They are here! They are here!" All Marjorie could think of was where is here?

When the bus slowed to a stop, Colonel Logan stood and faced the weary travellers, and, with a big smile, said, "Well my little Canadians, you are finally home."

The children clambered off the bus. Marjorie stood and stared. Clutching her little box of cake, the treasured symbol of her eleventh birthday, she felt quite alone standing on the side of the dusty farm road. All she could see was a landscape that looked scarred with recent logging and the tall, tall trees surrounding them. Where were Audrey and Joyce? Every time she thought of not seeing them again, a panicky feeling filled her. She had made friends with some of the girls on the journey over, but she wanted her sisters and she wanted her mum. They were her family, not these people. Without them, the loneliness threatened to swallow her up. Tears tried to come but she quickly squelched them. If she let her tears go, she felt she might cry forever.

UNIVERSITY OF LIVERPOOL ARCHIVES, SPECIAL COLLECTIONS BRANCH, FAIRBRIDGE ARCHIVES, D296.F4/1/1/6.

Finally, the children arrive at the Prince of Wales Fairbridge Farm School. Some of the school cottages are visible in the background. The new group is welcomed by anxious children who wait to see if they have a brother or sister in the arriving party.

SKIDMORE FAMILY COLLECTION.

Marjorie, far right, still holding onto the white box with her piece of birthday cake, and Kenny, third from right, are just off the bus at the Prince of Wales Fairbridge Farm School. The children without coats on the far left are the Fairbridge children, coming to greet the bus.

The little group of new child migrants stood near the bus, watching, wondering what to do next. Kenny stood not far from Marjorie. She scanned the crowd hoping to find her big brothers, Fred and Norman, but they were not there. She also looked for Joyce and Audrey, just in case. The children, who only a moment ago waited nosily for the bus to come to a stop, stood quietly and stared. Then suddenly they were waving and jumping up and down with excitement. Two brothers found each other. A girl shouted out "Johnny!" and ran to him. They were so happy to see each other. Their happiness saddened Marjorie as she watched the kids hug each other, and she turned away. She had never imagined that the Prince of Wales Fairbridge Farm School was like this. If her mum came looking for her, she would never be able to find her.

Fortunately, the children were not given any further time to stand and worry. There was a lot to do before the evening meal.

"Okay, boys and girls, quiet now. Pay attention. All the new children listen to me. I will call out your names and you can go and meet your cottage mothers. Then we will all meet in half an hour in the dining hall for a special tea." As Colonel Logan called their names, they gingerly walked over and lined up behind their assigned prefects, the older children selected to help the cottage mothers.

"Off you go now."

Picking up their suitcases, they followed their leaders. The younger travellers found their cases too much to carry and dragged them along in the dust. The older children offered to help the little ones, but Marjorie held onto hers; it was all she had that she could call her own now. She wanted to stop and put her box of cake in it so she could use two hands for her case, but she didn't dare break the line. It was all too bewildering. She had come this far — she had been sent this far — and now she was about to begin the next phase of her journey. It was a journey that neither she nor her mother would ever have imagined, but one that someone called Kingsley Fairbridge had envisioned for them.

The boys moved down the pathway away from the girls. Kenny, with guarded eyes, looked towards Marjorie and gave a slight wave. She waved back, and then turned to follow her group. As they walked, their prefect explained what the buildings were. The bus had stopped by the dining hall where the breakfast and noon meals were served.

"Most of the cottages at the farm school are duplexes," she said. When she saw puzzled faces looking back at her, she explained. "That is when you have two separate houses in one building, but our cottage is just a house on its own. Here is our cottage, called Atwood Cottage. If you ever get lost, just remember to ask for that name. All the cottages have names. That cottage duplex down the path next to ours is Pennant Cottage on one side and on the other side is our hospital, called Douglas Cottage." Marjorie looked up at her new home. It was a nice looking house, with a lovely white trim on all the windows.

She heard one of the Fairbridge girls say in a soft voice, "Should we warn them about the cottage mom?"

"Shh! She's on the porch," the other girl whispered back. A woman stood at the top of the stairs.

"Welcome home, girls. I am your cottage mother. How do you do?"

"Hello, ma'am," a quiet chorus of girls responded.

She told them to bring their suitcases in and opened the door, beckoning them inside. They climbed the stairs and entered the kitchen, then were shown the dorm, a large room directly off the kitchen. The newcomers had already been assigned to a cot. Marjorie counted twelve. It seemed cozier than the dorm at Middlemore, with each cot having a little shelf above for each girl's belongings. She liked that, but all their things wouldn't fit there. As if in response to Marjorie's unasked question, the cottage mother told the girls the shelves were for their nightclothes and other little personal things and the lockers in the basement were for storing the rest of their clothes. On the way to the basement, their new mother showed the new girls her sitting room and bedroom. She warned them that they mustn't ever go into her rooms unless invited, or unless it is was their duty day to tidy it up. She looked at the new girls and asked if that was clear. They replied, "Yes, ma'am."

Marjorie wondered how this could be her home if she was not allowed to go into some of the rooms. She yearned for a sense of belonging that had been missing ever since they took her from her own home. In the basement they were shown their lockers as well as the laundry tubs and the showers, a wood furnace, and the playroom. They were told that all the buildings at the farm school were heated with wood furnaces. In Marjorie's cottage, as in all the cottages, each child would share the various chores of stacking firewood and cutting kindling. Each week in the winter, one child was assigned to furnace duty, which meant waking up about three-quarters of an hour before everyone else to start the fire each morning. The house would then be warm when it was time for the rest to get up.

As they walked back up to the kitchen area, the cottage mother told them that dinner was usually prepared right there and served in the cottage by the girls, with breakfast and lunch being served in the main dining hall. But on Sundays and holidays breakfast was made in the cottage. She assured them that they would learn everything they needed to know as they went along.

"Now, a special welcome tea with hot buns and jelly is ready for you in the dining hall." The children were famished and it did not take much convincing to get them out the door.

Marjorie fidgeted in her cot that night. Her tiredness gnawed at her body, but sleep stayed away because her mind was in turmoil, thinking about her family and all that had happened in the last few days. Earlier, she had grabbed Kenny as they went into the dining hall. She just needed to be close to someone. He pulled away, embarrassed at her sudden show of affection. She was afraid of going to sleep; the nightmares would be lurking for her as soon as she closed her eyes.

The interior of the dining hall at the Prince of Wales Fairbridge Farm School, as shown in the Fairbridge Farm Schools Annual Report, 1936.

MIDDLEMORE EMIGRATION HOME, SEPTEMBER 22, 1937

Joyce was out of sickbay. She was angry — angry that they had left her behind, angry because Marjorie had her birthday without her, and angry because they took Marjorie and Kenny. And she was angry they had Audrey quarantined in sickbay. For the millionth time she tried to imagine where they had taken Marjorie and Kenny. She could not picture what Canada looked like. She hoped that they were okay. When she tried to ask the nurse, she was told to forget about them. But that was impossible! How could she forget about them? With this being her first day in the kitchen since getting out of sick bay, she tried to talk to Cook.

Cook was a little more helpful and told her that the children probably took a huge boat across the ocean. And then it takes quite a few days to get across Canada. "I should think that they have probably arrived at their new home now, as they have been gone over a fortnight." When she said that, Joyce's heart nearly broke a second time. She knew that the cook was only trying to make her feel better, but the thought of them happily settled somewhere else without her made her sad. No! It made her angry, and it made her afraid that they would forget her.

FAIRBRIDGE FARM SCHOOL

Marjorie tossed and turned. Finally she fell asleep, but was wracked with worried dreams. A bell rang. Where was she? Was it her school bell at Whitley Bay? No. She was in her new dorm and it was time to get up. The cottage mother was yelling for everyone to get dressed quickly.

"Make your beds. Breakfast is served in the main dining hall at 7:10 *sharp*! You don't want to miss breakfast do you?" The cottage mother's voice boomed out, shattering any illusion that this was Whitley Bay. Marjorie swung her legs over and stretched a bit, then let out a huge yawn. She jumped to the floor when the cottage mother shouted that she didn't hear any footsteps.

The dining hall was a beehive of activity. The children assigned to bring their cottage's cutlery and dishes ran to their tables to set them. The rest of the children sat down. Kenny was across the room. Marjorie gave him a little wave, but he did not wave back. He looked okay, but not happy.

It did not take long for the new children to figure out the farm school system. The farm had several cottages and each cottage had twelve to fourteen children and one cottage mother. They kept the boys separate from the girls — they even had their own pathways to walk on. Before Marjorie knew this, she started to run down the pathway when she saw Kenny. She just wanted to say hello to him, but an older girl yelled at her and asked her what was she doing.

"Don't go down there," she warned as she grabbed Marjorie's arm. "That's the boy's pathway and girls cannot go on that path and the boys cannot go on the girls' path. Those are the rules. You'll get a hiding if they catch you."

A group of Fairbridge girls standing at the side entrance to the Fairbridge dining hall. Marjorie is the third from the left post, back row. This photograph was quite likely used in a Fairbridge Farm School Annual Report.

This photograph of Marjorie, the girl holding the baby lamb, is labelled "Borrowed from the flock." It was used in the Fairbridge Farm School Annual Report, 1937.

Marjorie jumped back and waved at her brother. She had not been able to have a good talk with him for days. Looking after Kenny was impossible. She could only see him at meal times across the dining room, and that gave her no chance to talk to him. He always looked a little worried and during the few moments that they were able to talk, he whispered when he talked to her, as if he was afraid someone might overhear him.

The fall months passed quickly. Marjorie's days became a haze of farm chores and schoolwork. The winter months brought wind, rain, and mountains of snow, but soon there were signs of spring. Spring soon led to summer, and just when she had given up ever seeing her sisters again, her cottage mother told her that Audrey would be arriving with the next party coming in a few weeks. Marjorie stood there speechless. New kids had arrived last November, but the bus pulled away without bringing Audrey or Joyce to her, dashing her hopes. She had all but given up.

"You'll be catching flies if you don't close your mouth," her cottage mother told her.

"Really and truly, Audrey is coming? What about Joyce?" Marjorie was so excited that she could barely speak. "Does Kenny know? I have to tell Kenny!" Marjorie ran off before the cottage mother could ask her about Joyce. She had to find Kenny, even if it meant breaking the rules.

MIDDLEMORE EMIGRATION HOME, AUGUST 1938

Joyce crammed the blanket into her mouth. She wanted to scream but held onto it. She tried not to let anyone hear her. Their pitying looks were too much for her to take. Audrey had been out of quarantine for ages now, and she was as good as new. At first she looked awful with her head shaved and blue stuff all over her scalp because of the ringworm, but her hair had grown in now and it was thick and lovely.

Joyce spent as much time as she could with Audrey; it took away the pain of losing Marjorie and Kenny. The night times were wretched though, with horrid dreams where she lost Marjorie and Kenny and could not find them. She ran and ran and ran, looking everywhere until she felt her heart would burst. Her mum loomed overhead, scolding her for not keeping them safe. Frantically, Joyce continued her search, darting everywhere, looking into cupboards, under beds, behind the woodpiles. They had to be somewhere. She never found them, even though she could hear them calling out to her. Once her dream was so real that she woke up out of her sleep, sat up and listened. They have come back! "Marjorie, where are you?" she whispered.

"Oh, Joyce, go to sleep," a tired voice beside her groaned. "You are having another bad dream."

Joyce choked back the lump in her throat. Audrey had left that morning. A small group of children headed down the path with one of the nurses. Joyce knew what was happening. She now knew the routine. After her chores, she checked the dorm and looked at Audrey's cot. Her things were gone. She disappeared out of her life just like everyone else. Why did they keep leaving her behind? She had dared to dream that they kept her back so she could go with Audrey. Now Audrey had to go all by herself. Sisters need each other. Was there something wrong with her? What could it be? She was never sick, except for the time in sickbay with her broken heart. She had tried not to complain or be a bother to anyone. She tried to listen to Cook when she was working in the kitchen. She tried to be good. It was all she had left, but obviously, it was not enough.

Joyce crammed the soggy blanket further into her mouth and covered her head. She knew the others could hear her. But, what could she do? It was impossible to stop the tears. She wanted to run away, but where would she go? She had nowhere to run.

FAIRBRIDGE FARM SCHOOL, AUGUST 23, 1938

Marjorie waited for the sound of the bus turning into the farm school. Audrey should be on it. Earlier in the day she asked several times about Joyce. Was she coming too? But she was told to stop asking questions, as it was annoying. Her cottage mother looked down at Marjorie and asked why she always had a worried look on her face.

"Stand still, for goodness sake, and get your chores done. Is Joyce a friend of yours?"

"No, she's my sister too. She's my big sister, Audrey is my little sister." Marjorie was so excited that it was impossible to stand still and finish her chores properly. Her cottage mother said she didn't know anything about Joyce. All she knew was that Audrey was arriving today and that she was assigned to this cottage and that the group would arrive late in the afternoon.

"You better get your chores finished now so you will have them done when they get here. Help me get her cot organized." The cottage mother watched Marjorie. She hoped that having her little sister at the farm would be helpful. Marjorie had not settled in well, always seeming angry and quick to argue. She also thought Marjorie still acted as though she were homesick, although the girl had now been at the farm school for almost a year.

Thirteen

A Mother's Lament

Winifred wrapped her heart
Around precious memories of her babies
She never wanted to let them go
She never stopped needing
To hold them again.

SEPTEMBER 1938

Winifred sat up late into the night. There were days when life seemed almost normal, then, without warning, the sleepless nights would arrive and plague her. All she could think about was what went wrong and why had she lost her children. Six had vanished. She would always carry this loss with her, but she had no choice but to let them go. She loved them, but it was out of her power no matter how much she wanted them home.[1] Her children were her life and she would give them anything she could. But she had so little to give, and, in the end, her love had not been enough.

She looked at the photo of Marjorie that had arrived with the morning post. She spotted her little girl right away, as if she jumped off the paper at her. Marjorie looked quite smart and appeared to be happy, but her letter didn't give any information. "Dear Mum, I am fine. How are you? Love from Marjorie." That was it. Marjorie's twelfth birthday would be tomorrow. It made Winifred's heart ache to see her. She turned the photograph over.

A neighbour had accused her of not wanting them. Horrid woman. Of course she wanted them! They were her babies. By then Winifred knew that having your children taken from you could happen to any family. All you needed for disaster was to have your husband agree to let them go. She had no say. Didn't she do her best on her own for the four years that he was gone? The day that those men arrived with her husband's letter was still fresh in her mind, even though it was over twenty months earlier. After they left she had to force herself to go on doing her daily chores. But an important part of her spirit left with her children. As she stood, waving goodbye, something in her heart caved in and she'd had trouble filling it ever since.

However hard she tried, she could not erase the look of betrayal that passed across her children's eyes when the train pulled away. Their little faces, accusing her of disloyalty, came back to haunt her at the most unexpected moments. She could not forgive herself, so how could she expect her children to forgive her? Some nights she woke up in the middle of one of her dreams with her heart pounding. She had been running and running and running, trying to catch the train. If she could catch the train, she could save them. So close, and as she reached out, happiness filled her; she had not let them down after all! Then, with the final lunge, the train door disintegrated in her hands and that horrid man would be standing there, laughing at her. Those were the worst nights.

Marjorie, second from the left, full front, poses with a group of her cottage mates outside Pennant Cottage, her second residence at the farm school. The girls appear to have their Bibles and may be on their way to the Fairbridge Chapel.

SKIDMORE FAMILY COLLECTION.

Winifred knew that when you had no other choice, you had to find the strength to carry on. Even so, she kept going over the "if onlys": if only her country had wanted her children here, at home, and not so very far away; if only her parents were still alive, they would have helped; if only her husband hadn't been gone for so long, they wouldn't have taken her children; if only they hadn't sent her older boys away. Together, they may have kept this family together. Alone, she could not do it.

At first she did not want to believe that Fairbridge man when he said her husband's letter gave the Fairbridge Society control over her children. That could not be true! How can children, who have both a mother and a father, lose their parents because of a letter? Why did this have to be such a permanent thing? The schools had been on her back, the local council had pressured her, and the landlord had threatened to evict her because she had so many children. It was humiliating having no place to go and no one to turn to for help. The landlord's words still echoed in her mind.

"You can't have ten people living in this flat. It's not possible!" He was so furious that he was spitting when he found out that she had lied to him.

"We've been in a lot smaller places," Winifred pleaded with him. "We'll manage. It is not easy finding a place to live this time of year. I can't afford a larger place."

The landlord shook his head and walked away. Winifred was not sure what that meant. Could they stay? Did he mean for her to start looking for another flat? But what did it matter now? She only had three of her children left. That horrid Fairbridge man made sure of that. He had been very patient with her until she began to hesitate about signing his form. When she wanted assurance that she would not lose contact with her children, he began to get pushy. He urged her to get the papers signed and told her that she could write to them care of the Fairbridge Society office in Newcastle. He warned her that she must be very careful not to put distressing things in her letters, as letters from home could be very disturbing for some children and set back the adjustment to their new lives. He emphasized, "It would be best if you do not try to visit them while they are in Birmingham. Children who have settled in perfectly become quite a problem after an unnecessary visit from one of their parents. Best to try to forget them. In the long run you will be doing them a favour."

He brushed back his hair and looked at her. It appeared to Winifred that it was with the utmost effort that he kept his voice level. It was obvious that he wanted to get this over with as quickly as possible and leave her flat. How could he be so unconcerned about pulling this family apart? She looked around the room. She kept it as clean as she could. Could this wretched man understand that there were times when even soap was hard to come by? She looked at her little children. She tried to see them through the eyes of this well-dressed man. Did he have any idea of what it was like to be poor? Did he think that because she was poor that she had no feelings? Did he think that because she was poor that she cared less for her children than rich people did? Did he think that she liked living like this? That it was her choice to live like this?

"Visit them!" Winifred scoffed. She knew that she could never afford to visit them. She would even have trouble finding enough for the post to send them a letter. Forget them! Never! This ridiculous man kept going on and on without realizing that she did not want to listen. Winifred wished he would just go away.

"Do you have any children?" she looked directly at him.

"Why, yes. Yes I do," was his reply, smiling for the first time.

"Well, let's hope that you are never forced to be parted from any of them. Then you might just know how ridiculous you sound when you tell me to forget mine!" Winifred was so frustrated and angry that she was shaking. For a moment, she truly believed that he understood her.

The smile was instantly gone from his face. Her outburst had made him nervous. "Let's just get this done." His tone left no doubt about who was in charge.

Over and over she thought of the events leading up to that ill-fated day, searching for what she might have done differently. In the end, she knew there was nothing that she could change. Now she had to get on with her life — the two little ones needed her.

She had gone against that man's advice and visited the Middlemore Emigration Home only last week. It was her first visit and sure to be her last. She could understand now why he advised her not to go. It was a long and expensive trip to Selly Oak and then it wasn't easy to find her way from the train station to the Middlemore Home, but she was determined to find out if Joyce was okay. Maybe she could find out why they left this daughter behind.

She carried the "after-sailing" letter for Audrey with her. It was shocking that Joyce's name was missing. Imagine leaving her behind all by herself after taking the others! She was so certain that they had kept Joyce back to look after Audrey and then to accompany her to Canada when it was time for her to go. It was cruel to send such a young child overseas all alone. What was it like for her little children crossing the ocean all alone and then journeying all the way to the other side of Canada? When Marjorie and Kenny sailed they had each other, but Audrey had no one.

Her visit to the home turned out to be difficult for Joyce too, so Winifred made a promise to herself not to repeat such foolishness. When Audrey left for Canada last month, it was as difficult for Joyce as when Marjorie and Kenny left the year before.

Joyce had lashed out to her. "Why am I left behind? I want you take me home now! I hate it here! I hate you for leaving me here!"

How could she answer Joyce? It would be impossible to take Joyce back home, not now anyway. Winfred had followed her husband south to the London area. She missed Whitley Bay, it had been home for almost eighteen years, but she did not miss the constant reminders of her lost children on every corner. Was her life was any better in Plumstead? She and the children were crammed into a small lodging down on Bloomfield Road. She didn't know how she was going to manage with yet another child on the way. There certainly wasn't enough room for both Joyce and a new baby. Yes, Joyce was better off at the home for the moment. At least she had a bed to sleep in and decent clothes and plenty of food. Thomas was back again — but he had taken lodgings across the street because her flat was so crowded. Funny that, having your husband come back after four years, only to have him living across the street.

"Oh, Joyce." She felt so powerless when she unable to find the right answers. "Joyce, try to stick it out. We only have a very small flat right now. Maybe when we get into better lodgings I can come for you. We are all squeezed in. You have so much room here in this big building. Besides, the home does not want to let you go. They tell me you are a great help to them."

Joyce glared at her mother. Feelings of hopelessness consumed her. She ran off in tears and hid under her covers. She had prayed for the day when her mother would come to take her away. Here she was, but her dreams were forever shattered. She was not going home. She would never get away from Middlemore. Winifred knew that it was no use trying to comfort her. She had nothing to offer. Reluctantly she left Joyce in the dorm. Nurse was waiting for her in the hallway and it was obvious that she had heard everything.

"You are lucky that Canada agreed to take three of your children. This country has no room for all its poor children. They are much better off now. They have a chance of a good life in the colonies. Think of the opportunities they are being given, the education, and the chance to grow up in a beautiful clean country setting. They cannot get that from you."

"But children should be with their mother." Winifred's argument seemed weak, even to her.

"Who in their right mind would deny their children this chance?" Nurse looked at Winifred as she continued. "Be honest with yourself, what can you possibly give them? You were not even able to feed them properly. They have sunshine and plenty of food, and they will grow up to be strong and healthy in a country that wants them. Now that you have disrupted Joyce, it will take us ages to settle her down again. We feel it is best that you don't visit her again. I will show you out."

Who was she to judge whether her children would be better off without her! Were they really better off? Children should be with their mother, not sent off half way around the world or left in lonely institutions. An overwhelming need to go back in to comfort Joyce came over her, but now her way was blocked. She had come all this way and had only made things worse.

She knew that Joyce would be returned to her when she reached sixteen, and it comforted her to know that she hadn't lost her forever, but she wasn't so sure about the other three. She did not want to cause her children any more stress, and she knew it was wrong, but part of her hoped that her children in Canada missed her as much as she missed them. It was just too painful to think of the alternative. Could they simply forget her? She thought of them always. She hoped that Audrey would be placed near Marjorie. The girls could help each other, but there was no one for Kenny.

Winifred never got a straight answer from the home when she asked why they left Joyce behind. They said she was too old. Too old! My God, she was only thirteen now! She was only twelve when Kenny and Marjorie left. They had no idea how much the younger children needed Joyce and how much Joyce needed them. Imagine splitting the children apart! Well, what did she know? She was just their mother, and she had to rely on the charity of others. What right did she have to complain? They told her often enough over the past couple of years that she had little to offer her children. She was beginning to believe it.

She did not find the words to tell Joyce that her father had come home. That news would definitely make it difficult for Joyce to understand why she had she had to be left at the home. Thomas had walked in as if it had been the most natural thing in the world to be away for four years. He told her that he had been working in London and Ireland and even over in Spain for a spell. He seemed to be happier about stopping at home now that there were fewer children running about. She hoped he would see that they needed him and prayed that he would stop at home for good. Her hope was that once they were settled in Plumstead she would be able to bring this family back together again, at least as many pieces of it as she was able.

When she first discussed getting her children back with the society now that her husband had returned, they told her that the children were happy and settled in their new lives. Now that the Fairbridge Society had guardianship over the children, she no longer had any say in their care. There was no way to get them back. And, unfortunately, they were gone with Thomas's blessing. He thought they would be better off overseas. He could not understand why she was unable to see it. To him it was as plain as the nose on his face.

Winifred did her best to ensure that Joyce did not notice that she was going to have another baby.[2] She was not showing too much when she visited and had worn loose clothing. How could she explain a new baby to this abandoned child? Yes, the father of her children had waltzed right back into their lives, king of the roost! He knew the children were awaiting emigration but was surprised to hear that Fred had been sent to Borstal and Norman to a farm school at Castle Howard. He told her that had she been a better mother to his sons they might still be at home. He did not recognize the baby, Lawrence, who was over three years old already. He didn't know that she was pregnant with Lawrence when he left.

"Who's this? A neighbour's lad?" He walked in and ruffled Lawrence's head. The child hurried to his mother's side.

PHOTO BY PATRICIA SKIDMORE.

Marjorie and her younger brother Richard, who was born after Marjorie was sent to Canada, met for the very first time in May 2011.The photograph was taken moments after their first encounter. This meeting was sponsored and organized by the Family Restoration Fund.

Winifred looked at him and said, "You don't recognize your own son."

"Well, how could I? Was he born when I left? No! How come these two weren't sent to Canada?" Five-year-old Jean edged closer to her mother. She knew this must be her father, but she did not like the way he was talking.

Winifred sighed and thought that some things never change. "Because they were too young and I suppose the council felt that I could take care of them with Phyllis's help," she answered him.

Phyllis was a great help, but it was still difficult. There was never enough money for food and lodgings. Maybe her little children were better off in Canada. She looked at the photograph that Joyce had handed to her at the home. "Give it to Marjorie," was all she said.

She was going to write to the children in Canada soon. Joyce had been so worried that Marjorie, Audrey, and Kenny would forget her. Maybe having a picture of Joyce would help them to remember.

Joyce, third from top right, in a photo taken at the Middlemore Emigration Homes, circa 1938. Marjorie has held on to this treasure ever since Joyce had the photo sent to her in 1938.

SKIDMORE FAMILY COLLECTION.

Fourteen

FAMILY IS IMPORTANT

They say Home Sweet Home
Is the place to be.
My heart is not here
But I am forced to be.

PRINCE OF WALES FAIRBRIDGE FARM SCHOOL, FALL 1938

It was a momentous day for Marjorie when her little sister, Audrey, arrived at the farm school on Vancouver Island. Initially, it was difficult becoming sisters again. Over the past eleven months of separation their sisterly bond had been broken and both had changed as a result. It was not an easy repair, and they had to get to know each other all over again. Eventually, they found their former shared warmth as sisters and Marjorie felt that she had a little piece of herself back.

Luckily, the sisters remained housed together during Marjorie's remaining time at the farm school. She fell into the role of big sister, which gave new meaning and structure to her day. Kenny, however, remained at a distance, the Fairbridge farm rules making it difficult to get close to him.

Marjorie was less lonely, but much still remained missing for many, many years. As unrealistic as it was, Marjorie held onto hope during her entire five years at the farm school that they would send out her big sister,

Joyce, but they never did. It would be over thirty years before she would see Joyce again. All through that time she kept the picture of Joyce that her mum had sent in the fall of 1938.

The Arnison children, Kenny, Marjorie, and Audrey, at the Prince of Wales Fairbridge Farm School, circa 1940.

LIFE AFTER FAIRBRIDGE

In September 1942, shortly after her sixteenth birthday, Marjorie was placed as a domestic in a home in Victoria, primarily to look after an elderly, wheelchair-bound woman. Not having been trained to be the sole caregiver for an invalid, Marjorie found the placement, and the isolation, too difficult, and appealed to her after-care worker to remove her. Early in 1943, she found herself working in a family with a little boy, and soon after a little girl was born. This was Marjorie's first real experience of family life since being removed from her home in 1937 and she recalls, with great affection, that this family was a "lifesaver" for her. They have remained lifelong friends.

When Marjorie left this placement, she moved to Vancouver to work and roomed with a group of girls, some of who were from the farm school. She had met her future husband, Cliff, while she lived and worked with the family in Victoria. He was in the Merchant Navy and stationed in nearby Esquimalt when his vessel was in town. They kept in touch when Marjorie moved to Vancouver. In May 1948, they were married. Their first son was born on the last day of February 1949. In October 1957, their fifth child was born. Just a few weeks later, in early November of that same year, Marjorie was widowed.

The youngest was a newborn baby of just three weeks and the eldest was only eight years old. Without family support it was a struggle for Marjorie to raise her five young children on her own. Her younger brother and sister were both married, raising young families of their own, and her husband's family lived in Montreal, too far away to be of any help.

Clifford Scott Skidmore was the love of Marjorie's life. His death was tragic. Likely he was suffering from posttraumatic stress disorder and was misdiagnosed or perhaps it was not fully understood in the early 1950s — as, instead of being treated for depression, Cliff was one of the unlucky few that were experimented on in the early part of 1950s, and he was given a lobotomy. This erroneous event spelled the end for him, as the lobotomy heightened his depression and left him with blinding headaches. Soon after he took his own life — he was only thirty-two. Being left in this manner was incredibly difficult for Marjorie and her children.

Cliff had been working in Alberta at the time of his death and he was subsequently buried at the veterans section of the Burnsland Cemetery in Calgary. There was no closure for Marjorie, no service for Cliff. It took another eight years — until Marjorie's first-born son turned sixteen and he could drive her the almost 1,000 kilometres from Vancouver to Calgary — before she was able to visit her husband's gravesite and properly say goodbye.

Growing up in an institution had removed Marjorie from the experience of being parented. With few skills in this department and little in the way of education to fall back on, Marjorie faced the challenge of not losing her children as her mother had before her. She was told not to apply for a veteran's pension through her husband, but that welfare would give her better coverage for her children. The province's welfare agency next suggested she should give up some of her children. She refused and she fought to keep her family together. Her children recall her saying on numerous occasions throughout their childhood, "We may not have much, but we have each other." She instilled in her children the importance of family. "They took mine away once. I won't let them do it again."

Fear of losing her family and the shame of being rejected haunted Marjorie well into her adult years. The few photos from her mother were all she had connecting her to her family, to her past; the rest was locked away and inaccessible. Later communication with members of her English family would tell her that her mother never got over losing her children to Canada, but it took Marjorie nearly seventy-three years to realize that it was true. The most difficult part of coming to that understanding was the fact that she could not tell her mother that she forgave her and no longer blames her for sending her away.

Marjorie only saw her mother once after being sent away from Whitley Bay. In 1969, the sixty-nine-year-old Winifred travelled to Canada on her own to finally get to meet her grown children, over thirty-two years after having put her little ones on the train. The visit did not go well for Marjorie. She wanted answers and her mother felt at a loss to give her any. Marjorie's anger, which had festered for years, couldn't be contained, and her mother went to her grave without any resolution between mother and daughter. For years Marjorie thought being sent to Canada was the result of her family's failure and for years she had shrouded herself within an isolating sense of shame.

For the children of a child migrant it was also isolating. We had no roots to hold us together. It has taken a couple of generations, a formal apology, and a strong reconnection with our English family, to finally feel that we have a place of belonging, a sense of family pride, and a sense of family history. This healing didn't begin until my mother, Marjorie, nearing the age of seventy-five, returned to England for the first time in 2001, over sixty-four years after her removal in February 1937. The healing continued during her 2007 visit when she travelled to Whitley Bay. The feeling being loved and wanted by her English siblings, in spite of the great distances, has given Marjorie back a piece of what she lost so long ago — a sense of family, and a sense of belonging.

"What do you think?" I yawned, and hugged my manuscript, amazed we had both stayed awake.

"Well, that is my story — but it won't be complete until after this apology is over. Imagine, waiting all this time. I never thought that anything like this would ever happen."

"We should try to get a short sleep in before we land at Heathrow," I said while I packed away the manuscript. I looked over at my mother; she was already fast asleep.

Chapter 15

MARJORIE WAITED SEVENTY-THREE YEARS

Full circle at last.
Searching for our past,
Our lives more complete
New treasures we seek.

Eighty-three-year-old Marjorie never wavered once she accepted the invitation to attend the formal apology to the British child migrants to be held in London, England. Nonetheless, the prospect was still a nerve-wracking and exhausting business. She didn't know what to expect or how she might react.

I prepared a news release of our upcoming trip to London. Marjorie shied away from the attention, but I wouldn't let her hide from it. The local paper in her small interior British Columbia town of Oliver called for an interview and she was featured in the paper before, during, and after the apology. She was out in the open now. Her small town knew about her past. The *Globe and Mail* also called and interviewed Marjorie and myself. She felt awkward with all the attention and thought she sounded silly when reporters wanted her to speak into a microphone, but I told her afterwards that she was brilliant, that she spoke from her heart. She doubted the compliment until a reporter came up to her and hugged her, telling her that she was great.

It was not an easy switch for Marjorie to emote pride at being a child migrant when she had spent a lifetime feeling ashamed and uncomfortable about talking about her past. It also became apparent that she was concerned about what the others from her Fairbridge farm school family would think of her if she spoke out against her experience there.

I suggested that anybody trying to stop her story from coming out was quite simply continuing the bully system so prevalent at the farm school and contributing to the silence that has plagued the migration of children for centuries. Not everyone at the Prince of Wales Fairbridge Farm School had the same experiences or opportunities. Some had a wretched time and some had a marvellous time, and many others seemed to be unable to accept that anyone had a different experience from their own. Many felt that silence was the best route, that what happened to them was in the past and should stay there. But, in reality, the experience was very difficult for Marjorie and for many others.

I firmly believed that all the stories needed to be heard to give a balance and provide a true picture of life at the Prince of Wales Fairbridge Farm School: the good, the bad, and everything in between. When my mother found her truth difficult to confront and her pain of deportation difficult to share, I reminded her that her story was as valid as the next one. She was right to feel that what happened to her was wrong. Burying or ignoring her feelings wouldn't bring any closure. If there was nothing to apologize for, then why was the British government bringing her to London to give her an apology? This event would not be organized without solid evidence that the phenomenon of British child migration was fundamentally flawed and that many young children had suffered as a result.

Why were so many child migrants and their families finally talking about the issues that they faced as children? It was because the British government was finally listening. With the story now out in the public, many people find it difficult to believe that the migration of little children had continued for so long without a greater general awareness of the damage being done. Britain removed vulnerable young children from their support systems, from their families, from their communities, and from their country. Many of these children were not orphans and far too many were removed not because of parental abuse and neglect, but because of poverty. The migration of children did not just go on for fifty years, as the media so often portrays, but for over 350 years (see Appendix D).

A number of former child migrants have stated that they are thankful for the opportunities child migration gave them. I am really happy for them.

However, I wonder if some of these children may have left less behind in England, were not as attached to their families, or perhaps they had highly adaptable and adventurous personalities that stood them well in their new lives. Others have stated that they were told as youngsters that if they stayed in England they would have ended up in jail, so they are thankful to have been taken away and consider any difficulties encountered afterwards as justified. They believed themselves to be bad children and needed that badness knocked out of them. The only way to make them good people was to remove them from the bad influence of their families.

However, it makes me wonder if that really would have been the case. Had they been told so often during their young lives that they were fundamentally bad that they came to believe it? Possibly as adults they came to accept the loss of family and harsh treatment during their early years because they needed to believe that this was their only path. The truth may never be known. On some level they may have been "broken" much like wild horses, bent to the will of their masters. For some their scars are not as easy to distinguish, while many others carry them openly having never fully settled into their "forced" new lives.

When Marjorie was asked what she thought it would have been like for her had she stayed in England, she had no absolute answer. When young she felt that perhaps her leaving might have given the other children in her family a better chance, but that belief was shattered when two more children were born into her family after she was sent to Canada. She had been removed from England and sent to the colonies without ever understanding why. Not knowing why left a gap, which quickly became filled with shame.

In reality, Marjorie and her fellow child migrants had nothing to be ashamed of, but the country that sent the children out and the countries that accepted the children do have something to be ashamed of, especially if the child migration stories continue to be hidden.

LONDON: EVENING OF FEBRUARY 23, 2010

The first official event organized for the group of visiting former child migrants took place on February 23, the evening before the formal apology. The get-together, held at the Jolly St. Ermin's Hotel in London's city centre where the Australian contingent was housed, was a chance for the migrants sent to Australia, New Zealand, Canada, and former Rhodesia to introduce themselves, talk to one another, swap stories, and meet Margaret Humphreys, director of the Child Migrants Trust.[1] People, however, seemed hesitant to mingle and most sat quietly together in little groups. I tried to get to know some of their stories, but it wasn't easy. Many were obviously out of their comfort zone, and some seemed to be struggling with jet lag. For most of the Australians and the New Zealanders, the journey to London had taken as much as twenty-five hours.

Passing out information on the Canadian Prince of Wales Fairbridge Farm School, the Fairbridge Canada Association and its present-day programs[2] helped to break some of the ice. I met some former child migrants who were sent to Tasmania as late as 1974.[3] Few of those present realized that this had ever happened.[4] Another person I met during that evening was a man who had been sent to one of the Fairbridge farm schools in Australia with his sister, while his brother was sent to the Prince of Wales Fairbridge Farm School in Canada. The separation of the siblings remained painful, especially since his "Canadian" brother was unable to renew his passport in time to attend the apology gathering.

By the end of the evening, everyone seemed a little more relaxed. People were walking about and talking to others and new stories were emerging. They told a little of their lives, where they were born, where they had been sent, and where they were living today. However, no one seemed willing to discuss the apology itself. It was like the elephant in the room — the largest issue dangling before everyone and the reason all were in London, yet it was the least talked of that evening.

FEBRUARY 24, 2010: APOLOGY

The day of the apology arrived with a bit of sun to brighten the cool February morning. The day was expected to be long and full of emotion. I feared that this day might be too much for Marjorie. Reporters were in the lobby of the Cromwell Hotel, readying their equipment when we walked out of the elevator. Marjorie cautiously told a bit of her story. She was nervous; her early experience with authority made her unwilling to take chances, even now. It had been firmly entrenched in her as a child at the farm school that she was not to tell tales about the school. Having grown up with the knowledge that she had few resources to fight the system, she had learned early in life not to complain but simply accept things the way they were, aware that there was nothing she could do about it. Now that things were changing, she was not entirely trustful of this new attention. The reporters trailed the group as they left the hotel and headed for their bus that was waiting for them around the corner on Grenville Place. I grabbed my mother's hand, not to give her support, but to hold her back so that we might be able to answer more of their questions. Marjorie had travelled a long way and this was her moment to be heard. At the bus they asked one final question: "Marjorie, how are you feeling this morning?"

"I have butterflies," Marjorie replied, and quickly climbed aboard the bus, avoiding any further questions.

The bus pulled up to Portcullis House, the office building associated with Westminster Palace. The reporters from the hotel arrived before the bus did, which was surprising since our driver drove the large coach like a race car through the narrow streets of London. We sat on the bus for some time, looking at the unfamiliar sites and waiting for our guide to arrive to give us detailed instructions on what to expect for the day. Big Ben's clock chimed the hour. Boats travelled up and down the Thames. Vehicles and foot traffic jammed Westminster Bridge. Across the Thames, the London Eye was preparing for its daily routine of rotating tourists to soaring heights with the promise of a spectacular view of the city. When the guide finally boarded the bus, she handed each of us an envelope with our itinerary and a coloured nametag. The child migrants were handed an extra envelope with £75 spending money.

Once we were off the bus, the guide instructed us to line up along the building before being ushered single file into Portcullis House. It took a few moments, thus giving the reporters time to ask some final questions, much to Marjorie's consternation. Getting through the front door was just the first task, once inside we encountered a security barrier. We had our photos taken, our bags checked, our bodies scanned, and received a second tag bearing the newly printed photos to wear around our necks, proof that all had been thoroughly screened. Security was tighter than at the airport, making the gravity of the event most apparent. This apology was serious business.

Next, we were herded into a room set up with sandwiches and coffee. Most were hungry, but also nervous, so the food was not tucked into with any gusto. Following the refreshments, the guides took everyone on a tour of the child migrants' display at Westminster Palace, and then on to the House of Commons. It was a hasty tour, with little time to look at the display or to watch the proceedings of the house, however we did get a glimpse of the man we had all come to see, Britain's prime minister, Gordon Brown.

Soon, Marjorie and I, along with the other child migrants and their family support members, marched through the underground walkway back to Portcullis House. When we reached the second-floor conference room, only the former child migrants were permitted to go into the Boothroyd Room. Other family members were to wait in the hallway, but I refused to comply and stubbornly walked in beside my mother. It was now clear why the nametags were different. The child migrants had one colour and the family members had another. I was easy to spot with my wrong coloured nametag, but I had come a long way and I did not want to miss a moment. Besides, I had made a promise to my mother not to leave her side. I was ready to make a scene if asked to leave. We found seats and waited.

The room buzzed, but it was not with happy chatter. Some sat very still and others fidgeted. Those who talked talked quietly. We did not know what to expect. Suddenly, a screen at the front of the room sprang to life. It showed the House of Commons in Westminster Palace and there was Prime Minister Gordon Brown. Other business was discussed first and then, finally, the prime minster was talking about Britain's child migrants. The room became silent as everyone listened intently. *He is speaking about us*, their silence seemed to say. Necks craned, ears strained, whispers.

Everyone present in the room witnessed Gordon Brown as he went down in history saying:

> Until the late 1960s, successive UK Governments had over a long period of time supported child migration schemes. They involved children as young as three being transported from Britain to Australia, Canada, New Zealand, South Africa and Zimbabwe. The hope was that those children, who were aged between three and 14,

would have the chance to forge a better life overseas, but the schemes proved to be misguided. In too many cases, vulnerable children suffered unrelenting hardship and their families left behind were devastated. They were sent mostly without the consent of their mother or father. They were cruelly lied to and told that they were orphans and that their parents were dead, when in fact they were still alive. Some were separated from their brothers and sisters, never to see one another again. Names and birthdays were deliberately changed so that it would be impossible for families to reunite. Many parents did not know that their children had been sent out of this country.

The former child migrants say they feel that this practice was less transportation and more deportation — a deportation of innocent young lives. When they arrived overseas, all alone in the world, many of our most vulnerable children endured the harshest of conditions, neglect and abuse in the often cold and brutal institutions that received them. Those children were robbed of their childhood, the most precious years of their life. As people know, the pain of a lost childhood can last a lifetime. Some still bear the marks of abuse; all still live with the consequences of rejection. Their wounds will never fully heal, and for too long the survivors have been all but ignored.

When I was first made aware of this wholly unacceptable practice, I wrote to the Prime Minister of Australia to urge that together, we do more to acknowledge the experiences of former child migrants and see what we could achieve. It is right that today we recognise the human cost associated with this shameful episode of history and this failure in the first duty of a nation, which is to protect its children.

Shortly, I shall be meeting a number of former child migrants here in the Palace of Westminster to listen firsthand to their experiences, and as Prime Minister, I will be apologising on behalf of our nation. To all those former child migrants and their families, to those here with us today and those across the world — to each and every one — I say today that we are truly sorry. They were let down. We are sorry that they were allowed to be sent away at the time they were most vulnerable. We are sorry that instead of caring for them, this country turned its back, and we are sorry that the voices of these children were not always heard and their cries for help not always heeded. We are sorry that it has taken so long for this important day to come, and for the full and unconditional apology that is justly deserved to be given....[5]

When Gordon Brown was finished, everyone sat back. Just for the moment, silence permeated the room. The screen went off; the show was over. People began to talk, then to get up and move about the room, waiting. Gordon Brown's next stop would be in this very place. Having just been to the House of Commons, everyone knew it would take but a few moments before he would arrive. Emotions were ripe: ready to fall, ready to explode, and unpredictable. I watched and listened as I walked around the room.

"It took me twenty years to find me mum. Twenty years." One man emphasized.

"They should have told me I had family in England and instead they lied and told me they were all dead."

"When I finally located my mother, I learned that she passed away the month before." A sob escaped the man's lips. I found the free-flowing tears streaming down grown men's faces difficult to watch. I wanted to offer something, anything, but had nothing to give.

"I was sent in 1974. For God's sake, there was no need for that. What were they thinking?"

No, there was no need to be still sending children to the colonies in the 1970s, or at any time for that matter, but the program, once started, seemed hard to stop. Once again, I tried to find something helpful to say but I had nothing, so I said nothing. Besides, people did not appear to be looking for answers or even condolences. Their words seemed to be a way of releasing some of their building tension.

The pressure in the room grew with each passing moment. The emotionally charged atmosphere, mixed with the pain of years of waiting, was almost touchable. *Mister Prime Minister, you are a brave man*, I thought — this group could turn into an angry mob.

But, no, it did not. Gordon Brown walked into Boothroyd Room, and the relief was palatable. I breathed a sigh and watched Marjorie. This part — the child migrant's moment for a personal word and handshake from the prime minister — seemed to be the most unorganized event of the day. I thought that the child migrants would have been lined up to ensure everyone a turn, but instead the child migrants gravitated towards the prime minister from all corners of the room, pushing towards him, hoping for their moment. He was quickly encircled and, as people reached out to him, he barely knew which hand to take first. It wasn't frenzied, yet there was single-mindedness in the way everyone moved. I was concerned that my mother wouldn't persevere, so kept a close watch. When Marjorie was approaching Brown, I also pushed forward, apologizing, and explaining that I just wanted to get a photograph of my mother.

As Marjorie took Gordon Brown's hand, I heard her scold, "Now don't forget about Canada!" She needed to say this to him, as his apology was so heavily representative of the Australian migrants.[6]

Marjorie meets with British Prime Minister Gordon Brown in February 2010. David Lorente, founder of Home Children Canada, awaits his turn.

PHOTO BY PATRICIA SKIDMORE.

I stood on my toes, camera held over my head, unable to see what was in the viewfinder. A good shot would be pure luck; one chance, click, that was it. Brown moved on. I got it! I had my photo and Marjorie survived her brief meeting with the prime minister of Great Britain. Now she could begin to relax. I could see her shoulders loosen up, her face soften. The worst was over. When all had their brief encounter, the guides escorted us out of Boothroyd Room to the Attlee Suite, just across the hallway. It was all set up. Cameras and camera operators, two large screens showing a photo of a group of child migrants leaving Britain, a podium and seats for all.

"Please find a seat." No one knew for certain what would happen next.

Andy Burnham, British secretary of state for health, walked to the podium. He introduced himself and welcomed everyone. Following his brief speech, there was a short film showing some of the child migrants leaving Britain. Next, Gordon Brown took the stand, and gave his apology again but this time speaking directly to the child migrants seated in the room. It felt sincere. His face looked genuine.

PHOTO BY PATRICIA SKIDMORE.

British Prime Minister Gordon Brown giving a personal apology directly to the group of former Canadian, Australian, New Zealander, and Rhodesian child migrants brought to London for this occasion.

I believed him when he said sorry. I was moved and then shocked when tears moved down my cheeks. I glanced at my mother sitting beside me, but her attention was on Brown, her cheeks dry. I wiped away my tears, happy that my mother had lived to see this day; so many other Canadian child migrants were not present. A number of the Prince of Wales Fairbridge Farm School former child migrants are still alive, but the invitation had come too late to rally the group. It also came too late for the thousands of children who had passed on — from the first groups of children sent in the early 1830s, to the last group that arrived in 1948.

Gordon Brown continued, "This is your country...."

I wanted to stand up and yell out: "*It is not!* That right was taken away from my mother when she was just a little girl. She could never feel at home in England anymore because, at an early age, she was forced to find a home elsewhere."

Later, Marjorie would state that her life was in Canada now, with her children, grandchildren, and great-grandchildren. She could never leave her children. She now understands how difficult it must have been for her own mother. A family letter states that it was to her mother's "eternal distress" that she lost her children to Canada. In a sad way, hearing those two words made Marjorie very happy. She had always

PHOTO BY PATRICIA SKIDMORE.

Marjorie signing the Commemorative Book ensuring a permanent government record of the apology.

hoped her mother's distress equalled her own, and for the longest time she was angry with her mother because she thought her mum didn't care. It has taken a lifetime for Marjorie to fully understand that her mother did not willingly let her children go. They were taken. She never stopped wanting them back home with her.

Margaret Humphreys, director of the Child Migrants Trust, spoke after the prime minister, and the final speaker was Harold Haig from the International Association of Former Child Migrants and their Families. Once the formal speeches were over, Gordon Brown walked over and signed the Commemorative Book. Next, they invited everyone present to include their signatures. Each child migrant was given a special House of Commons pen set. After I signed my name, with a tremendous sense of pride, I added, "daughter of a child migrant."

Over the course of the day Marjorie continued to shed any leftover vestiges of shame and walked with an easier step, her head held high and dignified. Once she heard those simple words — "I am sorry. We were wrong" — she knew that she was no longer forgotten. Her childhood plight was now on a national stage, displayed for all to see, and her pain was no longer a shamefully hidden piece of her past. For her it was a release of the stigma secretly carried since childhood. Her family should not have been torn apart in such a way, and now the world knew it too.

With the formal part of the day over, it was time for the group to mingle and make their way over to the food and wine. The chatter was louder and happier than earlier. Reporters were allowed in and people appeared more willing to speak. Some of the dignitaries who attended the apology were introduced. One was James Wright, the Canadian high commissioner in London, who welcomed the Canadians. It was quickly arranged that the group of seven people representing Canada would be taken to James Wright's residence for a short visit before being driven back to our hotel. We expected to go to Canada House, by Trafalgar Square, but instead were taken to Macdonald House at Grosvenor Square, the former American embassy, where the Canadian high commissioner now resides. Mr. Wright explained that the room we were sitting in was a replica of the White House's Oval Office in the United States. The visit was quite informal with discussion mainly focusing on the little-known 115-year history of child migration to Canada.

It was disconcerting to discover that all the players in British child migration were not well-known. It was not just the British government that supported this scheme. The Royal Family had always been involved, along with many of Britain's wealthy, as well as many of the high-profile organizations, such as the Barnardo Homes, the Children's Friend Society, the Children's Aid Society, the Canadian Catholic Emigration Society, the Church of England Waifs and Stray Society, Big Brothers, the Salvation Army, Maria Rye and Annie MacPherson, as well as the Child Emigration Society, later known as the Fairbridge Society, to name but a few. Many influential people in Britain viewed the migration of its children as an outlet, a way to offset the country's high unemployment rates among its poor, a way to offset the financial burden of the children in its care, and a way to keep a steady stream of white stock to its colonies. They were simply moving "material" around and did not take into consideration the human toll of their scheme.

PHOTO BY PATRICIA SKIDMORE.

These seven Canadians at the Canadian High Commissioner's residence in London were the only members invited to represent the Canadian Home Children at the February 2010 apology in London. Back row (l-r): Patricia Skidmore, Elizabeth Mackay (wife of Roddy Mackay), Brian O'Malley (husband of Joan O'Malley), Dave Lorente (son of a home child and founder of Home Children Canada), Joan O'Malley (daughter of a home child and seamstress of the first Canadian flag). Front (l-r): Roddy Mackay (Prince of Wales Fairbridge Farm School child migrant), James Wright (Canadian high commissioner), and Marjorie Skidmore.

After our chat about child migration to Canada with the Canadian high commissioner, my mother and I were asked by CBC News to do an interview at their London studio. Marjorie had had enough for one day, so I agreed to go without her. The interview opened first with the explanation to their audience that Pat Skidmore was going to talk about the experience of being at the apology for the British child migrants who had been sent to Canada between the 1880s and the 1930s. These dates may have reflected the height of child migration to Canada, but, for me, they didn't tell the whole story, the one that started in 1619 and didn't end until the 1970s, or that Canada accepted children as early as 1833 and up until 1948. I felt it was important to correct the dates, since talking about British child migration between 1880 and the 1930s was misleading and left out much of the story.

Next, it was suggested that Gordon Brown's apology must bring some closure for my mother and our family. From my perspective: *Closure? NO!* But a new beginning, yes. His apology could be instrumental in raising awareness of the long history of British child migration and recognizing the need to get the stories of child migration into the history books of all the countries involved.

Marjorie weathered the day's events well, but it wasn't until after it was fully over and we were both safely in the hotel room, preparing to go to her brother's home the next day, that she truly began to enjoy what she had just witnessed. A reporter managed to get one comment out of Marjorie, when she was asked, "What was the best thing about the apology?" Marjorie didn't hesitate and smiled when she said that it was getting to see her family again. She was anxious to see her three brothers, David, Lawrence, and Norman, and her sister Joyce again. They all lived near London, except for a fourth brother, Richard, born after Marjorie was sent to Canada, who was living in Cyprus. She had never met this brother. It would take another year and Gordon Brown's Family Restoration Fund, with the help of the Child Migrants Trust, to bring these two siblings together for the very first time.

The following day, when Marjorie was safely ensconced at her youngest English brother's home in Dartford, Kent, outside of London, her happiness was unmistakable. She was with family — *her* family. David, the second child to be born after Marjorie and her two siblings were sent to Canada and the last to be born to this family, has been instrumental in providing Marjorie with a sense of belonging to her English family. He and his wife, Marion, and their three daughters have ventured to Canada regularly since 1986 to visit his two Canadian sisters. Through stories of his childhood and his growing up in the same household as their mother, a fuller image of the mother that Marjorie missed so desperately as a child took shape. Spending time with her English family helped remove the pain of rejection, as she came to fully understand the circumstances of her removal and her mother's role in it.

The day before flying back to Canada, Marjorie's younger brother Lawrence took us out for lunch. He was not quite three years old in February 1937 when his older sisters and his older brother disappeared from his life. He turned to Marjorie, putting his arm around her shoulder, and said, "It didn't just affect you, Marjorie; it affected our entire family."

"Yes, you're right Uncle Lawrence, and it affected the next generation as well," I observed.

MARCH 4, 2010, ABOARD THE PLANE HOME

We sat quietly during our plane ride home, at peace with our separate thoughts, processing what we had experienced over the past few days. It was so different from our plane journey over.

"It was a good apology, wasn't it?" Marjorie offered.

"Yes, it certainly was worth coming all this way." I replied. "The awareness of child migration is growing, and with perseverance and effort, the truth and the history can be finally documented. Your story deserves to be told. It belongs in the history of Canada."

For Marjorie, having heard Prime Minister Brown tell her that England was "her country" helped her to realize that, no, it wasn't, and it hadn't been for a long while. She could finally accept her life, her place in the universe. She was Canadian, as were her children, grandchildren, and great-grandchildren. Gordon Brown's apology had helped her see that she belonged in Canada and she could accept it more readily now that she felt that she had a choice in the matter.

"It's a nice change to find a place of belonging. I can fully accept my life if I can finally feel that I belong someplace."

"Well, you belong with your children and the rest of your family in Canada."

"Yes, I have been there for long enough. I must be entitled to call it home by now."

"I was told that your mother used to say, 'We will go when the ship comes over the hill.' She waited a long time for a ship that never came. Do you think your ship has finally come over the hill?" I sat back in my seat, filled with a feeling of contentment.

"You know, I think it has."

Afterword

PATRICIA'S PERSPECTIVE

As a researcher of child migration and as a daughter of a child migrant, I found that the apology heralded a new beginning for me. It allowed me to see the magnitude of what was missing from the history of the countries that accepted child migrants. Few of the stories of the more than 110,000 child migrants or home children sent to Canada between 1833 and 1948 are to be found. For 115 years, Canada encouraged and accepted children, yet you do not read about these children in the history books of Canada. My hope is that Gordon Brown's words will not be mere words but will signify a new awareness and an opportunity for the child migration stories to find a place of belonging.

Do we want future politicians to say "I didn't know?" This apology lends support to those who are working to collect information and establish a properly drawn timeline, so that this phenomenon of child migration can finally be fully documented. Many of the stories have been lost, but there are still a number of former child migrants scattered throughout the world who can give first-hand accounts of their experiences. Gordon Brown promised many things with his apology, most importantly, a Family Restoration Fund,[1] which gives funding for former child migrants to return to England to be reunited with their families. The Child Migrants Trust is administering the fund.

Brown also promised better access to the records for the former child migrants. Initially, the closed records of the various sending agencies were a stumbling block for many child migrants seeking their birth information and when making attempts to be reunited with their families. Restrictions are still in place on some of the Prince of Wales Fairbridge Farm School records housed at the B.C. Archives in Victoria and the University of Liverpool's Department of Special Collections and Archives. In 1962 the Fairbridge authorities in London ordered the headmaster of the Fairbridge Memorial College in Bulawayo, Rhodesia, to destroy all records of the college. One cannot help but wonder what they were trying to hide. The U.K.'s 1998 Data Protection Act restricts records for one hundred years for individuals whose sensitive personal data is held, for seventy-five years in respect of archives relating to the staff of the charity, and thirty years in respect of administrative archives. Individual child migrants can gain access to their own personal records.

There is always the danger of Gordon Brown's words being becoming *just words*. It is now the responsibility of those who can fight for the rights of the migrants and their families to pry open the door that Brown cracked and ensure that his promises come to fruition. The records compiled by the various sending agencies are a valuable portal into the past and a pathway to a greater understanding of child migration.

The Fairbridge Society was in a powerful position in the 1930s. The backing of the Prince of Wales strengthened the belief that they were doing the right thing for their country, the colonies, and the children they were removing. They worked on the assumption that they had enough children to work with until they got it right, but they failed to see that they were experimenting with young children's lives.[2] They failed to see that these children needed their families. They failed to see the flaws in their system, because they failed to see the children as people with full human rights, with rights to their families and their country of birth.

As noted earlier, the children were viewed as raw material, which, if moulded properly, could bring a profit. It was thought "within the wider imperial setting, destitute children were a sound political investment, both in terms of the future of the empire and the global spread of British values … Fairbridge once had the local Australian Bureau of Commerce and Industry appraise the boys at Pinjarra in the hope of publicizing just how dramatically the farm school system transformed Britain's slum children into valuable assets. They were priced at £1,000 a head."[3] They had value in the colonies if trained properly, but deemed valueless in Britain. They were shuffled about, reorganized, and transplanted.

Marjorie Skidmore standing by her personal history in the Child Migrant display, housed in Westminster Palace for the week following the apology. The words posted on the display board, quoting Patricia, say, "Some say that being sent to Canada was the best thing to happen to them, others say it was simply the worst. No matter what their stories are, they are mostly missing from the history books of both Canada and England. How can we fully understand who we are as a people and what we are capable of as countries, if we continue to deny and hide our past?"

Marjorie's coming back in 2010 for the apology, with its high media profile, allowed her English family to finally fully understand what had happened to their siblings and why they were sent away to Canada. Like Marjorie, who couldn't tell her children about her buried past, Winifred couldn't talk to the rest of her children about what happened to their siblings, other than they were in Canada. Was it too painful, or did she too bury the memories of losing her children in order to carry on? The honour of being brought back to the apology and personally meeting the prime minister removed the final vestiges of shame about her past, and Marjorie was able to speak openly to her English family concerning her feelings about being sent to Canada.

Now that I had rebuilt my mother's early years in England and her journey to Canada, I wanted her to tell me about her day-to-day life at the Prince of Wales Fairbridge Farm School. I wanted to know what growing up on the farm entailed, what chores she did, what helped her in her adult life, what held her back, what she liked, and what she hated.

Marjorie was at the farm school for five years, from September 1937 until the fall of 1942. She never forgot her family or stopped missing them. However, in time the pain of losing her family lessened and the other Fairbridge children became her substitute family. They did not have a lot of time to pine away at the farm school. Their daily life was strictly regimented; they worked hard and were tired at night. That was a blessing since nightmares plagued her, but when she was tired out, she slept better.

When Marjorie turned sixteen, she was placed as a domestic servant in a series of homes in Victoria, on southern Vancouver Island. The rest of her story was as important for me to uncover as her 1937 journey to Canada, so I asked her if she recalled how she coped, and what tools she used to survive her years at the farm school. She told me that it was difficult at times, but she and her siblings were just little children.

"We had no other choice but to just get on with our lives and accept where we were. If we used any tools, it was to use whatever we needed to stay out of trouble and survive. It was important to survive and to believe that one day there would be a different life for us one, far away from the farm school."

The human cost for children being sent to the colonies, often with people who could not or did not care to understand how they were feeling or have any idea of what they had lost along the way —their families, their countries, their identities — was rarely taken into consideration. The children were often referred to as "guttersnipes," "British trash," and "orphans" by the people put into place to guide them into their new Canadian lives. Kingsley Fairbridge expected his farm schools to run with high standards. He insisted "… men and women of the staff must be gentlewomen and gentlemen of culture and refinement, in order to bring up the children in a clean and wholesome atmosphere."[4] But the bottom line always remained an economic one. The program did not have enough money to attract or pay for Fairbridge's "ideal" and many of the farm school's more than 150 cottage mothers over a fifteen-year span were untrained and unfit for the job.

Perhaps the cottage mothers had one of the toughest jobs at the farm school. They were brought to the remote farm site on Vancouver Island, five miles south of Duncan, and placed at the head of a cottage housing twelve to fourteen children. Some children arrived as young as four years of age, and the age of the children in each cottage could range up to fifteen or sixteen. A cottage mother, terribly underpaid, was given the task of maintaining control over this large "family" of displaced children, and

PHOTO BY PATRICIA SKIDMORE.

Marjorie Skidmore and Roddy Mackay, the two representatives from Canada, both former Prince of Wales Fairbridge Farm School child migrants, wait for Gordon Brown's apology.

IN
LOVING MEMORY
OF
WINIFRED ARNISON
WHO DIED OCTOBER 20TH 1972
AGED 72.
ALSO
THOMAS FREDERICK
ARNISON
WHO DIED NOVEMBER 21st 1977
AGED 79.
"GOODNIGHT GOD BLESS."

PHOTO BY PATRICIA SKIDMORE.

Marjorie and David, her youngest brother, visit the gravesite of their parents in 2011. David has been a major force in supporting Marjorie's healing, particularly her coming to realize that her mother, Winifred, never wanted her children to be sent to Canada.

expected to create a sense of home in a very foreign environment. Their job hours were usually twenty-four hours a day, seven days a week, with little time off. If you were placed with a nice cottage mother, then your life could be a little easier than those placed with a mean one. A bad cottage mother and a cottage full of bullies prompted one little six-year-old Fairbridge boy, Roddy, to pray at night: "Dear God, please take these wicked people away from Fairbridge." His cottage was under the "care of a very harsh and cruel cottage mother. She also saw fit to turn a blind eye on the typical British Boy's School Bully system. The boy awakened daily wondering what new terrors the day held in store for him and his mates."[5]

Cottage life was an environment where young children instinctively knew that to survive they needed to fight for themselves in any manner that was open to them. The system produced survivors, but at times it was at the expense of emotional damage. One former Canadian Fairbridgian said that as an adult he could have a platonic relationship with people, but never an emotional one. That part of him was locked away as a youngster and he was never able to access it again.

Isobel Harvey, a B.C. child welfare worker, during her visit to the Prince of Wales Fairbridge Farm School in 1944, expressed concerned about the power that the cottage mothers had over the children, especially the younger ones. She also felt that many of the mothers "showed a lack of concern for the children under their care and she witnessed them yelling constantly at the children." What further concerned Harvey was the cottage mothers appeared to feel that the British child migrants were different from Canadian children. It prompted them to often raise their voices with the children and mete out strict discipline, and being kind to the children was seen as unnecessary.[6] The children had many obstacles put in their way, and when they lashed out against their treatment or faltered in an way, it was often thought to be because of their bad genes.

Harvey was not alone in her observations. A former duties master, Arthur Sager, began the chapter of his Fairbridge experience in his memoir with: "Had I known what I was letting myself in for I probably wouldn't have taken the job as Duties Master as those eight weeks at Fairbridge left me emotionally drained." Sager stated that the cottage system was at the "core of the Fairbridge philosophy and though in principle enlightened its successful application was completely dependent on the qualifications and character of the Cottage Mother. While required to adhere to School rules and regu-lations, they were given a wide degree of freedom in the running of their homes. Most were up to it though others were not as I was to discover later."[7]

Marjorie had an array of cottage mothers. Some were horrid, wicked, uncaring women, but, luckily for her, one or two were very kind and caring women. With the inconsistent care received, it is no wonder that many children had difficulty looking at their new home and new country as a place where they belonged. They were nobody's children and, as such, had to plough their own way into and through their adult life.

Appendix A

OUTFITTED FOR CANADA

Marjorie's Suitcase

One pair of thick pyjamas

Two pairs of thin pyjamas

Two vests

Two pairs of brown knickers

One gymslip

One woollen jumper

One thick skirt

Two handkerchiefs

Two pairs of socks

Two towels

One kitbag

One brush and comb with bag

Sponge bag with face flannel, toothpaste, toothbrush, and soap

Kenny's Suitcase

One coat or raincoat

Two vests

Three pairs of pyjamas

Two pairs of underpants

One belt

One pair of khaki shorts

One pair cotton shorts

Two khaki shirts

One jersey

One pairs of socks

One kitbag

One brush and comb with bag

Sponge bag with face flannel, toothpaste, toothbrush, and soap

One pair of sandals

Two cotton frocks

Two cotton knickers

One pair of shorts and sports vest

One Bible

The clothes she is wearing

Two towels

Two handkerchiefs

One pair sandals

One Fairbridge tie

One Bible

The clothes he is wearing

Appendix B

THE FAIRBRIDGE MARCH

Cheerio!
Here we are
Working hard
On the land
On our Fairbridge Farm.

Cheerio!
Here we are
Learning hard
The golden rule
At the Fairbridge School

Cheerio!
Here we are
Playing hard
In the fields
Where the skylarks sing
As we stroll along the country lane
And singing on our way
For the love of our Island home
In Canada
Our Empire home
For we love our Island home
Our Empire home in Canada.

God bless our home in Canada
And bless our Fairbridge School,
God bless our Alma Mater
Where we learn the golden rule,
God bless our home in Canada
And may we always sing
The Maple Leaf, O Canada,
God save our Gracious King.

Words and music by John Rowland, Victoria, British Columbia. This song was copyrighted in the name of the Fairbridge farm school. A copy of this song was accepted by His Majesty the King. Reproduced with permission of Gil Woods, Fairbridge Society contact in London, England.

Appendix C

BRIEF BACKGROUND OF THE PRINCE OF WALES FAIRBRIDGE FARM SCHOOL, NEAR COWICHAN STATION, BRITISH COLUMBIA

The Fairbridge farm schools were part of the British philanthropic scheme of resettling children of their poorer classes as farm and domestic labourers in the colonies. When Kingsley Fairbridge and his wife Ruby opened the first Fairbridge farm school in 1912, the migration of children from Britain had been an accepted practice for almost three hundred years.

It was as early as 1618–19 that the Virginia Company took one hundred street children from the City of London to Virginia in order to supply labour to the plantation owners at Jamestown, Virginia. The children, some as young as ten, were thought to be a nuisance and a burden to the taxpayers. This set a precedent and so the emigration of children to the colonies began.[1]

Kingsley Ogilvie Fairbridge was born in Grahamstown, South Africa, in 1885, the son of a land surveyor. His parents and grandparents were also born in South Africa. In 1896 his family moved to Umtali, Rhodesia, today known as Mutare, Zimbabwe. There he grew up in the relatively sparsely populated British colony. In March 1903, Fairbridge visited England for the first time, where he expected to find "stately processions of dignified citizens, conscious of the responsibilities of the Empire...." Instead he saw crowded streets filled with children, "dirty children, yet lovable, exhausted with the heat. No decent air, not enough food. The waste of it all! Children's lives wasting while the Empire cried aloud for men."[2] Fairbridge had a vision in which he saw a solution both to Britain's overcrowding and the lack of men in the colonies — it was to remove these children to the colonies and train them to be farmers. "Shift the orphanages of Britain north, south, east and west to the shores of Greater Britain, where farmers and farmers wives are wanted.... I saw great Colleges of Agriculture (not workhouses) springing up in every man-hungry corner of the Empire."[3] Long before Fairbridge was born, his great-grandfather, Dr. James William Fairbridge, had been involved in the setting up of the Children's Friend Society, which migrated children to South Africa, Canada, and Australia in the 1830s.[4] Being born into such a family, Fairbridge could see that the colonies continued to need a greater British population if Britain wished to maintain their control over them.

Settling the colonies and learning the skills needed to survive was a daunting task for most men, but it was felt that if children were taken out and taught the necessary skills — the boys to work on the land and the girls to have the domestic skills to work in households and eventually to become a farmer's wife — then it would be a start to solving some of Britain's problems.

Kingsley Fairbridge kept his dream alive and worked tirelessly towards his goal. He applied to Oxford for a Rhodes scholarship, failed, and tried again, and after his fourth attempt he was admitted to Exeter College. It was on October 19, 1909, while at this college, that he addressed fellow students with his idea, and as a result the Society for the Furtherance of Child Emigration to the Colonies was formed. He first approached the British South African Company with his plan for a farm school in Rhodesia, but was turned down because they considered Rhodesia unsuitable for child migration at that time.

The premier of Newfoundland offered "fifty thousand acres of good land,"[5] but Fairbridge felt the climate might not be suitable. He accepted Western Australia's offer of land and established the first Fairbridge farm school in 1912 near Perth. Fairbridge faced years of struggle to keep his farm school running, but in 1923 the Empire Settlement Act provided monies for the British Government to assist emigration, including child and youth migration. Fairbridge received substantial assistance from the Overseas Settlement Board in London, and, as a result, it placed his farm school at Pinjarra on a permanent footing.[6] On July 19, 1924, Kingsley

Fairbridge died at the young age of thirty-nine, but his farm-school scheme, now supported by the government and viewed as an ideal form of child migration, lived on.

On June 14, the Prince of Wales (later Edward VIII) launched an appeal to raise £100,000 to establish more schools in the British Empire on the model of the Fairbridge farm school in Western Australia. The prince told his audience that: "It is no exaggeration to say that the Fairbridge Farm School scheme is the only completely successful form of migration at the present time."[7] The prince donated £1,000 (£36,980 in today's money) and reiterated what Kingsley Fairbridge said in 1909, that "this is not a charity, it is an Imperial investment."[8]

His Royal Highness the Prince of Wales saw three outstanding merits in the Fairbridge scheme of migrating children:

1) Migrating children gave "a chance of happiness and of a successful career in healthy surroundings to orphan and poorer children of Great Britain, whose prospects in the present difficult times are … precarious."

2) The scheme of emigrating children overseas "makes a definite contribution to the solution of the problem, the great problem, of unemployment … to alleviate these conditions is one of the most valuable services which we can render to this country at the present time."

3) "By sending out these carefully selected children and training them for useful careers in the land which is to be their home the system should be capable of providing a steady flow of *good* citizens to the Dominions and to the Colonies."[9]

The appeal was a success, and, in early 1935, the Pemberlea Farm, near Cowichan Station on Vancouver Island, British Columbia, was purchased. The farm, comprised of 1,000 acres, with 250 acres cleared and cultivated, was named the Prince of Wales Fairbridge Farm School in honour of the Prince of Wales and his support of the Fairbridge Society and their work on child migration. The first group of forty-one children arrived in September of that year, officially marking the opening the second Fairbridge farm school.

Between 1935 and 1948 a total of 329 children were sent to the Prince of Wales Fairbridge Farm School. It is interesting to note that of this number, 95 percent were not orphans: 45 percent came from single-parent families, and 50 percent from two-parent families. It was believed that relatively few orphans were sent to Canada because Fairbridge officials and the immigration authorities did not want to bring out children who had spent most of their young lives in institutions or on the streets.[10]

Initially, close to 170 children were put forth for consideration for opening of this Fairbridge farm school. However, the Canadian officials in London rejected three quarters of the children on the grounds that they felt that these children were not up to the standards set for this program.[11] Thus, it appears that a trend developed to seek children who were living in their homes with parents who were caught in an economic struggle because of the years of unemployment during this time, which was especially acute in the Tyneside area of Northern England. This negates Kingsley Fairbridge's original "Vision Splendid" as it came to be known — his dream to shift the children from the orphanages of Britain to the farms of Greater Britain. Instead, many of the children at this farm school were removed from their families.

By the early 1940s, the Prince of Wales Fairbridge Farm School site was a little village unto itself. It consisted of the principal's house and office, the day school, the Howard Mitchell auditorium, the industrial arts building, the Kenilworth dining hall, a cook's cottage, a hospital, a chapel, a laundry, the farm manager's house, a horse barn, a cow barn and piggery, and eighteen cottages, each given a name plus a letter of the alphabet. Fourteen of the cottages were in duplex style. Each cottage was capable of accommodating twelve to fourteen children plus a resident cottage mother. During the fifteen years of the school's operation, there were over 150 cottage mothers hired to look after the children.[12]

Many former Fairbridgians have said that one's day-to-day life depended solely on who your cottage mother was. For some, the cottage mother they were placed with, "was a strict disciplinarian. She would beat you of you did something wrong.... If you were not liked by your cottage mother, your life was hell, really. She had complete control over us, she did not have to answer to anybody, she was our keeper. She had total dominance. I think I just got a bad one. There were some nice ones."[13]

Once again, the ideal and the reality were at odds. Kingsley Fairbridge's initial ideal set for a cottage mother fell short because of a shortage of women who were willing to take on the job of being a full-time "mother" to twelve to fourteen children. The farm school was isolated, the pay was low, and the war years opened up other jobs to women that offered better pay. The constant changeover of "mothers" would not have allowed for any sense of security among the children in these cottages.

The first principal of the farm school was Major F. Trew, who held the position from April 1935 to May 1936. Colonel H.T. Logan, an acquaintance of Kingsley Fairbridge from Oxford, was brought in next. He stayed until he resigned in June 1945 to take a position on staff of the Fairbridge Society headquarters in London. Mr. W.J. Garnett came next and was there from July 1945 to January 1949. The last principal was Major A.H. Plows, who held the post from February 1949 until the school's closing in January 1951. The farm school closed its doors in the early 1950s and the final twenty or so children still housed at the farm school were sent into foster care.

Today the property that once housed the Prince of Wales Fairbridge Farm School Village has been turned into a residential housing development. Many of the former cottages still stand and they have been remodelled into single-family dwellings. Several of the new owners have the former cottage name and alphabet letter proudly displayed. Newer homes have been constructed where the former dining hall stood and Fairbridge Hospital once stood. The Fairbridge School has been torn down. The Fairbridge Chapel earned its Heritage Building status and has been looked after by former Fairbridgians as well as interested residents on the property. A display board, with the names and dates of the arrival of the children as well as a bit of the history, sits under the trees to the left chapel. If one looks carefully past the shrubs to the left of the chapel stairs, the original 1939 cornerstone can be seen.

Every two years, several former Fairbridgians return to their childhood home to hold a reunion with their Fairbridge family. They come from around British Columbia, across Canada and the United States, and even some who returned to England to live make the trek out to see their old home near Cowichan Station. Memories of their Fairbridge years vary wildly from person to person, from the very, very good to the very, very bad, but regardless of their early experiences, many return simply to revisit their Fairbridge brothers and sisters.

Appendix D

CHILD MIGRATION TIMELINE

This timeline includes the first and the last documented groups of child migrants (home children) sent from Britain. However, this timeline is focused mainly on Canada and its involvement in British child migration between 1833 and 1948.

A. BRITISH CHILD MIGRATION: THE BEGINNING[1]

1618–1619: The Virginia Company took one hundred street children from the city of London to Virginia in order to supply labour to the plantation owners at Jamestown, Virginia. Jamestown had been established just over a decade earlier, in 1607. Some of these child migrants were as young as ten, and seen, like their nineteenth-century counterparts, as a nuisance and a burden to the taxpayers. Moreover, they were suspected of spreading the plague. In 1622, the Council for New England also asked for poor children to be sent to them. And so the emigration of children to the colonies began.[2]

1620: January: There was opposition to child migration and claims that the first group was sent illegally, but on January 31, the Privy Council authorized the scheme. A second group of one hundred children were sent to America.

1622: Several settlers in Virginia were victims of a First Nations raid. To replace them, another one hundred children were sent.

1645: The Corporation for the Propagation of the Gospel in New England arranged the emigration of some two hundred poor children (not "vagrants") to North American colonies. Members of the society escorted the children to the colonies. "Spiriting," or kidnapping children for work in Americas, had grown to meet the perennial labour shortage in the colonies. Bristol was the main port of emigration. Parliament passed an ordinance to make spiriting a felony.[3]

1698: August 30–September 1: A newspaper reporter claimed he observed "about 200" kidnapped boys held on a ship in the Thames awaiting departure for the West Indies.[4]

1740: Peter Williamson of Aberdeen, Scotland, was kidnapped along with about five hundred other youngsters and removed to the colonies in America.

1762:   Peter Williamson wrote a book about his 1740 kidnapping and subsequent adventures and misadventures: *French and Indian Cruelty, Exemplified in the Life and Various Vicissitudes of Fortune of Peter Williamson*. Bristol, England: Thoemmes Press, 1996 (reprint of the 1762 edition).

1810: *Caledonian Mercury* Edinburgh, Scotland. July 19, 1810: "Kidnapping Children." Newspaper article about a man selling children not his own to be sent overseas.

1830: The Society for the Suppression of Juvenile Vagrancy, later known as the Children's Friend Society, was founded in London in 1830 by a retired naval captain, Edward Pelham Brenton. His aim was to prepare destitute children for migration with training to enable them to support themselves.[5] He concluded that children were living off the streets because of poverty and lack of job prospects in England, and he saw emigrating the children as a solution to this problem. Dr. James William Fairbridge, the great-grandfather of Kingsley Fairbridge, was involved with the Children's Friend Society.[6]

1832: Society for the Suppression of Juvenile Vagrancy, later known as the Children's Friend Society, sent children to the Swan River Colony in Australia.[7]

B. TIMELINE OF CHILD MIGRATION TO CANADA[8]

1833–1837: The Children's Friend Society, founded by Edward Brenton, sent several parties of children to eastern Canada over this four-year period. The 1837 Rebellion stopped the migration of children.[9]

1834–1839: Increasing accusations of kidnapping and selling children were brought against The Children's Friend Society: "Children's Friend Society," *Morning Chronicle*, May 5, 1834; "The Kidnapping Society", *Champion and Weekly Herald*, January 27, 1839, Issue 38, page 4; "Transportation of Children by Parish Officers," *The Operative*, February 3, 1839, page 10; "The Children's Friend Society and Pauper Emigration," *Champion and Weekly Herald*, February 24, 1839, page 8; "Children's Friend Society, or, The Hackney Kidnappers," *Champion and Weekly Herald*, April 7, 1839, Issue 48; *London Dispatch*, April 7, 1839, page 1069; "Children's Friend Society," *London Times*, April 15, 1839, page 7; "The Kidnapping Society," *Champion and Weekly Herald*, April 21, 1839, Issue 50; "Transportation and Sale of Children of the Poor: Defense of the Children's Aid Society," *The Operative*, May 5, 1839, Vol. II, No. 27. The negative publicity, the loss of public support, and Brenton's death in 1839, resulted in the Children's Friend Society disbanding by 1842.

1853: The Gold Rush ceased the early phase of emigration of children to Australia. When conditions in Australia were deemed unsuitable for children, the young migrants were sent to Canada instead.[10]

1869: Maria Rye (1829–1903) was in the forefront of this wave of child migration. She established an Emigration Home for Destitute Little Girls in Peckham, London, to house her girls awaiting emigration. She took her first group of girls to Canada in October to her distribution house in Niagara-on-the-Lake, Ontario.[11]

1870: Annie Parlane MacPherson was a Scottish evangelical Quaker and philanthropist who pioneered child emigration to Canada. MacPherson took her first one hundred boys from London to Belleville, Ontario, in May 1870.[12]

Father James Nugent of Liverpool, England, pioneered Catholic child migration to Canada. He took his first group of twenty-four children to Montreal, Quebec, on August 19, 1870.[13] He continued to send children to Canada for another twenty years.

1872: William Quarrier established Orphan Homes of Scotland was at Cessnock, Glasgow, Scotland, in 1871. His first group left for Canada on July 2, 1872 and were taken to Annie MacPherson's receiving home at Belleville, Ontario, Canada.[14]

1873: Children were emigrated from the various children's emigration homes established in England by John T. Middlemore.[15]

Liverpool Sheltering Homes, run by a group of prominent Liverpool men and headed by Louisa Birt, Annie MacPherson's sister, sent children to Nova Scotia starting in August of 1873.[16] These children were placed with local farmers. Some 550 children were sent to Nova Scotia between August 1873 and the end of 1876.

The Children's Home in East London was established by Reverend Thomas Bowman in 1869. In 1908, the name changed to National Children's Homes and Orphanages. The first group of children was sent to Hamilton, Ontario, in May 1873. The institution continued to send children until 1934.[17]

1874: The Canadian Catholic Emigration Society was established by the Archdiocese of Westminster, London, England, with Father Richard Seddon as the secretary. British children were sent to Catholic families in the eastern townships of Quebec and the Ottawa areas.[18]

1880: The Liverpool Catholic Children's Protection Society sent child migrants to Canada for over twenty years, but due to financial pressures they stopped in 1902.[19]

1881: The Church of England Waifs and Stray Society, later called Children's Society, was established by Edward Rudolf of London, England, in May 1881. With the Archbishop of Canterbury as president, it became the Church of England's officially recognized organization for providing pauper children with homes. By 1883 emigration was underway, with the first group leaving with Annie MacPherson. By 1884 the society had established its own receiving home, Gibbs House, in Sherbrooke, Quebec. Its next group of children departed Liverpool on April 23, 1885.[20]

1882: Thomas John Barnardo sent the first of his children under Annie MacPherson's scheme. But when Samuel Smith, member of parliament for Liverpool and supporter of child emigration, donated money to both Barnardo and James Fegan, on the condition it be used to emigrate children, Barnardo complied and accompanied his first group to Canada on August 10, 1882.[21] The Barnardo organization sent over 20,000 children to Canada by 1930.

1884: The first of James Fegan's Homes was established in 1872 on High Street, Deptford, in southeast London. Fegan sent the first group of children to Brandon, Manitoba, in 1884. Fegan also established a receiving home in Toronto, Ontario, at 295 George Street. He died in 1925, but his wife continued his work until 1943.[22]

1885: Kingsley Fairbridge was born in Grahamstown, South Africa.

1886: The Salford Catholic Protection and Rescue Society was established.[23]

1887: The Southwark Catholic Emigration Society, London, England, was formed by Bishop Bunt and run by Canon Edward St. John. They opened a receiving home in Ottawa, Ontario, in 1895, and, in 1897, they established a home in Makinak, Manitoba. The society merged with the Canadian Catholic Emigration Society in 1898.[24]

Barnardo established an industrial farm in Russell, Manitoba. He gained the support of Sir Charles Tupper, the Canadian high commissioner in London. Barnardo asked Tupper to provide free transportation for the children, which he did, with grants and donations, and Barnardo was able to purchase a large farm. The Russell Farm in Manitoba was a forerunner to Kingsley Fairbridge's farm schools in Australia and Canada. The Russell Farm closed in 1908.[25]

1890: Barnardo submitted a "Scheme of Colonization" to the Canadian Department of Agriculture. This was a new development in the story of child emigration as it enabled young men to be sent from Britain to Canada to be trained in animal husbandry and crop management with the ultimate aim of settling the land. The Canadian government had an allotment scheme in place, offering every young man over eighteen years of age a small farm of 160 acres. Barnardo planned to link this with his training program at the Russell Farm. One problem was the lack of women. If more women were not sent out to Canada, farmers would not stay, but would move to the United States. The girls trained as domestics, but most left at age eighteen for work in factories, restaurants, and shops. Only a few married farmers.[26]

1891: The Custody of Children Act (the so-called Barnardo's Act) legalized the work of the private emigration societies where previously they had acted in a legal grey area.[27]

A "Boarding Out" scheme was established by Barnardo, where children under twelve were placed with foster families, who were paid to look after them.[28]

1896: Barnardo established a new home in Winnipeg, Manitoba, for boys between ten and thirteen years of age. There was a strong demand, for young boys to work on western farms. Initially, boys served as apprentices on Ontario farms.[29]

1901: The Salvation Army emigrated small groups in 1901. By 1903, the Army's emigration of children increased, and by 1905, it was chartering its own ships.[30]

1902: The Birmingham Diocesan Rescue Society for the Protection of Homeless and Friendless Catholic Children was established with Father George Vincent Hudson as its first secretary and administrator. It later became known as "Father Hudson's Homes."[31]

1903: Child-migration rhetoric was becoming less religious and more imperial. Mrs. Elinor Close of England advocated the training of workhouse children on farm schools *before* their placement with Canadian farmers. There was no support from the British Poor Law Board, but some private assistance did help.[32]

The Catholic Emigration Association was established. Father George Vincent Hudson of Birmingham, England, was the first secretary.[33]

1906: The Elinor Close Farm was established in 1904 near Rothesay, New Brunswick. The first children arrived in 1906. It closed eight years later with the start of the First World War. Kingsley Fairbridge was bitter over Close's farm as he felt it might jeopardize his first plans for a farm school in Newfoundland. This did not materialize.[34]

1909: The Society for the Furtherance of Child Emigration to the Colonies was formed by Kingsley Fairbridge. It was later renamed the Child Emigration Society (Inc.).

1912: The first Fairbridge farm school, the Kingsley Fairbridge Farm School, opened south of Pinjarra, Western Australia. The farm school closed in 1981.

1920s and 1930s: The Fairbridge farm school in Australia was visited by many, including the Duke and Duchess of York, King George, and Queen Elizabeth, who said, "I only wish there were more farm schools all over Australia and other parts of the Empire — but they must be run on the Fairbridge principle."[35]

1923: The Empire Settlement Act provided money for the British government to assist emigration, including child and youth migration. Kingsley Fairbridge received substantial assistance from the Overseas Settlement Board in London to place his farm school at Pinjarra on a permanent footing.[36]

1924: On July 19, 1924, Kingsley Fairbridge died at age thirty-nine, but his farm school scheme lived on. It served two purposes: child rescue and commonwealth migration.[37]

A British parliamentary delegation headed by Margaret Bondfield, MP for the Labour government, was dispatched to Canada to explore the whole process of sending young children to live and work there. Although the Canadian provincial child welfare associations opposed the practice almost without exception as professional childcare became more sophisticated, the Bondfield Report stated that "We have no doubt that the prospects in Canada for the average boy or girl are better that they would be in the U.K."[38]

Canadian government passed an order-in-council that effectively banned unaccompanied children under fourteen from entering Canada legally.

1925: The ban was made permanent.

1926: The following year as many as 4,000 children still sailed to Canada, but numbers declined by the end of the decade.

1931: There were only six girls and fewer than five hundred boys sent to Canada in 1931.

1932: Barnardo sent very few children to Canada after 1932. Britain needed alternative countries to receive child migrants and Australia presented the obvious choice.[39]

1933: The Children and Young Persons Act stated that the consent of the child and of the British secretary of state was needed, along with the consultation with the parents where these were deemed to be "fit persons." The intention was to manage migration in a more up-to-date and efficient way, but as the century progressed the limitations of the system were to be gradually exposed.[40]

1934: On June 14, the Prince of Wales (later Edward VIII) launched an appeal at the Grocers' Hall to raise £100,000 to establish more schools in the British Empire on the model of the Fairbridge farm school in Western Australia. It was also backed by His Majesty's government, represented by the prime minister, Stanley Baldwin.[41]

1935: The Child Emigration Society, founded in 1909 by Kingsley Fairbridge, changed its name to Fairbridge Farm Schools Inc.

The Prince of Wales Fairbridge Farm School opened near Duncan on Vancouver Island, British Columbia. The ruling of no unaccompanied migrants under the age of fourteen, passed in council in 1924, was quietly disregarded. The first forty-one children arrived in September. Close to 170 children were put forth, but the Canadian officials at Canada House in London rejected the majority of the children.[42] Many, such as the Quarrier Homes of Scotland, Bridge of Weir, protested this. They wrote to the Fairbridge Society secretary, Mr. Green, dated September 13, 1935, "of the 28 … only 2 children were passed by Canada House. What happened in London, I do not know, but we consider it nothing short of an outrage on a crowd of fine children … turned down in such a ruthless way.… [W]e spent days in preparation and a good deal of money … and all to no purpose. I do hope … when you go to Ottawa to knock some sense into the powers that be." They referred to the children presented to the Fairbridge farm school as "material": "the difficulties which confront the Society in the selection of material. If the Society turned down these children, then they would strike a blow at the source of revenue…. Strictly speaking, The Fairbridge Farm School is somewhat in the nature of a broker. They ask these public assistance authorities, who are like wholesalers, to supply the children, who are the retailers."[43] Numerous letters and newspaper articles about the children bound for this farm school refer to the children as "it," "material," "stock," and "culls," as if they were talking about a commodity and not about little children. Influential supporters at this time included Thomas Dufferin Pattullo, the Provincial Secretary's Department: "even in the Depression cheap farm labour and female household servants were in short supply."[44] Unwanted boys and girls from Britain were trained to become labourers and servants, which were two of the most despised occupations.[45] "A Canadian boy from the city does not take kindly to farm work." (From a letter dated December 23, 1935, the acting deputy minister, Department of Immigration and Colonization, to the Canadian Daughter's League.[46])

The Child Emigration Society, founded in 1909 by Kingsley Fairbridge, changed its name to the Fairbridge Farm Schools (Inc.).

1936: Harry T. Logan became principal of the Prince of Wales Fairbridge Farm School. He was a Rhodes Scholar and his appointment attracted attention and support.

1937: The Fairbridge Farm School of New South Wales is established at Molong, Australia. It closed in 1974.

The Northcote Children's Farm, associated with the Fairbridge farm school, was established at Bacchus Marsh, Victoria, Australia. The war suspended the migration of children and because there were not enough children to run the school at capacity, all Northcote children and a number of cottage mothers were sent to the Fairbridge farm school at Molong in 1944.

1938: Fintry Fairbridge Training Farm. Having no heirs, Captain Dun-Waters "sold" his Fintry Estate, located on the west side of Lake Okanagan, in the interior of British Columbia, to the Fairbridge farm school for one dollar.[47]

1948: The last group of child migrants was sent to the Prince of Wales Fairbridge Farm School. This was the final six child migrants sent to Canada. In total, 329 children were sent to the Prince of Wales Fairbridge Farm School near Duncan, on Vancouver Island.

1949-1952:   At some point during this time, the Fairbridge Farm Schools (Inc.) was changed to the Fairbridge Society (Inc.).

1970s: Child migration continued to Australia until the early 1970s.

1978:   Operation Drake was formed at the suggestion of HRH The Prince of Wales.

1980:   George Thurstan, one of the organizers of Operation Drake, formed the Drake Fellowship to help under-privileged young people from centres based in the heart of the inner cities.

1987: The Drake Fellowship merged with the Fairbridge Society to become Fairbridge Drake.

1992:   Fairbridge Drake was changed to Fairbridge.

2009:   November 16: Australia's prime minister, Kevin Rudd, gave a formal apology to all child migrants sent to Australia.

2010:   February 24: Britain's prime minister, Gordon Brown, gave a formal apology to all British child migrants sent to the colonies over the 350-year period of child migration.

The Canadian Immigration Minister, Jason Kenney stated that:

> There's no need for Canada to apologize for abuse and exploitation suffered by thousands of poor children shipped here from Britain starting in the nineteenth century.... [T]he issue has not been on the radar screen here, unlike Australia where there's been a long-standing interest. The reality is that, here in Canada, we are taking measures to recognize that sad period, but there is, I think, limited public interest in official government apologies for everything that's ever been unfortunate or (a) tragic event in our history.[48]

2011:   In April Fairbridge became part of The Prince's Trust. The united organisation was called The Prince's Trust.

Appendix E

TRANSCRIPT OF GORDON BROWN'S APOLOGY TO BRITISH CHILD MIGRANTS

House of Commons Debates, February 24, 2010, Volume No. 506, Part No. 44. U.K. Parliament: *www.parliament.uk.*

24 Feb 2010: Columns 301–308
Child Migration

12.33 pm

The Prime Minister (Mr. Gordon Brown): With permission, Mr. Speaker, I wish to make a statement.

Until the late 1960s, successive UK Governments had over a long period of time supported child migration schemes. They involved children as young as three being transported from Britain to Australia, Canada, New Zealand, South Africa and Zimbabwe. The hope was that those children, who were aged between three and 14, would have the chance to forge a better life overseas, but the schemes proved to be misguided. In too many cases, vulnerable children suffered unrelenting hardship and their families left behind were devastated. They were sent mostly without the consent of their mother or father. They were cruelly lied to and told that they were orphans and that their parents were dead, when in fact they were still alive. Some were separated from their brothers and sisters, never to see one another again. Names and birthdays were deliberately changed so that it would be impossible for families to reunite. Many parents did not know that their children had been sent out of this country.

The former child migrants say they feel that this practice was less transportation and more deportation-a deportation of innocent young lives. When they arrived overseas, all alone in the world, many of our most vulnerable children endured the harshest of conditions, neglect and abuse in the often cold and brutal institutions that received them. Those children were robbed of their childhood, the most precious years of their life. As people know, the pain of a lost childhood can last a lifetime. Some still bear the marks of abuse; all still live with the consequences of rejection. Their wounds will never fully heal, and for too long the survivors have been all but ignored.

When I was first made aware of this wholly unacceptable practice, I wrote to the Prime Minister of Australia to urge that together, we do more to acknowledge the experiences of former child migrants and see what we could achieve. It is right that today we recognise the human cost associated with this shameful episode of history and this failure in the first duty of a nation, which is to protect its children.

Shortly, I shall be meeting a number of former child migrants here in the Palace of Westminster to listen first-hand to their experiences, and as Prime Minister, I will be apologising on behalf of our nation. To all those former child migrants and their families, to those here with us today and those across the world-to each and every one-I say today that we are truly sorry. They were let down. We are sorry that they were allowed to be sent away at the time they were most vulnerable. We are sorry that instead of caring for them, this country turned its back, and we are sorry that the voices of these children were not always heard and their cries for help not always heeded. We are sorry that it has taken so long for this important day to come, and for the full and unconditional apology that is justly deserved to be given.

I would like to recognise the work of my right hon. Friend the Member for Rother Valley (Mr. Barron) as Chairman of the Select Committee on

Health, and of his predecessor the former Member for Wakefield, David Hinchcliffe. For their commitment to this cause, I would also like to praise all past and present members of the Commons Health Committee and the all-party group on child migrants. I would also like to pay tribute to the work of the Child Migrants Trust and the International Association of Former Child Migrants and their Families, which have campaigned for justice over many years. I know that the House will join me in paying special tribute to Margaret Humphreys, who founded the Child Migrants Trust and has been a constant champion and fighter for child migrants and their families.

Although we cannot undo the events of the past, we can take action now to support people to regain their true identities and reunite with their families and loved ones, and to go some way to repair the damage that has been inflicted. I can announce today support for former child migrants that includes the establishment of a new £6 million family restoration fund.

There are many painful memories as a result of the child migration schemes, and for many, today's apology will come too late for them to hear it. We cannot change history, but I believe that by confronting the failings of the past we show that we are determined to do all we can to heal the wounds. I commend this statement to the House.

Mr. David Cameron (Witney) (Con): On behalf of the Opposition, I welcome what the Prime Minister has said and the moving words of the Australian Prime Minister Kevin Rudd, who spoke last November of
    "the tragedy-the absolute tragedy-of childhoods lost."
This was something that happened under British Governments of all parties, and the apology made is on behalf of all of us.

We on the Conservative Benches join the Prime Minister in sending our good wishes to those affected, including those in London today and those attending events in other countries. We join him also in praising campaigners such as Margaret Humphreys and the Child Migrants Trust, as well as the work of the Health Committee.

It is hard to believe that this went on for so long that the last children sailed in 1967, after most of us in the House were born. Anyone who studies what happened-it happened systematically and for so long-will be profoundly shocked at the splitting of families, the lies and abuse that took place, the official sanction that made it possible, and as the Prime Minister said, the heartache that it caused.

In his apology, Kevin Rudd emphasised the projects that the Australian Government are supporting to provide what he described as a solemn reminder of the past. Bearing in mind our very close ties with Australia and the other Commonwealth countries affected, it is important that we do all we can to assist in that work.

It is right to judge a society on how it cares for its most vulnerable, especially our children, so should not our legacy to future generations be to do all that we can to make sure that the lessons from these appalling events are learnt and applied, so that such terrible mistakes can never happen again?

The Prime Minister: I am sure the whole House would want to thank the Leader of the Opposition for his eloquence in stating that there is not just Government support, but all-party support for the action that we are taking today. I believe that these sentiments will be shared in every part of our country.

Mr. Nick Clegg (Sheffield, Hallam) (LD): Of course, I add my own voice and that of my party to the Prime Minister's apology for Britain's role in the child migrants programme. An apology-we all know this-will never heal the extraordinary pain and hardship that was inflicted on thousands of vulnerable children and their families, but I hope today's apology will go some way to start to atone for Britain's record in this shameful episode in our history.

I join the Prime Minister in paying tribute to all involved in recognising the plight of those who suffered, including current and former Members of this House, but especially the Child Migrants Trust and the International Association of Former Child Migrants and their Families, which have done so much to try to heal the pain. I specifically welcome the Prime Minister's announcement that he will establish a family restoration fund-that is very welcome indeed.

I pay tribute to those child migrants in London today and, of course, those who are not. The suffering that they endured is simply unimaginable; the apology they are now owed is unlimited.

The Prime Minister: The child migrants who are with us today will be pleased to know that every main party-and, I believe, all the parties-in this House are supporting both the apology and the efforts that we are making to deal with some of the problems that they still have by the creation of the new fund. I thank the right hon. Gentleman for the eloquence of his tribute to what is being done.

Mr. Kevin Barron (Rother Valley) (Lab): On behalf of the Health Committee, may I thank my right hon. Friend for his statement and for the Government's continuing support for former child migrants? In 1998, when the Committee decided to do the inquiry under the chairmanship of the former Member for Wakefield, David Hinchliffe, two members of the current Committee were involved-the hon. Member for Poole (Mr. Syms) and my hon. Friend the Member for Dartford (Dr. Stoate). Does the Prime Minister agree that it was the independence and resources of that Back-Bench Committee which enabled this dark chapter in the UK's history to come out of the shadows and to make this day possible?

The Prime Minister: I do agree with my hon. Friend and I pay tribute to his personal work in making people aware of the problems that still had to be faced and the need for far further action than had been proposed. It was when he first came to me that I realised that the action we were pro-posing was insufficient to deal with the problem and that we had to work with the Australian Government to do far more. I acknowledge not only his work, but the work of all members of those Health Committees, and, indeed, the general work that Select Committees do to expose problems that need action.

Mr. Robert Walter (North Dorset) (Con): I was a member of the Health Committee that spent two weeks in 1998 in Australia and New Zealand hearing the life histories of hundreds of former child migrants. I must say that those were two of the most harrowing weeks of my life just hearing their stories.

The Catholic Church in Australia, some 10 years ago, led the apologies from the receiving agencies, and a number of others have done likewise. The Australian Government issued their apology last year, but I remind the Prime Minister that the report we presented to the House on 30 July 1998 said to the British Government that

"an apology is in order".

The apology is therefore long overdue, but none the less, it is very welcome.

I should like to ask the Prime Minister a question. Sending agencies in this country were complicit in this trade in children. Has he had discussions with them that they should join him in this apology?

The Prime Minister: I am grateful for the work that the hon. Gentleman has done and for his visits to Australia, which have helped to make what is happening today possible. I assure him that the reason that the apology has been made now is that we wished to consult the child migrants themselves about the form that the apology should take and how we should go about making it. That is why many child migrants are here in Westminster today, and I and other leaders will speak with them shortly and pass on the apologies of the whole House about what happened in our country. I agree with the hon. Gentleman that people made many mistakes in the implementation of this policy and in its design. We have to be vigilant to ensure that nothing like this ever happens again.

Frank Dobson (Holborn and St. Pancras) (Lab): May I join in welcoming the Prime Minister's statement? There have been several calls for public apologies for past events, and this one has the merit of being made to people who are still around to hear the expressions of regret. I am sure that other members of the Health Committee will join me in paying particular tribute to David Hinchliffe, the former Member for Wakefield and former Chair of the Committee. He became almost obsessed by the grotesque injustice of these events and, at one point, persuaded me as Health Secretary to sign over some money to help to fund the Child Migrants Trust so that it was better able to go about its task. I welcome the Prime Minister finding extra funds for the trust and I pay tribute to Margaret Humphreys and others. This is one of the most shameful incidents in modern times in this country, and when people say that we do not have the standards of the past, they should remember the standards of the people who did this sort of thing.

The Prime Minister: I am grateful to my right hon. Friend. He has taken a huge interest in this subject, and I join him in paying tribute to David Hinchliffe. As a Member of Parliament he took this issue up with great vigour, and since ceasing to be a Member he has continued to push for the changes that we are announcing today. The accounts that I have read of what happened to many of the child migrants are very harrowing indeed, and it is a reminder to us that we have to be vigilant and determined to eradicate injustice, wherever it may be found.

Mr. Robert Syms (Poole) (Con): May I welcome the Prime Minister's statement and agree with the comments about David Hinchliffe? More than 10 years ago, I went to Australia and New Zealand and heard the migrants' stories. It was very harrowing and horrible. I also welcome the additional money. The fact that we can now reunite some of the families will make some small amends for the troubles and difficulties that these children faced.

The Prime Minister: I am grateful to the hon. Gentleman.

Dr. Howard Stoate (Dartford) (Lab): I was one of the members of the Health Committee who visited Australia and New Zealand. I have been a GP for many years and I think that I have heard most stories, but never have I heard such harrowing tales of distress and loss as I heard from those brave migrants. I wish to place on record my tribute to those very, very brave people who were able to open their hearts to the Committee. We heard tales that I hope never to have to listen to again of abuse perpetrated by organisations whose job it was to protect children, but clearly failed to do so. I also wish to place on record my thanks to my right hon. Friend the Member for Holborn and St. Pancras (Frank Dobson). He was the first Secretary of State to take this situation seriously and, as he has already modestly said, to find money to allow some of these migrants to meet their families and pick up some of the threads that they had so cruelly taken away from them.

The Prime Minister: Both colleagues who have just spoken are right. These harrowing experiences about which we have read were the fate of so many children who should never have been sent from this country, who should have known about their true parents, and who should have had proper support and protection. We must never allow it to happen again.

Mark Pritchard (The Wrekin) (Con): In welcoming the Prime Minister's comments, may I encourage him not to forget a new generation of 65,000 children who reside in child care facilities in the UK, all of whom have huge potential that is so often unrealised? They all have God-given gifts and abilities that this nation needs. Can he reaffirm his commitment to the House to ensure that those children get the best support to realise their full potential?

The Prime Minister: I certainly can.

Mr. Parmjit Dhanda (Gloucester) (Lab): I welcome the Prime Minister's statement. The first time I came to know of this was a few years ago when I was a Minister and proposals were worked up by officials to reduce some of the funding for these child migrants. Thankfully, we saw that off. At one stage, I had to tell officials that I would resign rather than allow that to happen, so I welcome the extra funding pledged by the Prime Minister. Does he agree that, as long as any of these child migrants are still alive and with us, we must continue to fund and support them?

The Prime Minister: My hon. Friend is absolutely right, and I thank him for his personal efforts. Because we have failed in the duty of care for so many years, we have a particular duty of care to the child migrants.

John Hemming (Birmingham, Yardley) (LD): I, too, welcome the Prime Minister's statement. I must declare an interest as chair of the Justice for Families campaign, which resists injustices against families on the basis of the best interests of the child. The challenge always is that, when people say, "It's better for the child", it is quite difficult to question the injustice. Sadly, many things similar to the child migrant programme, albeit on a smaller scale, continue today, and families are emigrating from this country to escape the family courts. What confidence does the Prime Minister have that a Prime Minister in 20 years will not be making a similar, but smaller scale, apology?

The Prime Minister: I agree with the hon. Gentleman, and if he has any evidence of abuse that should be dealt with, he should bring it before us.

Mr. Geoffrey Robinson (Coventry, North-West) (Lab): The Prime Minister will have heard the remarks of my hon. Friend the Member for Gloucester (Mr. Dhanda), but even those of us who have not been deeply involved know that this has been a sorry and very sad saga. Will he ensure that the money, which is so appreciated, is found and willingly, usefully and generously disbursed to those who have had so much to bear over all these years?

The Prime Minister: My hon. Friend is absolutely right. We are disbursing the money as quickly as we can to those in the greatest need, and we are working directly with individual families to ensure that their needs are met.

Mr. Shailesh Vara (North-West Cambridgeshire) (Con): In order to appreciate the scale of the problem, can the Prime Minister give an indication of the number of children sent abroad, and does he have any idea of the number who might still be alive?

The Prime Minister: This information is being collected over time, so I think I should give a more updated report to the hon. Gentleman at a later date, rather than give him figures that might turn out not to be correct.

Judy Mallaber (Amber Valley) (Lab): My constituent, Pat Hewkin, who sadly died last year, lost her younger brother when she was six when child migrants were sent to Australia. I was honoured to be there when her brother came over for the first time and they were reconciled. I saw the joy, the sadness and the horror of their having to tell their stories, but it was absolutely wonderful to see how they were reconciled and able to meet each other-thanks to the work of the Child Migrants Trust and Margaret Humphreys. Pat was also able to go over and visit him in Australia. I hope, therefore, that the work of the Child Migrants Trust will continue to be supported because to see those families that were split asunder able to meet each other again was a very emotional thing to witness.

The Prime Minister: I am grateful for the work that my hon. Friend has done. Amid the tragedies of separation, we can see, in that particular family, the joy also of reconciliation, and we wish to make that possible for many more families.

Andrew Selous (South-West Bedfordshire) (Con): This was a very poignant statement for me, because, at the age of five-in 1967-I travelled to Australia for several months with my mother, who was an Australian citizen, to spend a very happy time with my grandparents. It is truly shocking to think that, at the same time, this country was officially sending children against their will to Australia where they had such a grim time. May I say that sorry is often the hardest word and commend the Prime Minister and my right hon. Friend the Leader of the Opposition for what they have said today? It was the right thing.

The Prime Minister: The hon. Gentleman is absolutely right. We have got to be prepared to say that this was wrong and completely unjustifiable, and do what we can to repair at least some of the damage done.

Charlotte Atkins (Staffordshire, Moorlands) (Lab): May I congratulate the Prime Minister on his apology today and congratulate the Child Migrants Trust? Many of these children not only lost their childhood and education, but worked as virtual slaves in Australia. Today's apology will be a small compensation for that terrible loss and experience. However, will my right hon. Friend guarantee that those surviving child migrants will not have to return cap in hand to the Government in a few years?

The Prime Minister: I hope that we will be able to continue the funding for as long as it is necessary to ensure that what reparation can be made, is made, and what damage can be reversed, is reversed. I know that we are dealing with the individual circumstances and stories of families now in very different positions, but we will do whatever we can to help individual families.

Dr. William McCrea (South Antrim) (DUP): I welcome the Prime Minister's statement and would like to associate my colleagues with it. It is a shameful part of our history, and we ought to make the apology with deep humility. Can he assure the House that the Government action of which he is speaking will extend to every part of the United Kingdom?

The Prime Minister: Yes, I can. I thank the hon. Gentleman, because every party in the House has now associated itself with the apology. I believe that I can now tell the child migrants when I meet them that it is the unanimous wish of the House both to apologise and to set up a new fund to help them.

Mark Durkan (Foyle) (SDLP): May I commend the Prime Minister's sincere apology and those from other party leaders in the House? They rang so poignantly with the very profound statement from Kevin Rudd last year. The Prime Minister will be aware that it was not just those children who were transported who suffered isolation, abuse and lies; many of their siblings left at home all too often experienced cruel care as well. Recently, many of them have come forward and had difficulty being received and believed. Their difficulty now is believing what they are being told: that there are no records available to settle their concerns, suspicions or beliefs that they have siblings in Australia and elsewhere. Will he ensure that this fund will help to unlock those difficulties that many of those people are now facing?

The Prime Minister: The fund is intended to help those families who were split up as a result of misguided decisions. Obviously, we shall look at what we can do to help reunite brothers and sisters or siblings, and at the same time ensure that they have proper provision for themselves in the future.

Sir Menzies Campbell (North-East Fife) (LD): Is it not clear, from what the Prime Minister has said, that one of the most reprehensible features of this policy was the systematic deception of children and their parents? Do we need any further indication of just how unreasonable this policy was other than the fact that it had to be cloaked in such deception?

The Prime Minister: First, the deception was unacceptable, but secondly the results of that deception were that parents thought that their children were in this country, when they were not, and children thought that their parents were dead, when they were alive. It is a most cruel deception for children to be made to believe that something that they should know about, or have the chance to know about, could never be told to them. When dates, birthdays and names are changed to conceal the truth, it is completely reprehensible, as the right hon. and learned Gentleman said in his eloquent way. We must make this apology, not just for that reason, but for the other reasons that I have cited.

www.publications.parliament.uk/pa/cm200910/cmhansrd/cm100224/ debtext/100224-0004.htm#10022460000003.

Printed with permission under Parliamentary Licence number: P2011000069. Start date: 09/05/2011. End date: 08/05/2016; PSI Licence number: C2011000157. Start date: 09/05/2011. End date: 08/05/2016.

Notes

PREFACE

1. My mother's birth records on her Fairbridge farm school form put her a year older as well. Various records for the children make comments such as "small for her age.... [B]ehind academically," which, of course, would be true if the records weren't incorrect, putting a child a full year ahead of its actual age.

CHAPTER ONE: BUTTERFLIES PREVAIL

1. Isobel Harvey, "Report on a Study made of Fairbridge Farm School during the Month of August 1944," 1–2. Harvey was superintendent of child care for the British Columbia Social Welfare Department of the time. Her report was not favourable towards the Prince of Wales Fairbridge Farm School. A copy of the report can be found at the Public Archives of British Columbia, GR 496, Vol. 58, file 1.

2. *One Hundred Years of Child Care: The Story of Middlemore Homes 1872–1972.* Birmingham: Middlemore Homes Committee (circa 1972), 30.

CHAPTER TWO: WINIFRED'S CHILDREN

1. Lucky tatties are a traditional Scottish treat that can still be bought in some candy stores in Scotland and England.

2. The Fairbridge Society, formerly the Child Emigration Society, was founded by Kingsley Fairbridge (1885–1924). Born in Grahamstown, South Africa, he moved to Rhodesia in 1896. Fairbridge grew up in an environment where imperial expansion was the norm, and he expected to live to see Rhodesia fully settled by the British.

The first Fairbridge farm school opened in Pinjarra, Western Australia, in 1912 (closed in 1981). The Prince of Wales Fairbridge Farm School on Vancouver Island opened in 1935 (closed in early 1950). The third Fairbridge farm school at Molong, New South Wales, opened in 1937 (closed in 1973). The fourth was the Northcote Children's Farm, which was associated with the Fairbridge farm schools, opened in Bacchus Marsh, Victoria, Australia, in 1937 (closed in 1944 and the remaining forty children were taken to the Molong Fairbridge Farm School). The Fintry Fairbridge Training Farm in the Okanagan Valley, British Columbia, opened in 1938 (sold in 1948). The Fairbridge Memorial College in Rhodesia opened in December 1946, near Bulawayo (closed in 1963). In 1957 a small school called Fairbridge House at Tresca, Exeter, Tasmania, was established, with the first group of children arriving in early 1958 (closed in 1976).

3. The Newcastle *Evening Chronicle*, September 24, 1935, "Empire Migration Conference at the County Hall, Newcastle, Migration only solution to unemployment. British Dominions suffer from lack of population while we suffer from overcrowding."

4. Mrs. Florence Booth (1861–1957) established the Life Saving Guards on November 17, 1915. She was married to Bramwell Booth, the second general of the Salvation Army and the eldest son of William Bramwell and Catherine Booth, who began the Christian Mission in London's East End in 1864, later the Salvation Army. Each girl worked to become a second-class and then a first-class guard. In 1921, a junior branch of the Guards, known as the Sunbeams with their yellow and grey uniforms, began. Ultimately, in 1959, the Guards and Sunbeams affiliated with the Girl Guide Association becoming Guides and Brownies and losing their link to the Salvation Army.

5. Borstal was a juvenile detention centre or reformatory, an institution of the criminal justice system, intended to reform delinquent male youths, originally those aged between about sixteen and twenty-one but raised to age twenty-three in the 1930s. The court sentence was officially called "borstal training." Borstal institutions were designed to offer education, regular work, and discipline.

6. Castle Howard is one of Britain's stately homes, located in the Howardian Hills, fifteen miles northeast of the city of York. Built in 1699, it is still the private home of the Howard family. An apprentice-ship farming program operated on the property in the 1930s.

CHAPTER THREE: ADRIFT

1. An excerpt from "The Innocents," printed in *Our Waifs and Strays*, the monthly paper of the Church of England Central Society for Providing Homes for Waifs and Strays, August 1887, 3. The editor of the paper, Rev. J.W. Horsley, is assumed to be the author of the poem. The paper was printed and published in London by Wells Gardner, Darton and Company. It was also reproduced in England's *TV Times*, May 6–12, 1989. This poem has often been cited in articles and in books about child migration.

2. The names of these two women are fictitious, but the story is based on Marjorie's recall of the horrors of that train ride.

3. The Fairbridge Society Office was located at 35 Dean Street, Newcastle, during the 1930s and 40s.

CHAPTER FOUR: WINIFRED'S SORROW

1. An excerpt from Honourable Sir Arthur Lawley's "Epilogue," in Kingsley Ogilvie Fairbridge, *The Autobiography of Fairbridge* (London: Oxford University Press, 1927), 179.

2. At this time, the Fairbridge Society sent children to both Canada and Australia and made the claim that they made every effort to ensure that members of the same family were sent to the same country, but this did not always happen.

3. An excerpt on page 2 of the Victoria *Times Colonist*, May 12, 1940, "Impressed by Island School. Malcolm H. Jackson Arrives From England With Party for Fairbridge Farm … It was not always easy to prevail upon the parents to part with their children but once they realized the benefits to the children themselves the transfer was not difficult." Malcolm Jackson was the branch secretary of the Fairbridge Society, Newcastle upon Tyne office.

CHAPTER FIVE: MIDDLEMORE EMIGRATION HOME, BIRMINGHAM

1. This Middlemore Emigration Home was located at Weoly Park Road, Selly Oak, Birmingham. For a brief history of the Middlemore Emigration Homes, see the website: *www.bifhsgo.ca/cpage.php?pt=13.*

2. The term Geordies refers to a native of or inhabitant of Newcastle upon Tyne, England, or its environs. Geordies also means the dialect of English spoken by Geordies.

CHAPTER SEVEN: OFF TO LONDON

1. A newspaper reporter interviewed Marjorie's group upon their arrival in Vancouver. His article included the following statement from a young lad in their group: "We are goin' to be taught to farm and that will give England a good name and Fairbridge a good name. We are to 'elp make the country British." *Daily Province* (Vancouver), September 22, 1937, 2. Numerous other articles, such as the following two by J.C. Johnstone, included statements about the importance at the time of keeping Canada "British": London *Morning Post*, July 1, 1935, "Nature abhors a vacuum.… If they are not filled with British stock they will be filled by the forcible occupation or peaceful penetration of aliens." And in the London *Morning Post*, July 2, 1935, "unless those territories [the British Dominions] are to be filled up with aliens and lost to the British Empire, we must find the means of replenishing them with British stock somehow."

2. Canada House is located across the street from Trafalgar Square, London, England. Constructed between 1824 and 1827, the original

building was designed by Sir Robert Smirke, a British museum archi-
tect. The Canadian government acquired the building in 1923. It under-
went restoration work in 1993, and was officially reopened by Queen
Elizabeth II, as Queen of Canada, in 1996. Canada House is the home to
the cultural and consular sections of the High Commission of Canada
to the United Kingdom.

CHAPTER EIGHT: THE LAST TEA PARTY

1. Letter dated June 10, 1937, (page 2) from Colonel Harry Tremaine
Logan, principal, Prince of Wales Fairbridge Farm School, Cowichan
Station, Vancouver Island, British Columbia, to F.C. Blair, assistant
deputy minister, Department of Immigration and Colonization, con-
taining Logan's ongoing appeal for funding for the farm school, stating
his firm belief that Canadian federal funding would "serve as a stimu-
lus and encouragement to the Fairbridge Society to extend to other
Provinces its work of building up our country." Library and Archives
Canada, Immigration Branch, Volume 375, RG 76, File 510340 Pt.2.

2. Canadian government officials in both Ottawa and London often
referred to the children presented for migration as "material," as if
they were removing the human element and seeing them as a commodity rather than young children. The following excerpts are found
in letters between Mr. Little, director, Department of Immigration and
Colonization, Canada House, Trafalgar Square, and FC Blair, assistant
deputy minister, Department of Immigration and Colonization, Ottawa.
Little to Blair, August 2, 1935, "I am not at all impressed by the material
that has already been submitted by the Fairbridge Farm School." Little
to Blair, August 13, 1935, "Mr. Green, [secretary of the Fairbridge Farm
Schools] … stated that he would present this week a party of better material from Birmingham." Blair to Little, September 19, 1935, "if the public
of the country knew the kind of material that is being put forward by
the Fairbridge Farm Schools for inclusion in their BC settlement, there
would be widespread and vigorous protest … if what we had examined
was a sample of what they really wanted to send, either they have a poor
appreciation of our standards or had a lot of very poor material that was

not worth sending." There are additional examples. The business end of child migration is discussed on page 2: "Strictly speaking the Fairbridge Farm School is somewhat in the nature of a broker. They ask these public assistance authorities, who are like wholesalers, to supply the children to ourselves, who are the retailers. I imagine, however, that the whole source of the trouble here is the fact that I have kept the Department advised of the material which was being submitted." Library and Archives Canada, Immigration Branch, Volume 375, RG 76, File 510340 Pt.2.

3. "Farm Schools for the Empire," *The Times* (Thursday, June 21, 1934), i.

4. *Ibid.*, i–iv.

5. Mr. William Alexander McAdam was acting agent-general for British Columbia, from 1934–58. He was present at many of the goodbye parties given to the children before they departed for Canada. The information stated here is taken from *The Times* (September 10, 1937), 9, and the Vancouver *Daily Province* (September 23, 1937), 19.

6. Telegram from the Duke of Gloucester, Prince Henry (March 31, 1900–10 June 1974), president of the Fairbridge Society, as published in the Vancouver *Daily Province* (September 23, 1937), 19.

7. "I saw great Colleges of Agriculture (not workhouses) springing up in every man-hungry corner of the Empire." From Kingsley Fairbridge, *Kingsley Fairbridge: His Life and Verse* (Bulawayo, Rhodesia: Books of Rhodesia Publishing Company, 1974), 159.

8. "Kingsley Fairbridge's Speech Read Before the Colonial Club at Oxford, October 19, 1909: The Emigration of Poor Children to the Colonies," Fairbridge, *Kingsley Fairbridge*, 229.

9. The children were all given suitcases to carry their new belongings to the colonies. I found my Uncle Ken Arnison's suitcase and it still has his name and destination on it. It is a rather large case, and I cannot imagine the small children carrying them. See the image on page 132.

10. Philip Bean and Joy Melville, *Lost Children of the Empire* (London: Unwin Hyman, 1989), 54.

CHAPTER NINE: JOYCE'S SORROW

1. Information related to Joyce (Arnison) Earl is based on personal letters and interviews from 1995 to 2011. Joyce was one of the four Arnison children sent to the Middlemore Emigration Home in Birmingham in February 1937 but was deemed too old for the Fairbridge farm school program at the time Marjorie and Kenny were shipped out to Canada.

2. Audrey contracted pertussis (whooping cough) and ringworm sometime in the summer of 1937 and was quarantined in the sick bay area of the home. Consequently she could not go to Canada with Marjorie and Kenny in September 1937. She was sent out to the Prince of Wales Fairbridge Farm School in August 1938.

3. In 2007, Joyce gave me permission to access her Middlemore Emigration Home personal files. There are a number of letters and documents showing that it was indeed the mistake in her birthdate that prevented her from joining her siblings at the Prince of Wales Fairbridge Farm School on Vancouver Island.

CHAPTER TEN: LEAVING LIVERPOOL

1. Philip Bean and Joy Melville, *Lost Children of the Empire* (London: Unwin Hyman, 1989), 78.

2. Marjorie has a vivid recall of the plight of this mother, who arrived to reclaim her daughter as the group was boarding the *Duchess of Atholl*. She unsuccessfully tried to prevent her daughter from being sent to Canada.

3. Stories about the sailors and their kindness to the children come from Marjorie's old and newly emerged memories. The sailors were very kind and generous. The men did rig up a jumping platform and always had treats for the children. There are many accounts of the seasickness and homesickness experienced during this time.

4. *Vancouver Sun*, Wednesday, September 22, 1937, and the Vancouver *Daily Province*, Wednesday, September 22, 1937.

CHAPTER ELEVEN: PIER D, PORT OF VANCOUVER

1. "On Their Way to Fairbridge School," *Vancouver Sun* (September 22, 1937), 3. This conversation and the ones that follow are a blend of the conversations that were reported in the *Vancouver Sun*, the *Daily Province* (Vancouver), and the *Vernon News* newspaper articles as groups of child migrants arrived on their way to Vancouver Island between 1935 and 1948. Many Fairbridgians have told me stories of how they were sent to Canada with strong apprehensions about the cowboys and Canada's First Nations people that they might meet in Canada. Numerous newspaper articles refer to this and many reporters did little to ease their fears.

2. *Daily Province* (November 13, 1937), 2.

3. *Ibid.*, 2.

4. *Daily Province* (Vancouver) (September 22, 1937), 1–2.

5. *Daily Province* (Vancouver) November 24, 1938), 9.

6. *Victoria Daily Times*, (November 10, 1941), 14.

7. *Daily Province* (Vancouver) (September 22, 1937), 2.

8. *Ibid.*, 2.

9. *Vernon News* (October 6, 1939, and January 29, 1942).

10. The ferry *Princess Elaine* was built at Clydebank, Scotland, by John Brown & Company, and launched on October 26, 1927. Designed specifically for the Vancouver to Nanaimo day run, she went into service in May of 1928, and made the crossing in just over two hours. She stayed on this route until 1952, when she was put on the Gulf Island run. It was soon determined that she was not suitable for small island ports, and the *Princess Elaine* was returned to the Nanaimo run in the summer of 1953. In the early 1960s, the *Princess Elaine* was sold to become a floating restaurant in Washington State (1963–71), but this venture failed and the vessel was scrapped in 1976.

CHAPTER TWELVE: PRINCE OF WALES FAIRBRIDGE FARM SCHOOL

1. "Fairbridge the Founder" was a school song written by Neil Morrison (age twelve), a boy sent to the Molong Fairbridge Farm School, New South Wales, Australia. Sung to the tune of "Marching Through Georgia." Located in D.A. Rutherford and the Molong Historical Society, "Follow Fairbridge the Founder: An Account of the Fairbridge Farm School at Molong, NSW," Forster, N.S.W: D.A. Rutherford, 1983.

2. The "Fairbridge March" was written by John Rowland of Victoria, British Columbia, and copyrighted in the name of the Fairbridge farm schools. See Appendix B for the complete verses. I would like to thank Gil Woods, Fairbridge farm school contact in London, England, for giving permission for the inclusion of the "Fairbridge March."

CHAPTER THIRTEEN: A MOTHER'S LAMENT

1. The theme that the children of the poorer classes of Britain were unwanted is in the forefront of many of the arguments put forward by the sending societies and used in the numerous pamphlets, appeals, and newspaper articles distributed to the public. The theme was so pervasive that I came to question who exactly did not want these children. My research suggested that many families did not want to lose their children. Perhaps it was simply part of an overall plan to populate the Empire and keep it British. Joy Parr suggests that, "When the economic distress of the 1880s receded, the advocates of child emigration as a safety valve for social unrest were replaced by proponents of an imperial mission to populate Greater Britain." See Joy Parr, *Labouring Children. British Immigrant Apprentices to Canada, 1869–1924* (Montreal: McGill University Press, 1980), 34. Kingsley Fairbridge emphasized that his scheme "will not be charity, it will be an imperial investment." See Kingsley Fairbridge, *Kingsley Fairbridge, His Life and Verse* (Bulawayo, Rhodesia: Mardon Printers, 1974), 197. Fairbridge proposed to "Train the children, from their earliest years, to follow an agricultural life. Train them in the Countries where they are wanted." (Published in "Child Emigration Society Pamphlet," circa 1912.)

Presenting these children as a burden on the country would allow the various sending agencies to justify their actions, plus gain the much needed financial support. Philip Bean and Joy Melville state that "The Board of Guardians calculated that emigration cost the equivalent of a year's maintenance in a perish workhouse, so a child sent away at seven saved the parish six year's keep." See Philip Bean and Joy Melville, *Lost Children of the Empire* (London: Unwin Hyman, 1989), 34.

The concept of unwanted children and the rational for shipping them abroad was not new. The migration of "idle youth" was seen as a solution in 1618 when King James I ordered a group of unemployed young people to be sent to the colonies, thus beginning the practice of migrating Britain's unwanted children, a practice that continued until the mid-1970s. The following is a transcript of a letter from King James I to Sir Thomas Smyth relating to the transportation of children to Virginia, dated January 13, 1618:

> Trustie and well beloved we greet you well, whereas our Court hath of late been troubled by divers idle young people, who although they have been twise punished still continue to followe the same having noe employment.
>
> We have noe other course to cleer our Court from them have thought fitt to send them unto you desiring you att the next opportunitie to send them away to Virginia, and to take sure order that they may be sett to worke there, wherein you shall not only do so good service, but also do a deed of charity by employing them who otherwise will never be reclaimed from the idle life of vagabonds.
>
> Given att our Court att Newmarket the thirteenth day of January 1618.

City of London, London Metropolitan Archives. Remembrancia V, no. 8 [LMA ref: COL/RMD/PA/01/005].

Kingsley Fairbridge, founder of the first Fairbridge farm school in 1912, stated: "The colonies should take something that England does not need…. In the crowded life of these islands pauper children are not wanted." Kingsley, *Kingsley Fairbridge: His Life and Verse*, 197 and 238.

2. This baby, born in February 1939, is the brother that the former prime minister, Gordon Brown, mentions in his foreword. The Family Restoration Fund was established by Brown as a result of his formal apology to all British child migrants in February 2010, and to enable all former home/children/child migrants to be reunited with their families. In May 2011, this fund was instrumental in bringing my mother, Marjorie, together with this younger brother Richard, who was born after she was sent away.

CHAPTER FIFTEEN: MARJORIE WAITED SEVENTY-THREE YEARS

1. The Child Migrants Trust was established in 1987 by Margaret Humphreys CBE, OAM, a Nottinghamshire social worker. The trust addresses the issues surrounding the deportation of children from Britain. Child migrants as young as three were shipped to Canada, New Zealand, former Rhodesia (now Zimbabwe), and Australia, a practice that continued as late as 1970. The Child Migrants Trust, a registered charity in both Australia and Britain, provides a range of social work services, including counselling and support for family reunions. The trust's offices in Nottingham, England, and Perth and Melbourne in Australia, also offer information, advice, and family research to former child migrants and their families. For more information, see *www.childmigrationstrust.com*.

2. Former members of the Prince of Wales Fairbridge Farm School have established the Fairbridge Canada Association (FCA), which attempts to keep the Canadian former Fairbridgians connected and informed of what the other members are doing and also up-to-date on what is going on in the larger child migration communities. A reunion is organized every two years. The FCA has established a Fairbridge Alumni Bursary Society and has given out close to $38,000 in bursaries from 1992 to 2012. The *Fairbridge Gazette*, first published at the Prince of Wales Fairbridge Farm School in 1939, is still published two or three times a year.

3. The Fairbridge house for orphaned British migrant children and/ or migrant children with one parent living was established at Tresca, Exeter, Northern Tasmania, in 1957. The home was closed in November 1976. In 1991, with the approval of the president of the Fairbridge Drake Society, London, England, the Tasmanian records of the society were deposited in the Archives Office. Access to the records is restricted for seventy-five years in line with the access determined for the British records of the Society, which are housed at the University of Liverpool.

4. I was surprised to learn that the Fairbridge farm school of New South Wales at Molong, Australia, established in 1937, didn't close its doors until 1973 (for more information, see *www.users.on.net/~quincejam/ farm.html*) and that the Kingsley Fairbridge Farm School in Pinjarra, Western Australia, established in 1912, did not close until 1981 (for more information, see *www.fairbridgekids.com/index.htm*). Rhodesia Fairbridge Memorial College opened at Bulawayo, in the then Rhodesia (now Zimbabwe) and ran from 1946 until 1962 (for more information, see *http://fairbridge-worldwide.com*). The Prince of Wales Fairbridge Farm School on Vancouver Island, British Columbia, established in 1935, closed in the early 1950s (for more information, see *www.fairbridgecanda.com*).

5. "Transcript of British Prime Minister, Gordon Brown's apology to all British Child Migrants," House of Commons Debates, February 24, 2010, Hansard, Volume No. 506, Part No. 44. For the complete speech, see appendix E, U.K. Parliament: *www.publications.parliament.uk/pa/cm200910/ cmhansrd/cm100224/debtext/100224-0004.htm#10022460000003*.

6. Margaret Humphreys, in her book *Empty Cradles* (London: Doubleday, 1994), 133, states that she felt that the Canadian child migrants were too old for her to help, so she concentrated on the Australian child migrants as they were sent to Australia and area until the early 1970s. "Canada was immensely sad for me, because it represented a generation of people I knew I could do little to help; it was far too late for them.... Events in Australia were so recent and appalling, and my resources so limited, that I decided I would immediately focus my attention there."

AFTERWORD: PATRICIA'S PERSPECTIVE

1. For more information on the Family Restoration Fund, see the website at: *www.childmigrantstrust.com/services/family-restoration-fund.*

2. Colonel Rawson, *Morning Post* (July 22, 1909), quoted in Kingsley Ogilvie Fairbridge, *Kingsley Fairbridge, His Life and Verse,* 237. It was believed that there was "room for any number of experiments on many different lines, and there are more than enough children to allow every method a fair and full trial."

3. Ellen Boucher, "The Limits of Potential: Race, Welfare, and the Interwar Extension of Child Emigration to Southern Rhodesia," *Journal of British Studies,* Vol. 48, (October 2009): 914–34. From Australian National Archives (ANA), Kingsley Fairbridge to the Commonwealth Superintendent for Immigration, October 1, 1921, A436, 46/5/597 Part 1A.

4. Fairbridge, *His Life and Verse,* 229.

5. Roddy Mackay, "Who Took the Fair out of Fairbridge?" *Fairbridge Gazette* (Summer 2000), 7–10.

6. Isobel Harvey, *A Report on a Study Made of Fairbridge Farm School During the Month of August 1944,* 5.

7. Arthur Sager, *It's in the Book: Notes of a Naïve Young Man* (Victoria, British Columbia: Trafford Publishing, 2003), 167–68.

APPENDIX C: BACKGROUND ON THE PRINCE OF WALES FAIRBRIDGE FARM SCHOOL NEAR COWICHAN STATION, BRITISH COLUMBIA

1. Bean and Melville, *Lost Children of the Empire,* 1; and Roger Kershaw and Janet Sacks, *New Lives for Old: The Story of Britain's Child Migrants* (Kew, Richmond, Britain: The National Archives of Britain, 2008), 13.

2. Fairbridge, *The Autobiography of Kingsley Fairbridge* (1927), 127, 142.

3. *Ibid.,*143.

4. Fairbridge, *Kingsley Fairbridge, His Life and Verse*, Publisher's Introduction, 6.

5. Fairbridge, *The Autobiography of Kingsley Fairbridge*, 171–72.

6. See the National Archives of Australia, "Child Migration: An Overview and Timeline," *http://poundpuplegacy.org/node/25832*.

7. *The Times*, (June 15, 1934), 11; (June 21, 1934), i-iv; and (July 25, 1934), 7.

8. *Ibid.*

9. *Ibid.*

10. Patrick Alexander Dunae, "Waifs: The Fairbridge Society in BC, 1931–1951," *Social History*, Vol. XXI, No. 42 (November 1988), 224–50.

11. Library and Archives Canada (LAC), Immigration Branch, RG 76, Vol. 375, File 510340, Pt. 2.

12. British Columbia Archives (PABC). Add. MSS 2121 Box 1 File 5 Roll of Farm School Staff 1935–1950.

13. *Ibid.*

APPENDIX D: CHILD MIGRATION TIMELINE

1. For more information, see the National Archives of Australia website at *www.naa.gov.au*.

2. Bean, and Melville, *Lost Children of the Empire*, 1, and Roger Kershaw and Janet Sacks, *New Lives for Old: The Story of Britain's Child Migrants*, 13.

3. For more information, see the National Archives of Australia website at *www.naa.gov.au*.

4. The last line of the article read: "he, and three others, have for some time made it their practice to kidnap boys, in order to sell them to the West-Indies." *The Flying Post: or Post-Master* of London, England, Tuesday, August 30, to Thursday, September 1, 1698, 2.

5. Kershaw and Sacks, *New Lives for Old: The Story of Britain's Child Migrants*, 15–17.

6. Fairbridge, *Kingsley Fairbridge, His Life and Verse*, Publisher's Introduction, 6. The Australian Dictionary of Biography, online edition at: *www.adb.online.anu.edu.au/biogs/A080485b.htm*.

7. Kershaw and Sacks, *New Lives for Old*, 17.

8. For more information, see "A Child Migration Timeline" at *www. goldonian.org/barnardo/child_migrationl.htm*, or "On Their Own: Britain's Child Migrants" at *http://otoweb.cloudapp.net*.

9. Marjorie Kohli, *The Golden Bridge: Young Immigrants to Canada, 1933–1938* (Toronto: Natural Heritage Books, 2003), 66–69. See also Geoff Blackburn, *The Children's Friend Society: Juvenile Emigrants to Western Australia, South Africa and Canada, 1834–1842* (Northbridge, Western Australia: Access Press, 1993), 239–40.

10. Kershaw and Sacks, *New Lives for Old*, 18.

11. *Ibid.*, 23.

12. *Ibid.*, 28.

13. *Ibid.*, 123.

14. *Ibid.*, 62.

15. *Ibid.*, 70–71.

16. *Ibid.*, 33.

17. *Ibid.*, 65–67.

18. *Ibid.*, 124.

19. *Ibid.*

20. *Ibid.*, 51–52.

21. *Ibid.*, 97–98.

22. *Ibid.*, 76–77.

23. *Ibid.*, 125.

24. *Ibid.*, 130–31.

25. *Ibid.*, 103–05, 108.

26. *Ibid.*, 105, 107.

27. The National Archives of Australia, "Child Migration: An Overview and Timeline," *http://poundpuplegacy.org/node/25832.*

28. Kershaw and Sacks, *New Lives for Old*, 107.

29. Corbett, *Barnardo Children in Canada*, 75.

30. Kershaw and Sacks, *New Lives for Old*, 60, 225–26.

31. *Ibid.*, 134.

32. See National Archives of Australia: *http://poundpuplegacy.org/node/25832.*

33. Kershaw and Sacks, *New Lives for Old*, 134.

34. *Ibid.*,143–44.

35. *Ibid.*, 152.

36. See National Archives of Australia: *http://poundpuplegacy.org/node/25832.*

37. Kershaw and Sacks, *New Lives for Old*, 144–51.

38. Bean and Melville, *Lost Children of the Empire*, 76-77.

39. Kershaw and Sacks, *New Lives for Old*, 192–93.

40. *Ibid.*, 197.

41. *The Times* (London), July 25, 1934, 7.

42. The follow are excerpts from letters between Mr. Little, direc-tor, Department of Immigration and Colonization, Canada House, Trafalgar Square, London and Mr. F.C. Blair, assistant deputy minister, Department of Immigration and Colonization, Ottawa, Ontario, dated

September–October, 1935. Library and Archives Canada, Microfiche Imm Pr., RG 76 Vol. 375 file 510340 pt.2. And letters between the Child Emigration Society, Canadian Immigration, and the various sending agencies, dated between March 1934 and October 1935, housed at the University of Liverpool Archives, Special Collections Branch, Fairbridge Archives, D296 K1/1/1- K1/2/6.

43. *Ibid.*, letter dated October 18, 1935.

44. Kershaw and Sacks, *New Lives for Old*, 153.

45. *Ibid.*, 162.

46. Library and Archives Canada, Microfiche Imm Pr., RG 76 Vol. 375, file 510340 pt.2.

47. See the Fintry website: *www.fintry.ca/history/index.php*.

48. "Immigration Minister Jason Kenney: No Apology for Abuse of Home Children," November 29, 2009. See the website at *http://informedvote. ca/2009/11/17/immigration-minister-jason-kenney-no-apology-for-abuse-of-home-children*.

Bibliography

ARCHIVES

Birmingham Archives & Heritage, England:
    Sir John Middlemore Charitable Trust, Middlemore Fonds, MS 517/25.

British Columbia Archives (PABC):
    Prince of Wales Fairbridge Farm School Records. PABC Add. MSS 2121 Box 1 File 5 — Fairbridge Farm School, Roll of Farm School Staff — 1935–1950. PABC Add. MSS 2121 Box 1 File 6, Fairbridge Farm School, Nurse King's Scrapbook 1940–1942.

Library and Archives Canada (LAC):
    Prince of Wales Fairbridge Farm School Files — 1936–1942 Immigration Branch Central Registry Files (RG 76, Volume 375, File 510340, Pt.2-4), microfilm reel C-10273.
    Middlemore Homes Records (MG 28, I 492) – Papers of the Middlemore Children's Emigration Home, Birmingham Archives Service, Birmingham, England, 1914–1937, Vol. 248 A-2079. Reference MS 517/248, Application Book No. 4.

University of Liverpool, Special Collections Branch, Archives:
    The Fairbridge Society (now Fairbridge)
    (b) Archives: D.296.E1, Children's Records, Case Files; D.296.F1, 1912-1982, Publicity and Fundraising – Appeal Leaflets, 1914-c1975; D296.F4, Publicity and Fundraising Photographs, 1912–1982.

ARTICLES, BOOKLETS, PAMPHLETS, REPORTS

Address by His Excellency, the Earl of Athlone, Governor General of Canada at the opening of the Prince of Wales Fairbridge Farm School Hospital, April 1, 1941. Printed by the *Cowichan Leader*, Duncan, British Columbia, 1941.

Dunae, Patrick. "Waifs: The Fairbridge Society in BC, 1931–1951." *Social History*. Vol. XXI, No. 42, November 1988: 224–50.

"Fairbridge Glimpses." Prince of Wales Fairbridge Farm School. 50th Anniversary of Founding. 1935. Booklet published in 1985 by members of the Old Fairbridge Alumni Committee.

Fairbridge Farm School Inc. London. "Fairbridge Farm Schools Twenty-Sixth Year, 1935." London: The Baynard Press. 1935.

_____. "Fairbridge Farm Schools Twenty-Eighth Year, 1937." London: The Baynard Press. 1937.

_____. "Fairbridge Farm Schools Thirty-Sixth Year, 1945." London: The Baynard Press. 1945.

_____. "Greetings From Fairbridge, 1947." London: The Baynard Press. 1947.

_____. "Fairbridge Farm Schools Thirty-Ninth Year, 1948." London: The Baynard Press. 1948.

_____. "The Fairbridge Story: 1908–1952. Forty-three Years of Successful Work for Children and the Empire." London: Watmoughs Ltd. 1952.

_____. "London Fairbridge Society." 1953.

_____. "The Fairbridge Society — London, 1986." 1986.

Harvey, Isobel, Superintendent of Child Welfare. "Report on study made of Fairbridge Farm School during the month of August 1944."

Logan, Harry Tremaine. "Fairbridge Child Care; A Key to Success and Happiness through Emigration." *National Council of Association Children's Homes*, Vol. 3, No. 3 (September–November 1949): 69 –76.

Mackay, Roddy. "Who Took the Fair out of Fairbridge?" *Fairbridge Gazette* (Summer 2000): 7–10.

Middlemore Homes Committee. "One Hundred Years of Child Care: The Story of Middlemore Homes 1872–1972." Birmingham: Kalamazoo Place.

Wharton, Carol. "Working Papers in Child Development and Care. The History of Fairbridge Farm School." Unpublished MA thesis, University of Victoria, March 1977.

BOOKS

Alexander, John. *Tynemouth and Cullercoats. Images of England*. Stroud, England: Tempus Publishing Ltd., 2001.

_____. *Whitley Bay: Britain in Old Photographs*. Gloucestershire: Sutton Publishing Ltd., 2000.

_____. *Whitley Bay: Past and Present*. Derby, England: Breedon Books Publishing Co. Ltd., 2007.

Amery, The Right Honourable L.S. "Preface." In Kingsley Fairbridge. *The Autobiography of Kingsley Fairbridge*. London: Oxford University Press. Original printing 1927. Fourth impression, September 1934.

Bagnell, Kenneth. *The Little Immigrants: The Orphans Who Came to Canada*. Toronto: Dundurn Press, 2001.

Bailey, Jo, with Ronnie Sabin. *The Long Way Home*. Rangiora, New Zealand: self-published, 2010.

Bean, Philip, and Joy Melville. *Lost Children of the Empire*. London: Unwin Hyman, 1989.

Blackburn, Geoff. *The Children's Friend Society: Juvenile Emigrants to Western Australia, South Africa and Canada, 1834–1842*. Northbridge, Western Australia: Access Press, 1993.

Buchanan-Brown, John. *The Book Illustrations of George Cruikshank*. North Pomfret, Vermont: David and Charles Inc., 1980.

Carrothers, William Alexander. *Emigration from the British Isles*. London: King Books, 1929. With special reference to the development of the Overseas Dominions.

Corbett, Gail H. *Barnardo Children in Canada*. Woodview, Ontario: Homestead Studios, 1981.

Douglas, Percy. *Geordie English*. London: Abson Books, 2001.

Dunae, Patrick A. *Gentlemen Immigrants from the British Public Schools to the Canadian Frontier*. Vancouver: Douglas & McIntyre, 1981.

Ensor, Rick. G.N. Clark, ed. *The Oxford History of England: 1870–1914*. Oxford: Clarenden Press, 1936.

Fairbridge, Kingsley Ogilvie. *The Autobiography of Kingsley Fairbridge*. London: Oxford University Press, 1927. With a preface by The Right Hon. L.S. Amery, P.C., and an epilogue by Hon. Sir Arthur Lawley, K.C.M.G.

_____. *Kingsley Fairbridge. His Life and Verse*. Bulawayo, Rhodesia: Mardon Printers, 1974.

Fairbridge, Ruby. *Pinjarra, the Building of a Farm School*. London: Oxford University Press, 1937.

Garrigue, Sheila. *All the Children Were Sent Away*. New York: Bradbury Press, 1976.

Granfield, Linda. *Pier 21: Gateway of Hope*. Toronto: Tundra Books, 2000.

Halls, Joan. *Miracle of Fairbridge*. Victoria Park, Western Australia: Hespian Press, 1999.

Harrison, Phyllis, ed. *The Home Children: Their Personal Stories*. Winnipeg: Watson & Dwyer, 1979.

Hill, David. *The Forgotten Children. Fairbridge Farm School and its Betrayal of Australia's Child Migrants*. Sydney: Random House, Australia. 2007.

Hiller, Harry H. *Canadian Society: A Macro Analysis*. Third edition. Scarborough, Ontario: Prentice Hall Canada Inc., 1996.

Hollerton, Eric. *Whitley Bay: Images of England*. Stroud, England: Tempus Publishing Ltd., 2001.

Humphreys, Margaret. *Empty Cradles*. London: Doubleday, 1994.

Jones, David C. "It's All Lies They Tell You: Immigrants, Hosts and the CPR." In Hugh A. Dempsey, ed. *The Iron Road and the Making of a Nation*. Vancouver: Douglas & McIntyre, 1984, 107–22.

Kershaw, Roger. *Emigrants and Expats: A Guide to Sources on UK Emigration and Residents Overseas*. Trowbridge, Wiltshire: Cromwell Press Ltd., 2002. Public Record Office, Richmond, Surrey, England.

Kershaw, Roger, and Janet Sacks. *New Lives for Old. The Story of Britain's Child Migrants*. Surrey, U.K.: The National Archives, 2008.

Kohli, Marjorie. *The Golden Bridge: Young Immigrants to Canada, 1933–1938*. Toronto: Natural Heritage Books, 2003.

Lane, John. *Fairbridge Kid*. Pinjarra: Fairbridge Western Australia. 1990.

Lawley, The Honourable Sir Arthur. "Epilogue." In Kingsley Fairbridge. *The Autobiography of Kingsley Fairbridge*. London: Oxford University Press, 1934. Original printing 1927.

Marriot, Sir John A.R. *Empire Settlement*. London: Oxford University Press, 1927.

Parr, Joy. *Labouring Children. British Immigrant Apprentices to Canada, 1869–1924*. London: McGill University Press, 1980.

Pettit, Mary. *Mary Janeway: The Legacy of a Home Child*. Toronto: Natural Heritage Books, 2000.

Rooke, Patricia T., and R.L. Schnell. *Discarding the Asylum: From Child Rescue to the Welfare State in English-Canada (1800–1950)*. Lanham, Maryland: University Press of America, Inc., 1983

Rose, June. *For the Sake of the Children: Inside Dr. Barnardo's 120 Years of Caring for Children*. London: Hodder & Stoughton, 1987.

Rutherford, D.A. and the Molong Historical Society. *Follow Fairbridge the Founder: An Account of the Fairbridge Farm School at Molong, NSW.* Forster, N.S.W: D.A. Rutherford, 1983.

Sager, Arthur. *It's In The Book: Notes of a Naive Young Man.* Victoria, British Columbia: Trafford Publishing, 2003.

Scholes, Alex G. *Education for Empire Settlement: A Study of Juvenile Migration*, London: Published for the Royal Empire Society by Longmans, Green and Co., 1932.

Sherard, Robert Harborough. *The Child Slaves of Britain.* London: Hurst & Blackett Ltd., 1905.

Sherington, Geoffrey. *Australia's Immigrants: 1788–1978.* Sydney: George Allen & Unwin, 1980.

Sherington, Geoffrey, and Chris Jeffrey. *Fairbridge. Empire and Child Migration.* Portland, Oregon: Woburn Press, 1998.

Sutherland, Neil. *Children in English-Canadian Society. 1880–1920: Framing the Twentieth-Century Consensus.* Toronto: University of Toronto Press, 1976.

Troper, Harold Martin. *Only Farmers Need Apply! Official Canadian Government encouragement of Immigration from US, 1896–1911.* Toronto: Griffin House, 1972.

Voas, Samuel Robert. *An Englishman's Lifetime in Canada.* Cowichan, 1974.

Wagner, Gillian. *Barnardo.* London: Weidenfeld & Nicholson, 1979.

_____. *Children of the Empire.* London: Weidenfeld & Nicholson, 1982.

Weaver, Jack W. *Immigrants from Great Britain and Ireland.* Westport, Connecticut: Greenwood Press, 1986.

West, Arthur George Bainbridge. *Fairbridge Farm School in BC.* London: A.R. Mowbray, 1936.

Wicks, Ben. *No Time To Wave Goodbye.* Toronto: Stoddart Publishing Co., 1988.

Williamson, Peter. *French and Indian Cruelty: Exemplified in the Life and Various Vicissitudes of Fortune of Peter Williamson.* Bristol, England: Thoemmes Press, 1996. Reprint of the 1762 edition.

Wymer, Norman. *Dr. Barnardo.* London: Cox & Wyman Ltd., 1962.

Wynn Jones, Michael. *George Cruikshank. His Life and London.* London: MacMillan London Limited, 1978.

Young, Beryl. *Charlie: A Home Child's Life in Canada.* Toronto: Key Porter Books, 2009.

MAGAZINES

Fairbridge Gazette. Magazine of the Prince of Wales Fairbridge Farm School, published by the Fairbridge Canada Association. February 1939 to mid-1950s and 1980 to present day.

NEWSPAPER ARTICLES

"18 Youngsters for Fairbridge School." *Vancouver Sun.* August 23, 1938. Page 1.

"28 Children for Fairbridge. English Society May Start Third School." *Vancouver Sun.* September 27, 1937.

"Are There Really Indians Here? Ask English Lads Bound For Island School." *Daily Province* (Vancouver). September 25, 1935. Pages 1, 3.

"Bennett Encourages Farm Boys For B.C." *Vancouver Sun.* November 11, 1938. Page 22.

"Boys 'to Keep Flag Flying' 13 English Schoolboys Coming to B.C. Farm to 'Freedom, Security,' Says Bennett." *Daily Province* (Vancouver). November 10, 1938. Page 1.

"British Train Child For Dominion Farms. Fairbridge Schools Seek 250 Pupils for Emigration This Year." *The New York Times.* July 24, 1938. Section C, page 4.

Brown, Edgar. "New Canadians At Fairbridge." *Daily Province* (Vancouver). December 18, 1937.

"Canada Whacking Big Country." *Daily Province* (Vancouver). November 24, 1938. Page 9.

"Canadian Pacific To Canada And U.S.A. Sept. 10 Duchess of Atholl depart from Liverpool." *The Times* (London). September 10, 1937. Page 2.

"Child Farmers to Meet Gov. General. Lord and Lady Tweedsmuir Paying Visit to Fairbridge Farm School Today." *Victoria Daily Times*. August 22, 1936. Page 18.

"Children Cheered As Farm Reached." *Victoria Daily Times*. September 26, 1935. Page 2.

"Children's Friend Society." *Morning Chronicle* (London, England). May 5, 1834.

"Children's Friend Society." *The Times* (London). April 15, 1839. Page 7.

"Children's Friend Society, or, The Hackney Kidnappers." *Champion and Weekly Herald* (London, England). Issue 48. April 7, 1839.

"The Children's Friend Society and Pauper Emigration." *Champion and Weekly Herald* (London, England). February 24, 1839. Page 8.

"Citizens For The Empire." *The Times* (London). July 13, 1939. Page 11.

"Classy Paper at Fairbridge." *Vancouver Sun*. May 20, 1941. Page 8.

"Commemorating Royal Tour. M.P.'s £5,000 For Fairbridge Farm School." *The Times* (London). May 31, 1939. Page 12.

"Doctor Paints Sad Picture of Childless World in Future. Britain's Declining Birthrate is Most Alarming According to Sir Leonard Hill." *Montreal Daily Star*. September 18, 1937.

"Duke of Gloucester Telegraphed B.C. Farm Party." *Daily Province* (Vancouver). September 23, 1937. Page 19.

"Earl of Athlone at Fairbridge Farm." *Cowichan Leader*. April 3, 1941. Page 10.

"Empire Migration Schemes Mooted in City. Dominions and Ministry Experts At Parley. Newcastle Plans to Solve Unemployment Problem." *Evening Chronicle* (Newcastle upon Tyne). September 24, 1935. Page 7.

"English Lads Here on Way To Fairbridge. All Ambitious to One Day Be Mounties." *Vancouver Sun*. November 24, 1938. Page 15.

"Enter New Life With Smile. Old Country Accents Blend As Children Acclaim Canada." *Daily Province* (Vancouver). September 22, 1937. Pages 1–2.

"Fairbridge Children Decide B.C. Rain is Just Usual Kind. Weather Doesn't Worry Them But Kenneth Dobbs, 6, Not So Sure About Indians." *Daily Province* (Vancouver). November 10, 1937. Page 2.

"Fairbridge Farm." *Daily Colonist* (Victoria). October 30 1936. Page 4.

"The Fairbridge Farm School." *Daily Colonist* (Victoria). March 13, 1935. Page 4.

"Fairbridge Farm School Departure of 28 Children Today." *The Times* (London). September 10, 1937. Page 9.

"Fairbridge Farm School Solving Empire Problem." *Daily Colonist* (Victoria). January 7, 1936. Page 7.

"Fairbridge Gets Estate. Older Boys of Vancouver Island School to Transfer to Fintry, B.C." *Victoria Daily Times*. July 6, 1938. Page 1.

"Fairbridge School for Island." *Daily Colonist* (Victoria). March 9, 1935. Page 4.

"Farm Schools for the Empire." *The Times* (London). Thursday, June 21, 1934. Page i–iv.

"Fintry Fairbridge School Closes Until Next April." *Vernon News*. October 6, 1939.

"Fintry Laird Tells of Hopes in Farm School." *Nanaimo Free Press*. March 22, 1939.

Furness, Adrian. "Lost Children of the Empire: The Children We Forgot." *TV Times* (England). May 6–12, 1989. Pages 22–23.

"The Girls of Fairbridge." *Daily Colonist* (Victoria). April 14, 1940. Magazine section, page 1.

"Grant Being Considered For Duncan Farm School." *Daily Colonist* (Victoria). February 13, 1948. Page 1.

"Immigration. A Protest From the Workmen of Hamilton." *The Globe* (Toronto). October 2, 1884, Page 2.

"The Importation of Waifs." *The Globe* (Toronto). October 9, 1884.

"Kidnapping Children." *Caledonian Mercury* (Edinburgh, Scotland). July 19, 1810.

"The Kidnapping Society." *Champion and Weekly Herald* (London, England). Issue 38. January 27, 1839. Page 4.

"The Kidnapping Society." *Champion and Weekly Herald* (London, England). Issue 50. April 21, 1839.

"Legion Presents Gates to Farm School." *Vancouver Sun*. November 2, 1938. Page 6.

"Little Empire Migrants." *Evening Journal* (Ottawa). February 23, 1939.

Logan, Harry T. "The Fairbridge Farm School — An Imperial Venture." *The Times* (London). May 15, 1939. Page x.

London Dispatch. April 7, 1839. Page 1069.

London Flying Post. No. 526. August 30–September 1, 1698.

"More Children At Fairbridge." *Victoria Daily Times*. September 22, 1937. Page 8.

"New Fairbridge Girls Declare They Won't Be Farmer's Wives." *Daily Province* (Vancouver). September 21, 1938. Page 3.

"On Their Way To Fairbridge School. 'Aw Joost Knaow Ah'm Goan Like Cawanada." *Vancouver Sun*. September 22, 1937. Page 3.

"Orphans of the Blitz Arrive at Fairbridge School After Hazardous Journey from Britain." *Daily Times* (Victoria). November 10, 1941. Page 14.

"Our Gutter Children." *The Times* (London). March 29, 1886.

"A Party of 28 children who will sail today for Fairbridge Farm School on Vancouver Island, were entertained at a tea party at British Columbia House yesterday." *The Times* (London). August 11, 1938. Page 11.

Reverend Arthur West. "More Children for BC. Big Man With Big Hands Comes Out to Start Fifty Boys and Girls at Farming." *Daily Province* (Vancouver). September 21, 1935. Magazine section, page 3.

Rodgers, Barbara. "Where Have All the Children Gone? Reunion Planned for August 26–27." *Times Colonist* (Victoria). August 7, 1983. Page 4.

"Royal Wedding Gift From Empire To Aid Fairbridge Schools." *Daily Times* (Victoria). September 14, 1948. Magazine section, page 13.

"School Scheme is Explained. Major H. Cuthbert Holmes Tells of Work of Fairbridge Among Children." *Daily Colonist* (Victoria). December 10, 1935. Page 10.

"Society Backs Farm School. Royal St. George Society Supporting Fairbridge Farm Scheme." *Victoria Daily Times*. Thursday, May 30, 1935.

"Steamship Arrivals. Duchess of Atholl at Montreal on the 19th." *Globe and Mail*. September 19, 1937.

"The Story of Founding of Fairbridge." *Vernon News*. January 29, 1942.

Taylor, Noreen. "Passage to Hell: Off to a Promised Land and a Poisoned Future." *Daily Mirror* (London). July 14, 1993. Pages 6–7.

"Tells Great Experiment. Major C. Holmes Describes Struggle Of Kingsley Fairbridge to Gyros." *Victoria Daily Times*. December 10, 1935. Page 5.

"Tillicum Traveller Visits Fairbridge Farm." *Daily Province (Vancouver)*. September 16, 1939. Magazine section, page 6.

"Transportation and Sale of Children of the Poor: Defence of the Children's Friend Society." *The Operative* (London, England). Vol. II, No. 27. May 5, 1839.

"Transportation of Children by Parish Officers." *The Operative* (London, England). February 3, 1839. Page 10.

"The Voyage of 28 Children. New Opportunities at Fairbridge." *The Times* (London). August 11, 1938. Page 13.

PERSONAL LETTERS AND INTERVIEWS

Arnison, David. Marjorie's youngest brother, born after she left for Canada. Personal letters and interviews. 1995–2012.

Arnison, Frederick. Marjorie's oldest brother. Interviews. 2001 and 2005.

Arnison, Norman. Marjorie's older brother. Personal letters and interviews. 1999–2007.

Earl, Joyce (Arnison). Marjorie's older sister. Personal letters and interviews. 1995–2012.

Lewis, Audrey (Arnison). Marjorie's younger sister. Personal letter, February 10, 1995, and interviews to 2012.

Skidmore, Marjorie. Personal letter, February 20, 1995, and interviews, 1999–2012.

VIDEOS: FAIRBRIDGE FARM SCHOOL IN PUBLIC ARCHIVES OF BC (PABC)

F1987:20/1: Prince of Wales Fairbridge Farm School: Miscellaneous footage ca. 1936–40. Alfred C. Lincoln "Fairbridge Pictures" Notes: Fairbridge children at work and at play; farm scenes; Guy Fawkes Day celebration; harvesting; cutting hay; swimming; baseball; picnic at Cowichan Bay; miscellaneous colour scenes on 1936, 1938 & 1939 stock. Black & white footage is largely Dupont stock some of which has turned sepia. Titled segments include: "Autumn Scenes"; "Hay Ho!"; "our Water Babies"; "Down by Kelvin Creek"; "and scenes from "The Day With Boy". The video's intention was to show a day in the life of a pupil at Fairbridge.

Video transfers: V1988 10/10.1 & 10.2 Provenance/Prev. no. Mrs. Dot Lincoln, Sidney, BC via Pat Dunae. MS + GR PABC Date of Accession: 1987 07   21. V1988 10/10 & 10.2 Prince of Wales Fairbridge Farm School: miscellaneous footage: ca. 1936–40.

V1980:76: Fairbridge Farm School, edited and narrated by Tom Turner. A home video production consisting of the films of Alf Lincoln (+1987:20 & V1987:30) edited and supplied with a sound track by Tom Turner.

V1987:30/1: Prince of Wales Fairbridge Farm School 1939–40 Credits: Alfred C. Lincoln Notes: Land clearing, construction and dedication of the Fairbridge Chapel; Lower Island Sports Meet, 1939; farming activities at Fairbridge; recreation; Boy Scout & Cub Troops; Christmas celebrations; visit of Our Lord and Lady Tweedsmuir; Royal visit to Victoria, May 1939.

WEBSITES

British Columbia Archives (BC Archives): *www.bcarchives.gov.bc.ca/index.htm.*

Child's Migrant Trust: *www.childmigrantstrust.com.*

Fairbridge Canada Association: *http://fairbridgecanada.com.*

Library and Archives Canada: *www.bac-lac.gc.ca/eng/Pages/home.aspx.*

Acknowledgements

To my mother, Marjorie Skidmore, whose patience and trust allowed me to uncover and recreate her childhood experience as a child migrant. My siblings: my sister Joan Skidmore, my brothers, Fred Skidmore and Rick Skidmore, and even the special lost one, Lloyd Skidmore (1951–2007), they all contributed to this story.

To my sons, Josh Havelaar, Fletcher Havelaar, and Jack Weyler, I thank them for growing up solid and allowing me to see that there is life and interesting projects to pursue after raising my three sons.

To my uncles and aunts, my mother's siblings who have now become part of our family story: Fred (1919–2006), Norman (1923–2012), Phyllis (1920–2007), Joyce, Kenny (1928–1983), Audrey and her husband Eric (1930–2012), Jean (1932–1989), Lawrence and his wife Pam, Richard, whom I met for the first time in May 2011, and David and his wife Marion, and to my English cousins — they have all made contributions to the story.

A very special thanks to the readers of my manuscript: Sally Campbell, Norm Gibbons, Christine St. Peter, Monica Turner, and Rex Weyler.

Thanks to Gil Woods, the Fairbridge farm school contact in London for allowing access to the Fairbridge files housed at the University of Liverpool. To the archivists at the University of Liverpool Special Collections Branch and the Birmingham Archives for all their help. To Reginald Corns, Birmingham, a former Middlemore Emigration Home child himself, who willingly shared his knowledge and his photographs.

A special thanks to Dave Lorente, Home Children Canada. His phone call to me in February 2010 changed the course of our lives and of this book.

To Sally Keefe-Cohen for her hard work on finalizing my agreement with the publisher. This book may not have reached this stage without her.

And last but not least, I am deeply indebted to Jane Gibson and Barry Penhale, who believed in this project from the start and their editing skills have seen it through to the finish. Thank you.

All have contributed in helping me to realize my dream of being able to hand to my mother — her story — never ending, never complete, but recreated for her and with her, to the best of my ability, now put into print, so it will never get lost again.

Index

About the Author

Patricia Jane Skidmore was born in Vancouver, British Columbia, and spent most of her childhood in the Vancouver suburb of Coquitlam. For her, being a daughter of a child migrant was a shameful and often worrying experience. She didn't feel that she belonged. There was no sense of family and no roots to ground her to her place of birth. Her mother's background, her past, her childhood, her family, were missing, and her mother would not tell her why. It worried her deeply. Her mother rarely spoke of her five years at the Prince of Wales Fairbridge Farm School or why she was sent there as a little girl. It took Pat well into her adult years to confront the issue — child migration and the role her family played in it — and try to understand it.

Today she is actively involved with the Fairbridge Canada Association (FCA) and its various programs: the *Fairbridge Gazette*, and the Fairbridge Alumni Bursary Society, which was formed by the former Fairbridge child migrants who were sent to the Prince of Wales Fairbridge Farm School on Vancouver Island, British Columbia. She also maintains the Fairbridge Canada Association website, *www.fairbridgecanada.com*.

Pat left the area of her youth in 1967, vowing never to return, and she raised her three sons on and around the small islands of Vancouver Island. But, never say never! Today Pat lives in Port Moody, British Columbia, right next door to where she grew up.

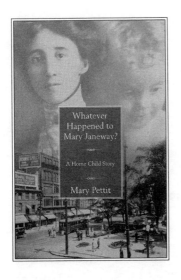

Whatever Happened to Mary Janeway?
A Home Child Story
by Mary Pettit

9781459701717
$26.99

Sixteen-year-old Mary Janeway, a home child, is desperate to escape from her rural home child placement and flees to London, Ontario, to find a domestic position. When conditions become unbearable, she moves on, vowing never to relinquish her freedom again.

After she arrives in Hamilton as a young bride, she quickly adapts to the urban conveniences and the marvels of new inventions, but even the latest technology can't stop the ravages of disease and other family tragedies.

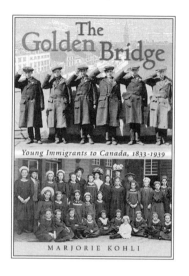

The Golden Bridge
Young Immigrants to Canada, 1833–1939
by Marjorie Kohli

9781896219905
$34.95

Author Marjorie Kohli has meticulously documented the incredible story of the removal of thousands of "waifs and strays" and young men and women, primarily from the U.K. and Ireland. They braved the perilous voyage to an unknown future in Canada, ultimately being placed throughout the Maritimes, Ontario, Quebec, and westward as far as British Columbia.

The most comprehensive resource of its kind, *The Golden Bridge* promises to be an indispensable tool for family researchers with a "home child" ancestor, and of interest to those unfamiliar with this aspect of Canadian history.

VISIT US AT

Dundurn.com
Definingcanada.ca
@dundurnpress
Facebook.com/dundurnpress